Taking Up Serpents

Taking Up

Snake
Handlers
of Eastern
Kentucky

Serpents

David L. Kimbrough

The University of North Carolina Press

Chapel Hill and London

The paper in this book meets the guidelines for
permanence and durability of the Committee on
Production Guidelines for Book Longevity of the
Council on Library Resources.

Library of Congress Cataloging-in-Publication Data
Kimbrough, David L., 1951–
    Taking up serpents : snake handlers of eastern
Kentucky / David L. Kimbrough.
      p. cm.
    Includes bibliographical references and index.
    ISBN 0-8078-2227-2 (alk. paper). —
ISBN 0-8078-4533-7 (pbk. : alk. paper)
    1. Snake cults (Holiness churches)—Kentucky.
2. Kentucky—Religious life and customs.
3. Saylor family.   I. Title.
BX7990.H6K46   1995
289.9—dc20   95-3593
                            CIP

99 98 97 96 95   5 4 3 2 1

In memory of my sister, Sue Ann Kimbrough

A "Baptist preacher," carrying a snorting blow torch, Saturday challenged the faith of snake and fire handlers during their biggest meeting at the Dolly Pond Church of God, where native converts promised the departing Rev. Raymond Hayes the weird cult would be perpetuated in the Grasshopper community, near Birchwood.

The man whom the "believers" later said was a Baptist preacher walked into the midst of snake and fire-handling rites, shoved a blazing gasoline torch into the hands of one of the brethren and declared, "Here, try this."

As the man stood looking at the noisy blue blaze a stooped, 90-year-old woman, one of the believers who had been sitting quietly on the sidelines, walked over and held out both hands into the flames, as she looked straight into the face of her challenger. "If you had the faith," she told him, her gaze unwavering, "you could do this, too."

The Rev. Mr. Hayes took the torch, turned the handle to let blazing gasoline splash against his shirt. Burning drops of the fluid fell to the floor, but his shirt did not catch fire.

During the handling of a large rattler and a copperhead the Rev. Mr. Hayes announced he had been bitten, displaying to the brethren two tiny red holes in his hands. Smiling and apparently unshaken, he held both snakes during an hour-long sermon, wrapping them first about his neck and head, then fondled them in his hands.

Once he laid them on a small stand on the pulpit where the Bible was lying open. He removed them when the rattlesnake persisted in making spine-tingling noises with its tail. "I can't preach with you making all that noise," he said, taking the reptiles again.

Several members of the same cult came down from Cleveland for the Rev. Hayes' last night at the meeting, raising the number of participants in Saturday night's rites to about 30.

During the ceremonies the rattlesnake's fangs were shown to the spectators. Using a match while another member forced the reptile's jaws open, Rev. Hayes displayed the snake's deadly needle-sharp teeth. "Are they there?" he asked the congregation.

One of the new converts, L. F. Ford, a native of the Grasshopper community, told the congregation that snake-handling rites would continue to be held at the church every Saturday night, Sunday morning and Sunday evening. "Bring your bad snakes if you want to see them handled," he told the spectators.

At the height of Saturday night's ceremony the Rev. Hayes laid two snakes on the floor and, removing his shoes and socks, he walked on them for several minutes. The meeting in the unfinished, floorless church continued until after midnight.

About midway of the ritual one of the believers gave the un-believers an opportunity to join their church and become snake handlers. Although the man continued to urge members of the congregation to "come up to the alter" no one made a move in the direction of the ropes behind which the snakes were lying.

No new believers were added to the rolls last night.

—"Snake Handlers Pass Challenge of Blow Torch,"
Chattanooga News—Free Press, July 23, 1945

Contents

Illustrations

Acknowledgments

I received no funding for this project but would like to thank the people in eastern Kentucky, Tennessee, and Fort Wayne, Indiana, for providing me with various forms of assistance. Nova Technologies of Austin, Texas, furnished me with an experimental shock device that is being used to treat snakebite victims, in case I was bitten. Fortunately, I never needed the apparatus, but I appreciated Nova's donation.

There are many people to thank for making this work possible. Arnold Saylor, who was pastor of the Highway Holiness Church of God in Fort Wayne, certainly made the greatest contribution to my knowledge about snake handling. After I attended his church on several occasions, he took me to eastern Kentucky to meet his people, who are very involved in snake handling. I would never have been allowed to do the research if he had not opened doors for me. His heart attack and death on January 3, 1992, were devastating for me. Park Saylor, one of the main subjects of this study, related events in oral tradition for many hours. Bradley Shell was also a very valuable contributor. He had run with the founders and played a large role in the snake-handling movement.

Brother Perry Bettis and his very kind and attractive wife, "Flo," of Birchwood, Tennessee, spent days helping me locate early snake-handling church members who were still living during the period of my research. Brother Perry passed away on December 11, 1991, and I certainly miss him. Another Tennessee snake handler who helped me was Liston Pack, who was minister of the church in Carson Springs, Tennessee.

Joyce Baker of Harmon's Lick, Kentucky, was very kind in giving me videotapes of certain snake-handling events that were very important to my work. She is also a very articulate person, with a deep knowledge of the Saylor family's history and snake-handling activities. Kale Saylor and his wife, Ada Lee, made me welcome in their home and contributed valuable materials to my work. Ms. Coots of Middlesboro was helpful in explaining the Holiness perspective on demon possession, as was Mrs. Marsee of Bean Station, Tennessee. Many other preachers and church members such as Denver Short, Austin Long, Bradley Shell, the Brocks, Shilo Collins, the Saylors, Ronnie Hoskins, and my good friend Benny Johnson were also helpful to me.

Scholars that helped me are almost too numerous to mention. Almost everyone in the Appalachian Studies Association gave me some type of assistance. Professor Dwight Billings of the University of Kentucky gave me numerous readings and suggestions. I would never have mastered Appalachian literature without his aid. Professor Ron Lewis of West Virginia University also provided help.

The Appalachian Ministries Educational Resource Center (AMERC), based in Berea, Kentucky, has made me feel like one of their own products. Dr. Mary Lee Daugherty gave me aspects of Appalachian religions as well as snake handling. Professor Helen Lewis of Berea College, who is a legend in Appalachian studies, was a valuable consultant as well.

Professor Bill Leonard at Samford University never let up. He was helpful to the time the work went to press. I certainly appreciate the many things he has done for me. Professor Jim Cox of Union College in Barbourville, Kentucky, is the person responsible for developing my knowledge of the Appalachian social structure and the stem family. Professor Ralph Hood Jr. of the University of Tennessee at Chattanooga was simply a godsend for all of his suggestions and help. Professor Tom Burton of East Tennessee State University's suggestions made life a lot easier for me in eastern Tennessee.

I cannot mention all the ways in which Dr. Steven M. Kane has helped me. Kane wrote a dissertation and many articles on snake handling during the 1970s and 1980s. He blazed the trails that virtually all snake-handling researchers embark on. Many times he receives no credit for his work. In going through the many archives, I found numerous newspaper articles and materials that Dr. Kane gave to libraries; I recognized them by the print of his trusty old typewriter, because he is not listed as the source or contributor. I will say in capital letters, THANK YOU, STEVE! You made this work so much easier with your willingness to share, and I certainly know the many contributions you have made to this field.

I would like to thank Warren Brunner, known as the "Norman Rockwell of Appalachia," for providing some pictures of snake-handling services. Richard Golden of Middlesboro, Kentucky, also provided valuable pictures, as did Bobbie Short, J. B. Collins, the *Tampa Tribune*, Reverend Jimmy Morrow, Park Saylor, and so many others. The *Louisville Courier-Journal* and *Chattanooga News–Free Press* contributed several articles, and I appreciate their unselfishness in letting me use them; *Courier-Journal* staff members Laura McCutchan and Joanna Gnau deserve particular thanks. My good friend Robert E. Royer, a CPA in Bloomington, Indiana, took time from his busy tax season to copy many of the photographs for me. Anthony Feyer of New York did some computer touch-ups on a few of the early snake-handling pictures and provided me with some excellent recordings of music in snake-handling churches. Becky Lucas and Quick Pic of Bloomington developed most of the pictures; also, David Moore of Middlesboro did some instant development of some pictures that were only loaned to me for a few hours.

Professor D'Ann Campbell was a tremendous help. Her critiques and suggestions were very valuable. She made herself available for assistance at all times. Professor Martin Weinberg and John Bodnar were responsible for teaching me my research skills. Perhaps Professor George Juergens was the most fun to be associated with during my work. On occasion he traveled with me to eastern Kentucky and Tennessee and viewed snake-handling services. He made many observations and comments that were helpful. I appreciate his concern for my safety when I handled serpents. Professor Paul Lucas was the biggest help. When I entered graduate school in 1986, he worked with me from the start to the end as my adviser. From the outset, I developed an admiration for his knowledge of religious history. He simply is the greatest.

I should also thank the editors of *Appalachian Heritage* for allowing me to adapt portions of my article "Solomon and Sarah Saylor: The Emergence of Lay Religion in Eastern Kentucky" (*Appalachian Heritage* 21, no. 3 [Summer 1993]: 49–57) for use in Chapter 4.

My wife, Elizabeth Kay Kimbrough, provided a major offering to this work. Her computer skills were essential in accomplishing this project. I would never have learned the various software packages associated with this work without her tutoring.

There are many librarians to thank as well. My good friend Clay Housholder simply researched every nook and cranny when I requested materials. I cannot express how valuable he was to this project. In all of my years in libraries, I have never found anyone that can top him. Julie Anderson and Cathy Gilbert were also helpful, as were Diane Hanson and Marty Sorury, who helped me with the miles of microfilm. Donna Lakes, Sidney Saylor Farr, and Gerald Roberts of the Hutchins Library at Berea College also deserve a tremendous thank-you.

My friend F. G. Summitt of Bloomington deserves thanks for his critiques, and all of my buddies at Rosie's Diner, the best restaurant in southern Indiana, were great. In fact, there are many people in Bloomington, too numerous to mention, who provided assistance in various ways.

Just after this work was completed, my friend Kale Saylor was killed by a rattlesnake bite in a church service in eastern Kentucky. This work would not have been possible without Kale's help, and I will miss him.

I certainly thank the tremendous staff at the University of North Carolina Press. I appreciate April Higgins and Christi Stanforth's efforts and hard work and David Perry's valuable suggestions and behind-the-scenes effort. Working with the UNC Press was a dream come true.

Finally, I would like to acknowledge Robert "Caruso" Remini's valuable suggestions.

Taking Up Serpents

Introduction

I write as a transplanted Appalachian. My parents left Tennessee in the late 1940s to join the great migration of Appalachian people to the industrial centers of the North. During my childhood visits to my grandparents in the small town of White Pine, Tennessee, I remember talk of religious groups in the area who handled poisonous snakes. My curiosity about the snake-handling churches never left me.

White Pine is located in the hotbed of snake-handling country. With the assistance of my cousin Bob Kimbrough, I located a snake-handling church at Carson Springs, Tennessee, in the summer of 1987. Carson Springs is in the vicinity of Newport, in the shadow of the Smoky Mountains. The pastor of the church, Liston Pack, was very open, friendly, and informative.

I developed a great respect for this man immediately. Over the period of my research, we developed a close relationship.

Initially, Pack was hesitant about letting me interview him. After we talked for a while, he became confident that I had no bad intentions, and he became very open about his church. He has been persecuted by the press, television producers, and the authorities, and has been the subject of much ridicule. In 1973, Pack's brother, Buford, and Jimmy Ray Williams died after drinking strychnine at Pack's church. In the early 1970s, Pack was jailed, because his religious beliefs broke a state anti-snake-handling law passed in 1947. Being incarcerated did not thwart Pack's snake-handling practices. He told me, "The very night they let me out of jail, I handled a copperhead. I won't back down. I believe taking up serpents is a command."[1]

Shortly after I made contact with the church at Carson Springs, I read an article in the *Indianapolis Star* about two men being bitten by rattlesnakes in a religious service at Fort Wayne, Indiana.[2] I approached the minister of this congregation, the Highway Holiness Church of God. From the beginning this preacher, Arnold Saylor, was very open with me. Some members of his congregation were apprehensive about me on my first visit, but they have displayed nothing but kindness and friendship since they have known me. I feel very much at home in the church, and the parishioners joke about adopting me.

After spending time with Arnold Saylor and attending several church services, Saylor said, "Dave, I'm going to take you to eastern Kentucky to meet my family." I was going to get to meet famous snake handlers such as Kale Saylor, the Brocks, the Longs, Park Saylor, Tess Walters, Bradley Shell, and many others who were so important and vital in the early years and beginning of the churches.

I will never forget the first time I met Arnold Saylor's Uncle Kale. He was a man who had stood in the pulpit with "Little George" Hensley—regarded as the person who initiated the snake-handling practices in Holiness churches—and with Sherman Lawson, another snake-handling preacher, who was said to have raised the dead on multiple occasions. Kale was standing in front of his church, located on Straight Creek, delivering a fiery message to a full church. He had his thumbs hooked through his suspenders and occasionally jumped up and down, exhibiting emotion and energy. As Joyce Baker, of Harmon's Lick, Kentucky, told me a few years ago, "If they wrote the Bible in today's times, Arnold would be seen as John the Baptist and Kale would be Moses." I feel her statement is accurate. Arnold Saylor would have gone to jail, given his life, or done whatever was required to defend his beliefs.[3]

I did not suffer from the common problems that many non-Appalachians find when they embark on these research trails. I am a native speaker with a suitable hillbilly accent. Others who have not had command of the mountain language have informed me that they had tremendous problems trying to understand the Appalachian jargon and accents.

Kale Saylor practically interrogated me when we first met. He said, "Dave, I prayed about you and I have a good feeling about you. Just don't do like others have and say things about us that isn't true."[4] I assured him that I had no intention of slinging mud on snake handlers. I simply wanted to do an oral history of the movement in eastern Kentucky. I had abandoned my plan to do a total history of snake-handling churches. I found that each denomination is ruled by local autonomy, and scriptural beliefs of the eastern Tennessee groups, other than the churches at Ferguson Ridge and Sneedville, are totally different than those in eastern Kentucky. Therefore, I concentrated my efforts on eastern Kentucky, with the Saylor family.

Accurate information about the snake handlers is rare, so I set out to collect materials that applied to my work. In May of 1988 I met Park Saylor, an articulate informant on snake handling and Saylor family history. In attempting to trace the origins of snake handling in eastern Kentucky, I focused on Park Saylor and his ancestors, who settled on Forrester's Creek, in Harlan County, around 1805.

Even though Appalachian Mountain people are relatively static in their lifestyles and beliefs, snake-handling Holiness / Pentecostal churches have been dynamic in many respects. Therefore, broad generalizations over long periods of time could not be made. Also, the local autonomy that exists in many mountain churches rendered standard survey techniques, such as statistical analysis, counterproductive. Before an investigation of the religion could be performed, it was necessary to examine the structure of the snake-handling churches. I have taken part in over three hundred religious services and visited approximately twenty-five snake-handling churches.[5] I did every ounce of the interviews to avoid losing the effect of the question-and-answer sessions—the problem that usually occurs in what one scholar calls "hired hand research."[6] My main goal was to limit error in interpreting responses to my inquiries. Many Appalachian expressions have different meanings and are difficult for non-natives to understand. It is also perplexing for someone with limited knowledge of the Bible to understand "scripture jargon," especially the varied interpretations found in many mountain locales. As historian Deborah Vansau McCauley explains, "It is fruitless to try to talk about the history of

Appalachian mountain religion unless a serious attempt is made to create a feel for the sights and sounds of mountain worship life."[7]

I entered this work into the snake-handling churches with no preconceived notions about the nature of their religion; I have always presented myself to the Holiness groups openly and displayed sincerity and respect for their beliefs. I participated in churches as far as my personal beliefs would let me. When asked, I played guitar in services or acted as a Bible reader.[8] I have handled poisonous snakes on many occasions, to the astonishment of the snake handlers.[9] During one "meetin'" I was asked, along with the congregation, to fast for a sick woman, who to my amazement improved. When I participated in the services, the congregations were more open and receptive toward me.

The oral history approach did present difficulties. A basic obstacle that surfaced was that of inaccurate statements, including the retelling of distorted rumors. One man who was associated with George W. Hensley for several years, during Hensley's middle age, informed me that Hensley's first wife (Amanda) left him for another man, who eventually killed her. This report is totally incorrect. Amanda did not leave George for another man, and she certainly was not killed; she died of natural causes.

The problem of consistency in response surfaced on several occasions. Not only does memory fade over time, but there are also profound differences regarding the accuracy of remembering one fact versus another during the same time.[10] The vividness of recall is related to various dimensions, such as the experience's original emotional impact, its meaningfulness to the person at the time, and the degree to which the person's ego was involved. Park Saylor, Kale Saylor, and other preachers have been very close to serpent handlers who have been killed in church service by snakes, but I found inconsistency in their reconstructions of the events. Even though the deaths had a tremendous impact on their lives, memory has been massively influenced by public attitudes and interpretations. These men, like all others, develop a script or standardized explanation and fit the basic facts to it in their memory.

The second problem that compounds memory is the simple issue of the time that has elapsed between the event itself and the interview pertaining to it. Historian John Bodnar found that "orally transmitted data has been shaped over a long period of time through considerable thought and discussion,"[11] and many times I have observed that historical events and personal biographies suffered from considerable revision over time. On occasion, this was a major quandary in my research. When a person was killed by snakebite, for example, most members replayed the event many times. George Hensley, Lee Valentine, and Raymond "Buck" Hayes were popular preachers who met death by snakebite, and the serpent handlers have recalled their deaths constantly. Their deaths have regularly been the subjects of sermons by various pastors. Therefore, the events have been kept fresh in people's minds. Nevertheless, public opinion has tainted memory concerning these incidents.

On occasion, chronological confusion was a problem. In order to minimize chronological confusion, I selected more than one person to relay the same information about a particular event. Also, I chose to interview people who had played a large part in the situation that I was gathering facts about. It appeared that ministers could remember the exact order of events because they were involved in constructing them. Park Saylor, Kale Saylor, Bradley Shell, and Perry Bettis were very informative, because they were involved in the early days of the Holiness serpent-handling movement. The preachers have continued with their doctrines from the beginning of the activity, but some memory has been lost. To minimize what historian Paul Thompson terms "selective memories,"[12] I asked the ministers the same questions concerning the founders, such as George Hensley and Sherman Lawson. I found much consistency in their responses. The preachers were very open toward deaths from snakebite, arrest, and other problems that they have suffered. I do not feel that I received exaggerated answers from either preachers or laymen, for it is a violation of their beliefs to be untruthful or to exaggerate.

Finally, I discovered changes in the snake handlers' collective memory. I found it puzzling that in a group which uses the Bible as its rule book and in which tradition and belief are deeply ingrained, allowing little room for change, there have been many changes in belief, ritual, and life histories concerning the early church leaders. For example, George W. Hensley was married four times. But most church members see divorce and remarriage (being double-married) as sinful, so they blotted out recollections of Hensley's marital and extramarital activities. A pastor's wife near Harlan, Kentucky, attacked me for even mentioning the subject: "You reporters come down here from trying to find dirt on us then you print it in the papers! Aren't you that man from *Hustler?*" I replied, "No. I am from Indiana University," but she went on, "Well, as far as I am concerned the Devil sent you. George Hensley was a fine man. He never had all of those wives."

Children are almost sacred, not only to the snake handlers but to all people in Appalachia. However, according to Hensley's son Loyal, George tried to persuade his second wife (Irene) to put their children in an orphanage. Again, this matter has been erased from the collective memory of the snake handlers. In short, even though many of the early church members are still living, and the historical events in question are relatively recent, one would expect little change in reconstruction of those events. However, I have found many changes in the snake handlers' collective memory.

I discovered that, as other social scientists have noted, many recollections of events emerged out of the social context of telling and retelling the stories.[13] This was particularly apparent when I had several preachers together. Interviewing the ministers collectively reduced the chance that a single informant would try to gain prestige by falsely claiming to have been an eyewitness of an event. In spite of my precautions, memory has its flaws, and I have seen much evidence of that fact.[14] I have spent the past eight years tracing and retracing the footsteps of the early snake handlers in attempt to gain accuracy, to clarify and refine early studies.

Numerous newspaper accounts also exist on the founding years of the snake-handling movement. Even though I found many good news sources, many newspapers and magazines have sensationalized events over the years and are often unreliable and inaccurate. They have ridiculed the Holiness serpent handlers and have made little effort to chronicle good and reliable historical facts. A good example is an article run in the *Chattanooga Daily Times* on September 21, 1914.

A rattlesnake from the mountains near Ooltewah was turned loose in the tent of the Holy Rollers here this afternoon and resulted in a general stampede of the audience, although the reptile was freely handled by the fifteen or twenty "believers" and none of them harmed.

Charley Robinson, who lives near here, brought the snake in. He caught it in the mountains and brought it to Ooltewah in a shoe box. When he released it in the tent of the Holy Rollers there was more than four hundred people there. Robinson turned his snake loose when the "believers" were talking in unknown tongues. The first one to see it was a woman with a babe in her arms. She picked the reptile up and fondled it. At times it was within six inches of the face of the baby, but the child was not harmed.

There was a babel of voices for a few minutes. All of the Holy Rollers jabbered in unknown tongues and they took time about caressing the snake. They thrust it in the faces of one or two members of the audience that did not believe, but one or two was all. Others left before the snake-bearer reached them.

George Hensley, leader of the Holy Roller band, will be put to a severe test tonight if he accepts the challenge of Ooltewah citizens. In a recent sermon he said that those who believed could drink poison and it would not harm them. Some local people will enter his tent with carbolic acid tonight and offer it to him it is said.

Hensley announces that there will be a "big day" here sometime this week, and that in order to show the unbelievers that he is the Lord's chosen prophet he will walk the waters of the Tennessee river.

He will go to a point near Harrison, he says, and walk across the top of the water. Someone in his audience suggested that it would be safer to try a "branch" first, but Hensley says that he can walk on water and do any other miracle he desires. If he drinks the carbolic acid and walks the river, he will find some converts in Ooltewah.[15]

Hensley was misunderstood by the newspaper reporters. He had actually stated "that if the power was on him he could do anything," including "raising the dead, walking on water (near Harrison where the river was the widest), or drinking poison." The next evening, when he was at an emotional height in the act of handling rattlesnakes, a gentleman from the crowd took Hensley a bottle of Coca-Cola that had not been tampered with and told him it was carbolic acid. Believing that Coke bottle contained deadly poison, Hensley consumed its entire contents. In several episodes, Hensley did in fact drink strychnine, battery acid, and other lethal liquids, as well as handling snakes and fire.

Even though newspaper accounts of snake handling are generally sensationalized, much information was gained by many reporters such as Joe Creason of the *Louisville Courier-Journal*. The *Courier-Journal* has covered Kentucky's snake-handling movement in great detail. There was hardly an event that they did not report. Richard Golden of the *Knoxville News-Sentinel* also provided valuable insight into the events associated with the snake handlers. Golden took the classic pictures of the snake handlers in eastern Kentucky during the late 1940s and 1950s. He is also a wealth of information, since he knew many of the movement's founders.

Most historians use oral history primarily to fill in the gap left by written sources.[16] Oral history was my primary means of collecting information on the Holiness serpent handlers. Folklorist William Lynwood Montell states that "oral traditions can be utilized in historical writings, provided that these recollections are approached with proper caution." Montell also maintains that "accuracy of local historical legends is not the most important question to be faced by the person who gathers and analyzes them, but rather the essential fact is that these folk narratives are

The author handling a snake for the first time, Highway Holiness Church of God, Fort Wayne, Indiana, 1988 (Photo courtesy of the author)

believed by people who perpetuate them."[17] It is not so much a matter of fact versus fiction, he writes, as the social acceptance of traditional history.[18] This method, in conjunction with historical events in the life of Park Saylor and the Holiness serpent handlers, provides the nucleus of this study.

Despite its difficulties, my work has been fun and exciting. I have made many friends who have influenced my life. And despite my participant observation, some churches did remain suspicious of my presence and informed me that Christ had warned them about the dangers of outsiders: "Take heed to yourselves and to all the flock, in which the Holy Spirit has made you overseers, to care for the church of God which he obtained with the blood of his own Son. I know that after my departure fierce wolves will come in among you not sparing the flock; and from among your own selves will arise men speaking perverse things, to draw away the disciples after them" (Acts 20:28–30). Nevertheless, I have fond memories of my research on the snake handlers and continue to have close relationships with them.

This book centers on the emergence of the snake-handling movement in eastern Kentucky, focusing on the Saylor family. The first chapter reconstructs a snake-handling service that I observed near Hazard, Kentucky, in September 1988. Snake-handling meetings are not uniform; the congregations' practices vary. I used this gathering to illustrate the Holiness worship service because almost all of the "signs" were followed at this particu-

The author handling a snake, Highway Holiness Church of God, Fort Wayne, Indiana, 1990. Arnold Saylor Jr. is standing in the background. (Photo courtesy of Arnold Saylor)

lar church. The second chapter covers George W. Hensley's emergence in 1910 near Chattanooga, Tennessee, along with the rise of snake handling, and follows him during his troubled years in Ohio. Hensley is regarded as the founder of the snake-handling movement, and his constant evangelizing resulted in the movement's spreading throughout Appalachia, the South, and some industrial centers in the North. He was found in many key issues and controversial matters during the early years of the snake-handling churches, such as problems with the law or denominational differences.

Chapter 3 continues with Hensley after his move to Kentucky in the early 1930s and covers the Saylor family's entry into the movement. Since so much variation in belief is found in snake-handling churches "from holler to holler," I decided to focus on the Saylors and trace their religious history, from the family members' settlement in eastern Kentucky in 1805 to their present-day convictions and practices.

Chapter 4 recounts the pioneer era of Harlan County, Kentucky, and the settlement of Solomon and Sarah Saylor. It examines the Saylors' communal and noncapitalist lifestyles and their close reliance on family for assistance in times of hardship. Exchange of goods and work is also considered, along with the Saylors' religious practice. Upon settlement they were

Park (far right) and Alma Saylor with a friend, 1987. Park is holding a picture of his grandfather. (Photo courtesy of Park Saylor)

traditional Scotch-Irish Presbyterians with a deep Calvinist heritage. Due to the influence of Baptist farmer preachers and of Methodist circuit riders that reached the Saylor's isolated home, a folk religion developed in which preachers emerged from the laity. Religious practice was groomed to fit the circumstances at hand. Chapter 4 closes and Chapter 5 continues with Solomon Saylor's son, John, and grandson, Josiah, who practiced the same lifestyle as their ancestors. During Josiah's lifetime, pressures on subsistence farming and the Saylors' traditional kinship practices began to transform the family's life in the years after the Civil War. Customary farming methods were gradually obliterated by the growth of the native population, together with the advent of capitalist land barons. Due to the shortage of land, Josiah Saylor and his son, Zachariah, could not rely on subsistence farming for security, as their fathers had. Traditional self-sufficient agricultural practices had failed to teach them the importance of accumulating capital, thus they were destitute and could not buy land. Out of necessity, Zachariah Saylor's son, John Austen, like many other mountaineers, moved into the coal camps that were built in the 1920s. This was the final stage of transition from a noncommercial economy to a capitalistic economy. The rapid changes that occurred in the mountains with the introduction of capitalism caused problems such as massive population growth, increased homicides, malnutrition, and many other horrors. Even the conventional forms of religious practices had been altered, leaving mountaineers largely unsatisfied with their churches. During this era of great upheaval, Holiness preachers emerged, restoring customary worship habits, such as emotionalism, and ancestral preaching methods. The Holiness preachers were given credit for "working miracles" and giving hope in the brutal world that had emerged. During the 1930s Holiness religion intensified further when George W. Hensley arrived preaching snake handling, as described in Mark 16. Hensley's snake handling was what impressed mountaineers most, and he gained many converts, including the Saylor family. From the introduction of Hensley's snake handling until the present, the Saylors have clung to the practice of snake handling.

Chapter 6 continues with the struggle between the capitalists and the mountaineers and describes how snake-handling religion intensified as times got worse. Hensley's evangelizing in the South continued, although he had suffered snakebites himself and had witnessed the snakebite deaths of other church members. Due to the snakebite deaths, several states passed anti-snake-handling legislation in attempt to stop the practice. However, the laws were unsuccessful.

Chapter 7 covers the period after Hensley moved back to Tennessee, when he became involved in arrests as a result of his snake-handling exercises. On July 24, 1955, Hensley was killed by a rattlesnake bite while evangelizing in Florida. Chapter 8 returns to eastern Kentucky and observes the persecution that the snake handlers were subjected to by the authorities, while Chapter 9 examines the religion in eastern Kentucky up to present times.

Chapter 10 surveys the outmigration of Appalachians from the eastern Kentucky coalfields to industrial centers like Detroit, Chicago, and Fort Wayne during the 1940s. These people were unsatisfied with the religious practices they found in such cities and established their own churches. In some cases, snake handling was brought to the industrial centers. For example, Arnold Saylor established a church in Fort Wayne that was passed on to his son following his death. Church members there handle snakes almost weekly. The Fort Wayne church has kept strong ties to family members who have remained in eastern Kentucky—people who represent what some Appalachian sociologists refer to as the "stem family." These strong bonds back to eastern Kentucky constantly reinforce religious convictions in the cities, preserving the snake handlers' heritage.

One. Snake Handlers
Pass Challenge of Blowtorch

The Holiness serpent handlers, who originated in 1910 among the Church of God Holiness, are one of the most controversial religious groups in American history.[1] For the most part, all the general public knows about this religious group are the highly sensationalized events reported by magazines, television, or newspapers. Generally, the media makes little effort to explore the heritage of the snake handlers' beliefs, instead leaving the public to conclude that they are freaks or weirdos. In fact, the snake handlers are not weird or strange. They have a strong fundamentalist base firmly grounded in a religious heritage that can easily

Brother Kale's church in Kentucky, 1988 (Photo by the author)

be traced to the revivals conducted at Cambuslang, Scotland, in the seventeenth century.

The snake handlers have also been persecuted by the authorities, and this persecution has given the general public a bad impression of their religion. Throughout the history of the movement, law officials have badgered church members by ridiculing them, jailing them, and using other means to break up snake-handling religious gatherings. However, the religion has endured the attacks, and meetings continue to be conducted—every night, in some locations.

Adopting a form of old-line fundamentalist Appalachian religion, snake handlers believe that the Holy Ghost grants them the power to heal the sick; perform exorcisms; speak in new tongues; drink poisons like strychnine, battery acid, or lye; and handle deadly serpents. They base their beliefs primarily upon a passage from Mark that reports the words of Christ before his ascension into the heavens: "And these signs shall follow them that believe; in my name shall they cast out devils; they shall speak with new tongues; They shall take up serpents; and if they drink any deadly thing, it shall not hurt them; they shall lay hands on the sick and they shall recover" (Mark 16:17–18; all biblical quotations are from the King James version).

They also cite several other passages to sanction their beliefs and practices, including Luke 10:19 ("Behold, I give unto you power to tread on

Old Rural Street church in Austin, Indiana, 1987 (Photo by the author)

serpents and scorpions, and over the power of the enemy: and nothing by any means shall hurt you"); Acts 28:3–6, which says that Paul shook off a viper that was "fastened on his hand" without suffering any ill effects; and Exodus 4:2–4, which tells how Moses, at God's command, transformed his rod into a serpent and picked it up by its tail.

Some believers argue that Jesus was a serpent handler, citing 2 Timothy 2:6 as evidence: "The husbandman that laboureth must be first partaker of the fruits." Anthropologist Steven M. Kane, who spent many years doing research among the snake handlers, states that he was given an additional text—John 20:30: "And many other signs truly did Jesus in the presence of his disciples, which are not written in this book."[2] After quoting these passages, the snake handlers add, "He wouldn't tell you to do something he didn't do himself." From the pulpits of eastern Kentucky the signs are preached on nightly, along with reports of other miracles, such as levitations and raising the dead.

The Sunday morning service is conducted at 11 A.M. In one service that I witnessed, members began to gather around 10 A.M. in order to socialize and to discuss events that had transpired in the mountains during the past week. On many occasions the congregations have visitors from Alabama, Michigan, and Indiana. As more of the faithful arrived, members of the same sex shook hands, hugged, and occasionally kissed each other on the lips, as dictated in Romans 16:16 ("Salute one another with an holy kiss").

Praying at a Saylor Cemetery Homecoming, 1990. Note the snake boxes under the bench. (Photo by the author)

Men and women exchanged only handshakes. Some younger male members affectionately hugged older women who were special to them.

Many people arrived with a variety of musical instruments, including acoustic and electric guitars, fiddles, steel guitars, bass guitars, pianos, harmonicas, drums, banjos, and cymbals. Generally, the musicians in the churches play with great skill. As more people entered the church, the musicians began to tune their instruments. When the preacher entered the building, he hugged people and welcomed the gathering. Some members of the congregation greeted him with statements such as "Bless him, Lord," or "Be with him, Jesus." The pastor displayed considerable fondness toward the young children in the gathering. He asked one young boy, "Are you married yet, son?" The young man blushed and replied, "No, I'm not even out of school yet." The congregation laughed, and the preacher moved to the next child to pick on. All of the children appeared to love the pastor and joked back with him.

Around 10:30 the church began to fill, and members began to get serious. As in most snake-handling churches in eastern Kentucky, men sat on one side of the building and women on the other. A few male members brought in wooden boxes covered with wire mesh; these boxes contained rattlesnakes, copperheads, and cottonmouths. Some boxes housed a single

Joshua Saylor displays a snake box containing a rattlesnake, 1991. (Photo by Warren Brunner)

snake, while others held up to five. The boxes were placed under the deacon's bench.[3]

As the church filled, some musicians began to play hymns, and a few female members started singing and clapping their hands. They were soon joined by the whole congregation. The sound was deafening. Cymbals clashed, tambourines jingled, feet stomped, hands clapped, as the worshipers sang a song called "Feel Like Traveling On":

My heavenly home is bright and fair,
I feel like traveling on,
Nor pain, nor death, can enter there,
I feel like traveling on.

Yes, I feel like traveling on,
I feel like traveling on,

My heavenly home is bright and fair,
I feel like traveling on.

Its glittering towers the sun outshine,
I feel like traveling on.
That heavenly mansion shall be mine,
I feel like traveling on.

Let others seek a home below,
I feel like traveling on,
Which flames devour, or waves o'erflow,
I feel like traveling on.

The Lord has been so good to me,
I feel like traveling on,
Until that blessed home I see,
I feel like traveling on.

Some members raised their hands in the air during the music and began shouting and talking in unknown tongues, as described in Mark 16. A few jumped up and down, screaming phrases like "Praise the Lord" and "Halle-lujah, precious Jesus." One young man jumped up from his seat and ran to the front of the church. He reached into one of the snake boxes, removed a large rattlesnake, and shouted, "Glory, thank you, Lord." An elderly gen-tleman clad in bib overalls opened a box and handled five rattlesnakes simultaneously. The music continued, and some of the congregation danced and shook uncontrollably. Many communicants focused their at-tention on the snake handling, while others were involved in their own spiritual experience.

The young man who first handled the snake passed it to another man. This member began to cry and jump up and down, screaming, "Thank you, Jesus!" The minister took a rattlesnake and placed it on an open Bible that sat on the lectern. The snake immediately coiled, as if it was ready to strike the pastor. The preacher then laid his head on the reptile without being bitten. Church members shouted, "Bless him, Lord." The preacher started talking in tongues: "Oh-shana-dee, oh shana-dee-la-inter-dee-cors." He picked up the snake and rubbed it in his face, again escaping injury. A man in his mid-forties placed his bare feet in a box of copperheads, while a thirty-five-year-old man opened a box of snakes and placed it over his head and danced ecstatically. Neither man was bitten.

A young woman shouted, "Sweet Jesus," and grabbed a snake from a fellow member. She jumped up and down several times and also spoke in

Joe Short, near Manchester, Kentucky, 1988 (Photo by the author)

tongues. A young child started walking toward the front of the church, where the snakes were being handled, and was stopped immediately. (Snake handling is usually performed in the front of the building in order to protect those who do not participate in the ritual.)

After forty-five minutes of singing and snake handling, the excitement began to subside. Then an elderly woman jumped up and testified to the congregation, "I love the Lord today. He is so good to me. He has healed my body many times. I praise him for it. Lots of times I got down and out but the Lord has always come to my rescue. He healed my body many times and I love him so. Hallelujah to God! Pray for me that I will never get out of the Lord. Hallelujah!" Other members shouted, "Bless her, Glory to God." The woman returned to her seat, and the minister cheered, "Hallelujah! If you people have something to say, say it! I said, say it! Praise the Lord!"

The preacher then asked the congregation if any prayer requests were needed. A gentleman from Alabama stood and said, "Brother, a woman from Fort Payne lost her son in a terrible automobile accident. She is so hurt. Please remember her in your prayers." A woman stood and stated, "My father is getting weaker every day. I beg you all to pray for him." Other members made special prayer requests in regard to catastrophic events, illness, and hope for "sinners who have done wrong." When the prayer began, many worshipers went to the front of the church, to a clear area between the pulpit and the first row of seats. Other members stayed at their benches. They turned to the back of their seat and knelt, resting their

Sister Hall, near Manchester, Kentucky, 1988 (Photo by the author)

arms on the seat and bowing their heads. Some members of the congregation knelt on the floor. All of the congregation prayed aloud in unison. Again, some members spoke in unknown tongues. This ritual lasted for approximately fifteen minutes. The minister then asked for someone to rise and "sing us a song." A woman rose and sang,

Can't nobody hide, can't nobody hide,
Can't nobody hide from God.
You may hide it from the preacher,
But you shore can't hide it from God.

Can't nobody hide, Well can't nobody hide,
Can't nobody hide from God.
You may hide it from the deacon,
But you shore can't hide it from God.

Can't nobody hide, Well can't nobody hide,
Can't nobody hide from God.

The instrumentalists joined in, and the hymn lasted for about ten minutes. One man opened a snake box and handled a copperhead. After the song, the preacher walked to the front of the church and began to deliver his message. "I'm glad to see you all here today. We have people from Florida, Alabama, Georgia, and Indiana with us Kentuckians today. Isn't that wonderful, praise God. I wish we could be in church all of the time. Praise God. There will be a day that we can, if we continue to live right. I tell you, Brother Bob, it has got to be Holiness. Peter didn't say, I build these churches on these rocks. He said, On this rock I build this church." Many members shouted, "Amen." The preacher continued,

> You can't live like other people and make it to heaven. The other day, I was in a woman's house and she had a television playing. Her children was watching that thing, Ah. No good can come from that, Ah. When I questioned her about it, Ah, she said she only had it on for the news, Ah. Brother Jim, you must keep away from evil such as television, Ah. They contain every kind of filth known to man, Ah. You should never let your children watch television, Ah. I tell you, many of you care more about your dogs than you do your children, Ah. You chain up your dogs to keep them from getting hurt, Ah. You turn your babies out on the street to get hurt, Ah. When they are watching television or on the street, they see prostitution, homosexuality, drugs, and every kind of evil there is.[4]

The preacher began to shake and cry frantically. He screamed, "You've got to keep your babies in church, Brother Ben. Some of these preachers say they have a vision. The only vision they have is television. My own son came home from school one day with an earring in his ear. When I saw that, I threw him clear out of the house. Now many of you say that little earring can't hurt anything. Let me tell you this. That little earring will only lead to worse things. Before long the spirit of the homosexual will be on you. I want to live clean and not look like some sissy."

The crowd shouted, "Amen," and the preacher continued with a fiery message that lasted an hour. After he completed his sermon, he pulled out a handkerchief and wiped the perspiration from his face. He then said, "Thank God. Now let's hear one of you brothers testify. Come on, Brother Bob." Brother Bob walked to the lectern and preached for fifteen minutes on the evils of the federal government. He concluded, "I tell you brothers something. They may be in power now, but they will have to answer for the evils for all eternity, and eternity is forever."

Everyone was given a chance to testify, and ten people did so, on various topics. Some declared that they have been blessed with miraculous cures.

One woman stood and asked the congregation to pray for her. Many members walked to the front of the church and placed their hands on the woman. They formed a circle around her and rubbed olive oil on her forehead. All of the members prayed aloud and in their own words. Three other people then walked to the front of the church and asked to be "prayed over."

The preacher proclaimed, "The Lord will heal you if you believe. The Bible says, 'These signs will follow those who believe. They shall lay their hands on the sick and they shall recover.'"[5] As the service draws to an end, the pastor said, "Come on, boys. Do your job. Let's hear a song." The service had lasted for four hours. A young man rose and began a hymn, and the instrumentalists joined in.

I wanna live so God can use me,
Oh, anywhere Lord anytime.
I wanna live so God can use me,
Well, anywhere Lord anytime.

I wanna sing so God can use me,
Oh, anywhere Lord anytime.
I wanna sing so God can use me,
Well, anywhere Lord anytime.

I wanna pray so God can use me,
Oh, anywhere Lord anytime.
I wanna pray so God can use me,
Well, anywhere Lord anytime.

The congregation then began to handle snakes again. One man rolled over coiled rattlesnakes that he had placed on the floor; he escaped unharmed. Another man grabbed a fire bottle, lit it, and held it to his face for sixty seconds. He received no burns; various parts of his body were smoke-blackened, but he showed no other signs of having been in the fire. One by one the worshipers started to leave the building, as the musicians continued playing various songs. Later in the evening, the congregation would return for Sunday night service.

Archie Robertson suggests that hymns such as the ones performed in the service are a "better clue than the remarks of preachers to what the people in the pews are really thinking."[6] This is especially true of the snake handlers. The following is a song composed by an unknown snake handler, titled "I'm A Holiness Child," which mentions the five Bible signs that the snake handlers in eastern Kentucky practice. Other versions of this hymn are found throughout the mountains. The verses are generally rewritten to fit the particular situation.

I believe in the Bible. I believe it's right.
I believe you got to live holy, live a good clean life.

[chorus] I'm a Holiness Child, yeah, I'm a Holiness Child—
If anybody asks you who I am tell 'em I'm a Holiness Child.

You have to have the Father, you have to have the Son,
You have to have the Holy Ghost, baptized, speaking in tongues.

The Holiness train is loaded, so try to get on board, and
Holiness without, no man will ever see the Lord.

I read about ol' Moses, and what he had in his hand,
Oh, yes it was a serpent and not a sinner man.

I believe in Mark 16, and every word is true,
I believe in casting out devils, and taking up serpents too.

The Bible says one Spirit and Jesus paid the cost
and you can't say Jesus is Lord, but by the Holy Ghost.

I went down to the altar with a hunger in my soul,
I did not care what the people said for the Spirit had control.

I went down to the altar and went down in a run,
I came up from the altar with the Holy Ghost, speaking in tongues.

No, you can't make me doubt it, you've come to late to change,
The Bible means just what it says and it's gonna stay the same.

I believe in casting out devils in my Savior's name, it's true.
I believe in laying hands on the sick and speaking with new tongues too.

There's no way I'll doubt it, they've come too late to change.
The Bible means what it says, and it's gonna stay the same.

They say it's wrong to carry the [snake] box, but if it's in our Savior's
   will
If they would try to move so fast they'd be taking up serpents still.

The signs have come a long way and many have been killed,
Because they tried to move too fast and got out of God's will.

Now the signs are right no matter what the people say. "He that
Believeth not shall be damned and he that believes shall be saved."[7]

Bruce Helton handling fire, near Hazard, Kentucky, 1988 (Photo by the author)

One additional practice of the snake handlers, not covered in this hymn, is the ritual handling of fire. Fire handling emerged almost simultaneously with snake handling among the Church of God congregations. Members invoke several biblical passages in order to sanction their use of fire in religious services, including Isaiah 43:2 ("When thou walkest through fire, thou shall not be burned; neither shall the flame kindle upon thee"); Hebrews 11:34 ("Faith quenched the violence of fire"); 1 Peter 1:7 ("That the trial of your faith, being much more precious than of gold that perisheth, though it be tried with fire, might be found unto praise and honour and glory at the appearing of Jesus Christ"); and Daniel 3:20–27, which reports the release of Shadrach, Meshach, and Abednego from the "fiery furnace."

According to Steven Kane, between the years 1914 and the early 1920s, fire handling exceeded snake handling in frequency. By the middle of the 1930s the practice was almost nonexistent in the Church of God. It was still occurring in "various independent or 'Free Pentecostal' Holiness groups, which earlier had adopted the rites, continued to carry them out. They have done so up to the present."[8] He described fire handling thus:

The torches used consist of soda pop bottles or brake fluid cans filled at least halfway with "coal oil" (kerosene) and provided with tightly twisted, cotton-rag wicks. They give a very sooty, bright orange-yellow flame 6 to 20 inches high. At the emotional peak of a religious gathering, amidst the din of vigorously strummed guitars, clashing cymbals and tambourines, shouting, and singing, communicants light the torches and put the flames to various body parts and articles of clothing. More men than women take part, and their demonstrations are usually more dramatic. Among both sexes there is considerable variation in frequency and manner of handling. Virtually all fire handlers also handle snakes, though not always at the same meeting. The great majority of snake handlers, however, never handle fire, and in every church there are members that abstain from both practices.[9]

As Kentucky snake handler Bradley Shell once said, "They wrote a story about us one time in *Foxfire*, but its not foxfire, it's real fire. The Holy Ghost fire."

Church members who handle fire and serpents speak of receiving the power to do so by "anointing," "faith," and "innocence." The most common method is by anointing—the state that occurs when God transfers spiritual power to an individual. Worshipers believe that the Holy Ghost at that point takes control of their faculties and allows them to carry out God's works, such as handling serpents, fire handling, prophecy, healing the sick, raising the dead, and so on. In three separate interviews, the preachers Liston Pack, Arnold Saylor, and Kale Saylor described the anointing to me:

Liston Pack: If you saw me get anointed you would think I was having a stroke. My hands start drawing and I get a warm feeling all over.
Kimbrough: Is that how everyone acts?
Liston Pack: No, everyone is different. If I told you how you should feel, I might tell you wrong. When I'm anointed, I can see into the future, talk in tongues, and tell when someone is lying to me. You might not be able to do that. When I'm anointed, even my complexion is pale.
Kimbrough: Does the music get you excited enough to get anointed?
Liston Pack: No, you cannot pump up for anointment. The Spirit moves on you.

Arnold Saylor: When you are anointed, colors look different, people look different, sometimes you can see into the future. It is hard to describe. When the power is on me, I can handle any snake. I have had them to strike me, over and over, and not be able to get a fang into me. It is a wonderful thing, Dave, it is hard to describe.

Kale Saylor: It is like someone poured cold water over me when I'm anointed.

Church members have reported that the Spirit has moved on them while driving a car, walking in the woods, or doing other activities. Arnold Saylor said that once while he was en route to Kentucky from his home in Fort Wayne, Indiana, he and the other passengers in his car began singing and playing gospel music, and the Spirit moved on them. "As we were singing and passing through Cincinnati, the Spirit moved on us and we actually began to pass serpents. . . . As we crossed the big bridge in Cincinnati, we were passing snakes."

Many have mistakenly believed they were under the anointing and received lethal bites. One example is Walter Henry of Cleveland, Tennessee. On August 25, 1946, Henry was killed by a rattlesnake after he declared that "the power and anointing would guard him from the serpent's fangs."[10] Only days earlier, the same snake had killed eighteen-year-old Harry Skelton, who was also supposed to be anointed. Several others have perished believing that they were "protected by God's shield."

The second means is by faith. Church members have confidence in God and believe that God will not allow any harm to affect them, even if they receive snakebites, provided that they are living a "good life." On occasion, after someone receives a severe bite, church members will enjoin, "Just hold your faith, brother. If your faith's strong enough, that bite ain't gonna hurt you."

A fifty-year-old Newport, Tennessee man said "If you have enough faith the Lord isn't going to let you get hurt." Reminded that many snake handlers have been killed by snakebite, he responded, "Yes, and the reason is because they lost faith. See, you are going to eventually get bit, but you don't have to die. Just keep your faith that God will help you. Jeremiah 8:17 says, 'For behold, I will send serpents, cockatrices, among you, which will not be charmed, and they shall bite you, saith the Lord.' " From the earliest days of snake handling, the "faithful" have received bites. In September of 1939, Mrs. Alvie Weaver was bitten by a copperhead at the McGhee Street Church of God in Knoxville, Tennessee. Mrs. Weaver declared that she was bitten because of her "lack of faith" and as a way to "make believers out of some people." She also stated that a group of Kentuckians from Middlesboro, who had visited her church a week prior to the bite, had had more faith: "Why them women made hats out of those snakes—they quiled 'em in their hair and wrapped them around their necks. Them people over in Kentucky have more faith in the power of the Lord than we have. They even had a baby handling those snakes—why he wasn't no bigger than my little one here. Yes sir! he picked that snake up and put it back in the box."[11]

The final source of power for handling serpents is innocence. Some church members believe that children can handle serpents because they are young and do not commit sin willfully. I have watched children freely handle rattlesnakes without being bitten. However, it is very rare for children to handle snakes; most preachers will not allow children to go near the snake-handling activity. Children have not always escaped injury, either. The *New York Times* reported on August 1, 1940, that a copperhead struck five-year-old Leitha Ann Rowan of Adel, Georgia, along with six to eight other believers.[12] The bites occurred at an outside meeting in the family's yard.[13] The others were not harmed by the bites, but Leitha became ill.

The child's father, Albert Rowan, described as a "mild-mannered tenant farmer," was arrested and held in jail on a misdemeanor charge, along with Reverend W. T. Lipham, who was booked for malicious mischief. Lipham was reported to have handled serpents for thirty years. When the men were jailed, they fasted for divine deliverance. Sheriff W. I. Daugherty had no tolerance for the snake handlers and told reporters, "These people handle snakes promiscuously and it is against their religion to accept medical treatment."[14] Superior Judge Smith also had little patience for the believers and issued a temporary countywide injunction against such rights, pending a hearing on a permanent order.

Leitha's mother hid her for over seventy-two hours to prevent medical treatment, believing the Lord would heal her. Relatives then turned the child over to authorities and permitted a medical examination, because Judge Smith had "ruled that Lipham and Rowan would face murder charges if the child died."[15] The relatives claimed that the girl had already "practically recovered." Dr. H. W. Clements disagreed, announcing that the bite was serious. Solicitor General Homer Nelson said the girl might lose an arm. The following is a description of Leitha's examination: "Leitha Ann sat upright on the physician's examination table, but did not talk as Dr. Clements examined her. The child's arm was still swollen from the effects of the bite, [and] her palm and her body were discolored."[16] Eleven days after the bite, Dr. Clements determined that Leitha was out of danger, and the child's father was released from jail on a $3,000 bond. Leitha recovered fully from the bite.

In an incident that occurred near Nashville, Tennessee, authorities intervened to prevent a child from handling serpents. On September 1, 1934, Reverend Deway Dotson declared at the office of the *Nashville Tennessean* that he would "handle all the rattlesnakes anyone would bring to an upcoming revival that was to be held on the night of Sunday, September 9."[17] His ten-year-old son, Deway Jr., announced that he would handle them also. His father interceded and said, "If the Spirit moves on him." George W. Brown, secretary of the Humane and Juvenile Court Commission, would not accept the boy's statement. He proclaimed, "That man can let a rattlesnake bite him all he wants to, but if he dares put that boy in a cage or near a box where there is a snake he will be arrested."[18] As Dotson left for a fishing trip with his brother-in-law, he encouraged reporters to attend the upcoming revival. "I won't catch any rattlesnakes while on my fishing trip," he said. "I want other people to bring their own rattlesnakes. If I bring one they would say I took the poison sacs out of it."[19] In October 1947, Joe Creason of the *Louisville Courier-Journal* wrote a convincing article arguing that the snakes at a recent snake-handling meeting had not been tampered with: "One look at the rigid, swollen, right hand of Faye Nolan, the 12-year old handler who was bitten by a rattler at a Cawood, Ky., meeting September 28, will convince even the most skeptical that the snakes do have fangs and that they pack a powerful, often deadly, wallop."[20]

In the late 1950s, the *Middlesboro Daily News* ran an article on an Arjay, Kentucky man named James Estep, who had been bitten by a rattlesnake after a religious service at a Pineville radio station. While Estep was convalescing at his home and being interviewed by the newspaper, he asked a friend named Frank to pray for him as he fondled a four-foot rattlesnake; his injured hand "hung at his side in a blood-stained cloth."[21] In the past three years, Estep had been bitten thirty-one times on his face, stomach, arms and hands. One frightening feature of the interview was that Estep had also allowed his two-and-a-half-year-old son to handle serpents. He said, "I let Donnie have a hold of a few, but I never let him go with them."[22]

I have found no documented reports of a child dying from a snakebite in a religious service, but in 1983, M. C. Garrott of the *Murray Ledger and Times* stated that he recalled a "case of a little girl who had been bitten on the hand by a poisonous snake during one of the meetings and whose parents refused to permit medical attention for her." She did recover, Garrott said, but he thought she was left with a "withered hand and arm."[23]

Generally, adults are arrested if a child is bitten, as Leitha Rowan's father was. Sixty-four-year-old preacher Reece Ramsey of Chattanooga,

Young girl handling snakes at the Kentucky/Virginia line meetings in the early 1950s (Photo courtesy of Richard Golden)

Tennessee, was apprehended by authorities after fourteen-year-old Pauline Barbee was bitten at a brush arbor meeting near Dolly Pond in 1948. The girl suffered no ill effects from the bite. Pauline absolved Ramsey of blame "and said she reached for the snake while 'shouting under the power.' "[24]

Snakes have also perished after biting believers. On July 23, 1945, the *New York Times* featured a story titled "Snake Bites Man and Dies," about a snake handler named Luther Morrow in Grasshopper, Tennessee. On July 22, Morrow was bitten by a large rattlesnake in a church service. The following morning, the snake died, while Morrow put in a full day's work in the hot sun at his farm.[25] I have seen many rattlesnakes die in the hands of a believer. Snake handlers tell me that the primary reason a snake dies in their hands is because they are in such an anointed state that the "power" kills the reptile.

Pentecostal, Holy Roller, and Free Pentecostal are only a few of the labels applied to Holiness groups in the United States. The snake handlers are one of many subgroups found in this branch of the Christian religion. Perhaps only 2,500 people nationally are actual snake handlers. They are found primarily in the southern Appalachian states. Most Holiness people do have common beliefs, such as an individual "working to be filled with the Holy Ghost." Evidence that this has happened is seen in glossolalia, or speaking in tongues, as described in the second chapter of Acts. Many Pentecostals who believe they have been given other supernatural gifts, such as the ability to heal, to give prophecy, and interpret the act of speaking in tongues, are still violently opposed to snake handling. One Harlan County Pentecostal preacher was fiercely opposed to snake handling, even after I cited to him the scriptural basis of the practice. "I'm telling you they are wrong! They are crazy! The Lord does not want you to play with snakes," he said.

When I told Park Saylor of this conversation, he responded very stoically:

> See, many preachers today are against the Bible signs. They will have healing in their church, but there is no sting in healing. They won't have serpent handling. I want you to get this in the back of your mind. If you find a man that tells you he follows the signs, but won't have serpent handling, then he is not full-gospel. If you ask a man if he believes in serpent handling and he says no, then he has denied the word of God. Foolish things confound the mighty. Well, it looks foolish to anoint a man with oil. It looks foolish to this world for a man that God has moved on to flip the lid on a snake box and say God has moved on him to lift up a serpent. The problem is, people who condemn us doesn't know any better because they haven't been taught. . . . So many people, including preachers, only want to practice certain parts of the Bible. They only want to preach on what suits them. They leave out what doesn't suit them. That will get them in trouble. The word of God stands to every man. It is for our learning and teaching. Many men have tried to change it. There was a man named Bud Pfaff, who witnessed people getting the Holy Ghost. He rejected it and joined the Methodists. I feel he missed the line.

On occasion some ministers have to curb the practice of serpent handling in their congregations. Various pastors have informed me that some members attend church only to handle snakes and do not follow the other signs, such as healing. The wife of a Middlesboro, Kentucky preacher made the following comment: "My husband has stopped serpent handling for a while. Before and after that sister got bit, a lot of the people were only interested in serpent handling. He told them that he wanted to see other signs followed, such as healing the sick, before he allows snake handling again. We must understand the real reason we are in church. It is to worship God. Snake handling is secondary. We believe in it [serpent handling], but it is our duty to make the people understand the real reason we have church."

Park Saylor agreed. "If people only come to church to handle serpents, then they are doing it for the wrong reason. I have instructed people for years to be fully anointed by God before they stick their hand in that snake box. Don't just do it because others do it. Make sure God's power is on you before you do it."

The snake handlers are divided into two factions in respect to their interpretation of the Godhead: they are known as either Jesus' Name or Trinity people. The Saylor family is of the Trinity belief, and Reverend Kale Saylor recited this song to sanction his position:

There is a strange doctrine in our land today
Deceiving our people and leading them astray
They teach there is just one in that beautiful place
But when they come to judgment there will be three they must face.

The Father, the Son, and the sweet Holy Ghost
The Apostles, and Prophets, and the Heavenly Host
The books will be open to see what they've done
They'll be cast into darkness for teaching just one.
While Stephen was stoned by a murderous mob
He saw Jesus standing at the right hand of God.

Jesus' Name, Jesus Only, Unitarian, Oneless, or Oneness churches believe that the Father, Son, and Holy Ghost are the same being and that the titles are used only to specify diverse features of Christ's person. The Trinitarian or Three God people argue that the Father, Son, and Holy Ghost are separate. Both snake-handling and non-snake-handling Pentecostal and Holiness denominations have had bitter arguments over the issue. The Jesus Only churches use Acts 2:38 to sanction their position: "Then Peter said unto them, Repent, and be baptized every one of you in the name of Jesus Christ for the remission of sins, and ye shall receive the gift of the Holy Ghost."[26] They also cite Isaiah 9:6 ("For unto us a child is born, unto us a son is given: and the government shall be upon his shoulder: and his name shall be called Wonderful, Counsellor, The mighty God, The everlasting Father, The Prince of Peace"); Matthew 1:23 ("Behold, a virgin shall be with child and shall bring forth a son, and they shall call his name Emmanuel, which being interpreted is God with us"); and John 14:8–9 ("Philip saith unto him, Lord, shew us the father, and sufficeth us.

Jesus said unto him, Have I been so long time with you, and yet hast thou not known me, Philip? He that hath seen me hath seen the father; and how sayest thou then, Shew us the father?").

The Trinity churches also use biblical evidence to justify their stand. They cite Mark 16:19 ("So then after the Lord had spoken unto them, he was received up into heaven, and sat on the right hand of God"); John 3:16 ("For God so loved the world that he gave his only begotten Son, that whosoever believeth in him shall not perish but have everlasting life"); and Matthew 28:19 ("Go therefore and make disciples of all nations, baptizing them in the name of the Father and of the Son and of the Holy Spirit").

Most snake handlers avoid wearing any type of jewelry and refrain from extravagant dress. In many churches, even a person who bears just a wedding ring or watch is seen as sinful. The snake handlers argue that 1 Peter 1:18 justifies this position: "Forasmuch as ye know that ye were not redeemed with corruptible things, as silver and gold from your vain conversation received by tradition from your fathers." The women wear long print or solid-colored dresses and abstain from makeup or other cosmetics. They do not artificially curl or cut their hair; It is usually pulled to the back of their head and bobbed. They cite 1 Corinthians 11:14–15 as support for their belief: "Doth not even nature itself teach you, that if a man have long hair it is a shame unto him? But if a woman have long hair, it is a glory to her: for her hair is given her for a covering."

Arnold Saylor told me,

After my wife was saved she took off her wedding rings and flushed them down the commode. I am against women cutting their hair, and I will tell you why. If a woman says she is just cutting the dead ends off her hair, the next thing she does is cut it off to her shoulders, because she claims it is hot. Then she cuts it off like a man's next. The next time you see her she will be wearing britches. I believe that cutting off the first dead end of hair is a gradual, step-by-step process to developing the spirit of a homosexual. It is a sin for a woman to act like a man. One thing leads to another. Even the small things. Before long you get away from God. I certainly don't believe an angel cuts her hair.

In a similar vein, Perry Bettis declared in a January 31, 1988 sermon at Middlesboro, Kentucky, "I tell you women, it is easy for you to get led astray with all of these ads for makeup. Let me tell all of you this, there is no beauty in some women running around here all painted up, and looking like some Jezebel."[27]

Male communicants are clean-shaven and neatly groomed, with short hair. They wear long-sleeved shirts with dress slacks. Some Holiness men wear blue jeans, and many older male believers wear blue denim bib overalls. Neckties are frowned on in most churches because they suggest that one may be getting "proud and worldly." George Hensley's son, James Roscoe Hensley, informed me that wearing detachable shirt collars in churches used to be prohibited.

In Wesleyan fashion, the Saylor family is violently opposed to the use of alcohol and tobacco. Kale Saylor recited this song, called "Tobacco Song," about women using tobacco:

Now when you confess you are angry, cross, and all wrong,
Craving a chew and your plug is all gone.
Oh, where does your patience and religion lie,
On a plug of tobacco or a home in the sky.
A very small babe sitting on his mother's knee,
A-chewing tobacco, a sad sight to see.
While the filthy ol' snuff and the fair lady's dip,
Has spoiled her great beauty by filling her lip.

Local autonomy does prevail in these matters; some churches give men and women the freedom to express their own opinions about their appearance. However, the Trinitarian churches in the Pineville / Harlan area, where my work focused, follow the strictest line and cling to very traditional beliefs. Pastors such as Kale Saylor are stern in their values, even on the question of women wearing shorts in their own homes: "To start with, if a woman only wears shorts in her own home, the next thing she will do is just run down to the grocery store for a minute. Before long she will be running around all over the place looking like that. If she has pretty legs the men will be looking at her, and that's when the trouble starts. It's best to just stay covered up."[28] Opel Lawson added, "You are always in view of God." Lawson, who now lives in the Cincinnati area, is the daughter-in-law of the famous evangelical preacher Sherman Lawson. The woman is credited with having tremendous healing powers and the gift of prophecy.

Local autonomy governs the church service itself. An example is the variety in interpretations of Romans 16:16 ("Salute one another with a holy kiss"). Other scriptures that appear to sanction kissing among church brethren are 2 Corinthians 13:12−13 ("Greet one another with an holy kiss") and 1 Peter 5:14 ("Greet ye one another with a kiss of charity"). Arnold Saylor understood the verses to mean that only members of the same sex should kiss each other: "You have to use wisdom. Men shouldn't be kissing women other than their wife. If I would encourage that kind of stuff, it wouldn't be long before they would be kissing for reasons other than religion." Reverend Oddie Vieu Shoupe, on the other hand, encouraged kissing between different sexes in his church. In 1973 he told reporters at his church in Monterey, Tennessee, "We've talked it over in our church and brothers and sisters agree the kiss demonstrates true love among us. . . . There is no jealousy."[29]

Steven M. Kane and I have traced seventy-five persons who died as a result of snakebites. This is not a high number, considering the frequency with which serpent handling is practiced. Most snake handlers have been bitten at some point in their lives. Atrophied fingers and hands, paralyzed limbs, and a variety of other physical disabilities are not uncommon among those who regularly handle snakes. When a bite occurs, members generally refuse medical treatment.

Kentucky snake handler Tess Walters related that he had lost two fingers, one to a copperhead and the other to a rattlesnake. Asked why he did not go to the doctor, he answered, "If it is God's will for you to get bit, there's no need to run to the doctor. It is in His hands then. No doctor can help you."

Mrs. Alvie Weaver, who was bitten at a church in Knoxville, Tennessee, in 1939, expressed similar convictions concerning physicians: " 'I haven't done a thing but wash the blood off,' she said. 'I couldn't even move my arm Sunday and the pain hurt all down my side. . . . That shows you the difference in trusting in doctors. I would have died down there at the church the other night if I had depended on medical aid. Why, they gouged that other woman's fingers to pieces—her fingers are still swollen tight together.' (Mrs. Weaver was referring to Mrs. Winnie Miles Johnson, who was bitten first by the copperhead . . . [and] treated at General Hospital)."[30]

Observers have put forward several theories for why members are not struck more often during services. One common belief is that loud, rhythmic music hypnotizes or "charms" the snakes. But in fact, snakes are deaf and can hear no sounds. As Shilo Collins said, "A man said to me, you people can't handle them snakes unless that music is playing. At that point, I felt the power come over me, and I grabbed a serpent. There wasn't any music playing."

It has also been alleged that repeated handling tames the snakes. However, while it is possible that serpents will become accustomed to routine handling, snakes cannot be tamed. There is no guarantee that the serpent will not bite if it is accidentally frightened or injured. A 1990 snakebite

Lee Valentine at the Kentucky / Virginia line meetings shortly before his death in Alabama in 1955 (Photo courtesy of Richard Golden)

death in Georgia was inflicted by a snake that reportedly would "lay in your arms like a baby." The snake had never before exhibited aggressive behavior, but suddenly it inflicted a lethal bite on an unsuspecting snake handler.

Another assumption is that the serpents are drugged by the warmth of the snake handler's hands; but warm hands actually should serve to make the cold-blooded reptile more active. And according to yet another theory, repeated snakebites make the snake handler immune to venom and reduce life-threatening danger when future bites occur. However, repeated bites do not produce immunity in man. In some instances, in fact, victims of snakebites develop an allergy that makes subsequent bites more dangerous. In nonallergic people, the severity of a bite depends on such factors as the length of the fangs and the amount of venom the snake manages to inject.[31]

Nonbelievers have suggested that the snake handlers milk the snakes before a service to remove their venom. My own examinations of the reptiles prior to a church meeting tended to disprove this idea. On one occasion I opened a rattlesnake's mouth and placed a pencil behind its

Raymond "Buck" Hayes at the Kentucky / Virginia line meetings, early 1950s (Photo courtesy of Richard Golden)

fangs. As I squeezed its venom sacs, a yellowish liquid drained from its fangs. A preacher commented, "He's as deadly as a shotgun, isn't he, Dave?" And even if attempts were made to milk the snakes, it would be impossible to extract all of the poison.

Finally, it is common belief that the snakes are fed before a service and that this keeps the snake handlers from being bitten. But snakes do not eat often. Most snake owners inform me that their snakes only eat once a month or so. Besides, snakes do not bite because they are hungry; they attack out of fear and other causes not associated with hunger.

Church members who see God's agency in everything that happens believe that God allows a snake to bite to punish them for sins in their daily life; to prove to unbelievers that the snakes have not been tampered with; to try the faith of the victim and his or her fellow worshipers; or to show His healing power. Today's believers do not condemn a worshiper who has been bitten and swells or gets sick, although in the early years of the movement such people did receive criticism. Shilo Collins relates, "When we first got started, if you got bit, people wouldn't even talk to you. They thought you had done something wrong. It's·not like that anymore."

Today it is commonly held that a bad bite can happen to anyone, even the most devout member, and experiences vary widely. "I have been bitten 119 times. I have suffered bad bites and good ones. I guess it's up to the Lord how ill I get," reports Dewey Chafin of Jolo, West Virginia. Bradley Shell says, "I have been bit fifty-four times and they never put nothing on me. I drink strychnine like cold pop and have handled a bunch of fire. I have never got sick or been burned." But Louise Ferguson says that her husband "handled serpents for forty years and never received one bite." And Park Saylor says, "They have never stuck a tooth in me. You must wait on God."

Two. The Beginning

During an outside church service in 1910, near Cleveland, Tennessee, George W. Hensley watched a man handle a poisonous serpent without being bitten.[1] This event caused Hensley much spiritual trouble. He dwelled on it constantly. He believed that the disciples acted exactly as Jesus instructed in Mark 16 before the Ascension. Hensley also believed that Mark 16:18 ("They shall take up serpents") was a command. In order to receive eternal life after death, he felt it was essential for him to risk his life on Earth.[2] Anthropologist Weston La Barre reports, "He then climbed White Oak Mountain, which rims Grasshopper Valley on the east,"[3] and at an area referred to as Rainbow Rock, he found a large rattlesnake and captured it.[4] J. B. Collins's *Tennessee Snake Handlers* alleges,

He approached the large reptile, and, disregarding its buzzing, blood-chilling warning, knelt a few feet away from it and prayed loudly into the sky for God to remove his fear and anoint him with "the power." Then suddenly with a shout he leaped forward and grasped the reptile, and held it in his trembling hands. . . . Snake-handlers believe that God granted Hensley a strange power that day to render the reptile harmless. And from that hour, Hensley was to become a voice crying in the wilderness.[5]

A sixty-seven-year-old Harlan County, Kentucky snake handler informed me that Hensley was anointed by God to perform such a feat: "On that day, Little George Hensley was protected like he was wearing a suit of armor. Nothing could have hurt him."[6]

A few days later, while preaching at Sale Creek, Hensley cited Mark 16 to the congregation. He picked up the serpent that he had caught and ordered the gathering to handle it also, in order to prove their faith and spiritual superiority or be "doomed to eternal hell."[7] Hensley established a church at Dolly Pond called the "Church of God with Signs Following." The congregation first met in such places as members' homes, barns, or brush arbors. Park Saylor contends that Hensley could preach serpent handling from a variety of texts: "Jeremiah, Isaiah, Amos, or Zechariah, George Hensley could preach serpent handling out of any book in the Bible. He had great power. Hensley could get the Lord to move where others couldn't."[8]

During the first decade of the twentieth century, the Church of God, Cleveland (Tennessee), was beginning to attract a significant following in the Appalachian region. Church of God congregations were found "in the mountains of southeastern Tennessee, northern Georgia, and extreme western North Carolina."[9] Around 1908, during the dedication of its church in Owl Hollow, Tennessee, a small congregation invited A. J. Tomlinson,[10] the general overseer of the Church of God, Cleveland, to attend the ceremony. He was also asked to preach the dedication sermon. Tomlinson was unable to attend the event but sent his sixteen-year-old son, Homer. Homer had to walk twelve miles to get to the ceremony, which was scheduled for 11:00 A.M.

The church at Owl Hollow was a small building with homemade pews. On the day Homer Tomlinson dedicated the building, "more came than could be seated inside."[11] After his sermon a dinner was held. He then

George Went Hensley
in Florida, 1936 (Photo
courtesy of the *Tampa
Tribune*)

spoke at an afternoon service to another large crowd, which included
George W. Hensley. Homer stated:

I stood up to preach, began only to read, beginning at the first verse of
St. John, third chapter, in the wonderful story of Nicodemus, to whom
Jesus spoke alone, of how he could be born again, of the water, and of the
spirit. The wonder of it all overwhelmed me, I read through tears of
worship streaming down my face, closed with the sixteenth verse saying, "For God so loved the world, that he gave his only begotten Son,
that whosoever believeth in him should not perish but have everlasting

life." This is spoken as the greatest verse in the Bible. . . . Yet in tears, I made my first call for sinners to come to the altar.[12]

Tomlinson earnestly asked the sinners to beg the Lord's forgiveness for their evil ways. George Hensley and four other "sinner men" approached the altar, knelt in prayer and, in fundamentalist terms, were saved. In less than two years' time, Hensley started receiving the "gifts of the Holy Ghost," such as speaking in tongues. Hensley gave up moonshining, tobacco, and other things that his church brethren considered evil. It was during this period that he claimed God moved him to be a minister. Hensley began his ministry as a free Pentecostal evangelist. He preached not only in churches but also in brush arbors, barns, or the homes of people who wanted to hear the Word. After Hensley began "following the signs," he developed a modest following of Christians and of "sinners" who wanted to see him handle serpents or drink poison. Hensley claimed the fact that he could not read did not hamper his ability to deliver God's Word. His sermons were totally unrehearsed; he claimed that the Lord told him what to say.[13]

Hensley's fame spread rapidly throughout Appalachia. In 1912, A. J. Tomlinson invited him to become a minister in the Church of God.[14] Hensley accepted and continued his evangelical work as a Church of God minister. In 1918, he established the East Chattanooga Church of God, located at the corner of Dodson and Glass streets. He also continued to conduct his evangelical work by holding revivals and tent meetings and by visiting nearby churches.[15]

George Hensley's serpent-handling ritual was followed in many of the Church of God congregations, but he did find opposition in many sects. J. B. Ellis, a missionary, attacked the practice in the church newspaper, the *Church of God Evangel*, shortly after snake handling began:

> I would like to say a few things to the saints who handle fire and serpents. These things that come under the head of miracles, and Paul says "All do not work miracles." I have had considerable experience with those who take up serpents and have studied the matter carefully. Only the mercy of God has kept some of them out of the grave. God has given them several object lessons that ought to teach them there is a limit to it. For instance two brothers came across a copperhead; the power came on one of them and he took up the reptile. It bit him on the back of the hand. Evidently he received the full force of the poison. He felt no pain then nor thereafter. The second was only slightly bitten once on the finger. Immediately his hand and arm became swollen. He suffered great pain and did not work

for four months. . . . These no doubt have the gift of miracles, and could as easily command the lame to walk, the blind to see, and the deaf to hear if they would only use their gifts to profit withal. . . . Let us get the gifts and use them as God directs and be sure we are in the more excellent way; for if we had all gift(s) and not charity we would amount to nothing.[16]

Local newspaper articles were also critical of Hensley and his followers. The following is an article from the *Chattanooga Daily Times*, September 24, 1914:

Oscar Igou, who lives across the state line in Georgia, attempted to bluff the Holy Rollers, who are holding meetings here, by bringing in a five-foot rattler, with five rattles and a button, but George Hensley and his believers handled it with impunity. . . . A 10-year-old child, the daughter of one of the corps of preachers, while in an apparent trance from the influence of Hensley, picked up the evil-looking reptile and played with it for several minutes. She was not harmed. . . . "It is the work of the devil," said Hensley, when he was asked about the snake that Igou brought in. "The devil is tempting us and the Lord gives us strength to handle snakes. We will handle any that are brought in and they will not harm us."[17]

An editorial in the *Cleveland (Tenn.) Herald* on September 24, 1914, claimed that the snakes' fangs had been removed, making them "no more harmful than a dog or cat." The commentary continued, "[The] snake business marks the degradation of worship and prostitution of religion." The writer maintained that snake handling was a diversion used by the Devil to take the attention of the people away from Jesus Christ.[18] The *Pentecostal Holiness Advocate* also asserted that members of the Church of God were "deceiving followers."[19] Others simply stated that Hensley and the Church of God were misinterpreting the Bible and what Jesus meant as the signs.[20]

Hensley found unbelievers and hecklers in almost every meeting. In one gathering a group of rowdies dumped a box of water moccasins (cottonmouths), copperheads, and rattlesnakes in front of Hensley while he was preaching. The audience fled in fear, but Hensley stepped out of the pulpit and gathered the snakes in his arms "like a boy would gather stovewood in his arms to carry into the house."[21] Following this event, Hensley was invited by A. J. Tomlinson to preach in his Cleveland, Tennessee church. Homer Tomlinson described the scene:

Hensley was invited to come to Cleveland by my father, and when it was announced that he would come, it was just to preach, and give his testimony of how the Lord had blessed him. Enemies, however, took this occasion to bring in deadly serpents, seeking to discredit the Church of God in Cleveland. Only a single serpent was brought in, tempting Hensley, when of a sudden the power of the Holy Ghost came upon him, and he reached into the box and took up the vicious rattlesnake, and it became docile in his hand. Others, including my sister, Iris, in some amazing testimony that this sign would follow them that believed, anointed by the Holy Ghost, and acting beyond their own volition, one by one took the serpent, and from hand to hand. The serpent remained docile, and before hundreds of witnesses, all without hurt, the four-foot rattler was then returned to the box, and was later taken out and destroyed.[22]

A. J. Tomlinson recorded, in the *Church of God Evangel*, an event that occurred in September of 1914:

The sensation was so great that outsiders got enthused and wanted to test the matter further. So on Sunday night Sept. sixth they took in a "Copperhead." This was handled with as much success as the first, and many were made believers on account of the demonstration of God's power. The meeting went on after that with seekers in the altar and good results until Thursday night, September 10. Outsiders determined to give the matter a thorough test secured two snakes for the occasion. These were believed to be very poison, so much so that those that took them in were exceedingly careful and fearful lest they should be bitten. Nothing was done with the snakes in the meeting until the power came on the saints, then both snakes were taken up, but as soon as they were touched by those under the power they wilted and never offered to bite any one. One was a poisonous Adder and the other a rattler, both believed to be very dangerous. At the close of the demonstration with the snakes several came forward with tears in their eyes begging for prayer. When the altar call was given others came forward pleading for salvation.[23]

Mountaineer Charlie Robinson, intent on having fun with the Holiness believers, took a rattlesnake in a shoe box to a tent meeting near Ooltewah, where Hensley was preaching to a crowd of four hundred. At the height of the meeting, when believers were preaching in unknown tongues, Robinson released the snake. The first person to see it was a woman with a baby in her arms. She picked the snake up and fondled it. "At times it was within six inches of the face of the baby," the *Chattanooga Daily Times* recounted, "but the child was not harmed." All of the crowd then handled the snake; reportedly, though, no one suffered injury.[24]

The following evening, unbelievers decided that they would put Hensley to the test. They announced that they would enter his tent with highly poisonous carbolic acid and offer it to him to drink. The unbelievers took the preacher a bottle of Coca-Cola, telling him that it was the poison. As the meeting progressed Hensley grabbed the bottle and emptied its contents, believing that it was lethal. The unbelievers were shocked that Hensley had enough faith to drink a liquid that he believed to be toxic.[25]

Most newspapers and scholars contend that snake-handling services continued for ten years—until 1918, when one of the members was bitten by a rattlesnake. J. B. Collins stated that Garland Defriese "fell to the ground at the feet of his fellow worshipers, the fangs of the reptile still fastened to his flesh. Moved to frenzy, the believers began shouting their prayers toward heaven while Defriese writhed in agony on the ground." Collins added that Defriese "recovered after a few weeks, but the experience dulled his enthusiasm for the practice, and snake handling that day lapsed into a state of suspended animation that was to last for twenty-three years."[26]

In fact, though, this was far from the first time one of the believers had been bitten. In one of many such accounts, the *Chattanooga Daily Times* from September 16, 1914, featured an article titled "Proselyting with Snakes: 'Holy Rollers' of Cleveland Scorn Bites of Reptiles." The article stated that on the previous evening, at a "barn-like affair" with a sawdust floor, Reverend Tom McLain of the Church of God had been bitten on the thumb by a rattlesnake. And before McLain was bitten, another man named Finley Goodwin had been struck by a copperhead.[27] The ritual of handling serpents in religious services did not, as Collins claimed, lapse "into a state of suspended animation" after the Defriese bite; people continued the practice. But snake handling did decrease in Tennessee during this period, because George Hensley left the area due to marital problems with his wife, Amanda.

By all early indications, George and Amanda Hensley were very religious people who labored hard in their evangelical work. The following is a church newspaper article praising Hensley and his wife for their "war against sin and the devil":

We had the pleasure of attending the Ooltewah meeting Saturday and Sunday night. Bro. George Hensley and his wife assisted by Bro. M. S. Haynes and others have been waging a relentless war against sin and the devil. Two large rattlesnakes have been taken up under the power of God. Fire has also been handled twice during the meeting. We found the attendance large, and the best of attention and order. In spite of the ridiculous falsehoods published through local papers, people are seeing the truth. Praise God.[28]

Because George Hensley could not read and write, Amanda filled out his examination certificate for the Church of God ministry.[29] In addition, Amanda appeared to play an active role in Hensley's ministry. The following is the full text of a letter she wrote from Ooltewah, Tennessee, that appeared in the *Church of God Evangel* on April 4, 1914:

I want to find room in the little paper to tell what the Lord has done for me. I had consumption and was in the last stage. The doctor said one of my lungs was almost gone. I could not sing or talk long at a time. I began to pray for God to save my life and my soul, for I didn't feel ready to die. I asked him to spare my life till I found out what was the matter. Then I heard Bro. Homer Tomlinson preach and saw they had more of the Lord than I did. I began to trust the Lord from that time and he has healed me, sanctified me and given me the Holy Ghost. He has called husband and me out into the work. We held a 13 days meeting at Evansville. A boy was healed that the doctors had about given up. Three were saved and two sanctified. They rocked us several times but we had God with us. Pray for us. Your sister under the blood. Manda Hensley[30]

Although George and Amanda Hensley worked together in church, their marriage suffered. Hensley did not support his family adequately because of extended evangelical trips. Also, another man, a neighbor, started paying attention to Amanda.[31] George Hensley reportedly carried a pistol during this time in case Amanda's suitor got too forward with his intentions. According to a source close to George Hensley, the neighbor asked Amanda to leave her husband, but she refused. One evening when George was returning home from a church meeting, the neighbor and his cousin waited along the road and beat him severely. The cousin held Hensley while the neighbor cut him with a knife. John Roberts, who lived in the area, found Hensley lying by the roadside, bleeding profusely. Roberts and his family nursed him back to health. For the rest of his life Hensley bore an ugly scar across his face, and numerous other scars on his back and arms, from this event.[32]

After the attack Hensley resigned from the ministry and also left his wife and family. The reason stated on his Church of God revocation of

George Hensley with
his second wife, Irene,
in Kentucky, early
1930s (Photo courtesy
of Jean Hensley Potts)

ministry form, signed by Tennessee overseer M. W. Litzinger, was "Re-signed—has much trouble in the home." When he left, he told Amanda, "I'm leaving you a good farm and a boy big enough to run it." He did not own the farm, though; he only rented it. In the next few years, Hensley "backslid" and "returned to his sinful ways."[33]

In the spring of 1923 he resumed making and selling moonshine whis-key and was indicted by the grand jury of Hamilton County, Tennessee, on three charges of selling liquor.[34] Hensley was found not guilty on two of the charges, but guilty of the third. He was fined one hundred dollars and ordered to pay court costs and was also sentenced to four months in the county workhouse. He was put to work on the chain gang, building county roads, but because of his "likable personality," the prison guards made him a trustee. As a trustee Hensley was responsible for running errands, such as getting water for other prisoners. One day while getting a bucket of water, he escaped. For a brief period, he hid from the authorities at his sister's farm near Ooltewah. The prison guards failed to recapture him, and he made his way to Cleveland, Ohio, to live with relatives—probably with his sister Bertha Weaver.

Hensley worked various jobs while in Cleveland. Shortly after his ar-rival there, he began to preach again. He held tent meetings, conducted revivals, and preached the gospel wherever he could. During one of those meetings, conducted at the Salvation Army in Cleveland, where Hensley was also working at the time, he met his second wife, twenty-two-year-old Irene Klunzinger of North Royalton, Ohio. (Hensley was forty-seven then.) Irene had not been married previously. She was described as a small, very intelligent, and "sickly" woman.[35]

Irene believed that she had been cursed by a witch at birth. The sorceress was her aunt, who had a particular score to settle with the family. Irene's father informed her of the malediction when she was a young child. She always lived in terror of this curse. When Irene married George Hensley, she believed that he could cast the demon out of her and relieve the spell. It appears that Hensley never accomplished this feat, however.[36] Irene's belief that she was hexed followed her to the grave. After George and Irene were married, they moved to Washingtonville, Ohio, where George's brother helped him find employment in a coal mine.[37] On March 3, 1928—shortly after they had relocated—Irene gave birth to their first child, an infant named Faith Lillian.[38]

Three. The Move to Kentucky

On a crisp Sunday morning in October 1929, Sherman Lawson, a Free Pentecostal evangelical preacher who lived in the vicinity of Path Fork, Kentucky, told his wife, "You go on to church without me, because I feel the need to go up on the mountain and pray."[1] The mountain that Lawson prayed on was located above the Path Fork church. When members of the congregation entered the meetinghouse, Lawson could be heard praying, screaming at the top of his lungs.

Later in the afternoon, when the congregation left the church, Lawson could still be heard from the mountain. As darkness approached, Lawson came down from the mountain and said to his wife, "Look up Mark 16 in the Bible and read it to me. I saw a vision when I was up there and don't

Sherman Lawson, ca.
1940 (Photographer
unknown)

know what it means."[2] She opened the old family Bible and began. Lawson listened earnestly, but it was not until she reached verses 15 through 18, concerning "following the signs," that he demonstrated a profound interest.

"That's it," replied Lawson. "When I was in prayer on the mountain I had a vision that people were handling serpents. God has shown me that in a short period of time people will be handling serpents in these mountains." Sherman Lawson was unaware that the ritual of serpent handling in church services had already begun in 1910, at Sale Creek, Tennessee, through the efforts of George Hensley, who would be moving to eastern Kentucky three years later.

In early 1932, George Hensley and his family left Ohio and relocated to Pineville, Kentucky, which lies in the mountains in the eastern part of the state. Hensley's move was influenced by a native Kentuckian named Jim Jackson, who had observed him handling serpents in the Chattanooga area.[3] Upon his arrival, Hensley worked in a Pineville coal mine for a brief time at the rate of seventy-five cents per day, because he was destitute.[4] Jackson, George, and Sill and Harve Eads had been conducting church meetings in an old schoolhouse at East Pineville. In the spring of 1932, Jackson built a small three-room church at East Pineville with materials gathered from a mining camp that was being torn down at Rella, Kentucky. The church was known as the East Pineville Church of God. Hensley was immediately invited to join the worship services. At the first gathering Hensley attended, he preached on the "signs." Hensley stated to the congregation, "The Lord has given me the power to handle serpents, fire, and drink strychnine, and I praise him for these gifts."[5]

Park Saylor informed me that some members of the service were not convinced that Hensley had the power to "follow the signs." A man named John Dash was particularly skeptical of Hensley's claims. Later in the week, after Hensley made his declaration, Dash was cutting a power line in a rural area around Pineville. He found two large rattlesnakes, one yellow and the other black, and put them in a lard can. The black rattler was four feet in length; soon after it was captured, the snake gave birth to eleven infants. Dash took all of the snakes to George Hensley before a Sunday church meeting and asked him if he would handle them in church. Hensley replied, "If the Lord moves on me, I will." During the church service Hensley handled all of the serpents, including the newborns.[6]

After the meeting, Harve Eads and Bill Blanton walked to a nearby town named Harbell. When they arrived at the old sawmill there, the men started to discuss the good time they had experienced at church. Eads stated that he would have "enjoyed handling the serpents." Blanton informed Eads, "Harve, you went all through those people with a serpent." Eads replied, "If I did, I never knew it," referring to the intense state of "anointing" that he had experienced.[7]

In the late 1920s and early 1930s it was a common practice for religious groups and evangelists to meet at the yard of the Pineville courthouse on Saturday mornings and deliver gospel messages for three or four hours.[8] Large crowds gathered in an almost carnival atmosphere. On one Saturday morning in the summer of 1932, George Hensley was preaching and handling serpents in front of a large assembly. A group of hecklers led by several brothers started to ridicule the evangelist, but Hensley ignored the men; it was routine for unbelievers to taunt him while he preached.[9] Park Saylor remembers that "the Devil had some men there that day. They also were handling serpents, but had ran yellow copper wire through the snakes' mouths so they could only stick their tongues out, but not bite. They made a mockery of God and went up above East Pineville and drowned. . . . They just went swimming in the river and drowned. See how God wiped them out? The Lord said 'Vengeance is mine.' "

George Hensley preached in many of the Holiness churches in eastern Kentucky as an evangelist or guest pastor.[10] At a place known as Mill Creek, Hensley was holding a large rattlesnake that "sinners" had brought to church and was delivering a fiery message about "following the signs" when a lady named Francis ("Fancy") Brock jumped from her seat, apparently in an anointed state, and took the serpent from him. Brock handled the snake without being bitten. Many of the church members were astonished that a woman could accomplish such a feat. One young man named James Simpson was reluctant to believe that God had anything to do with snake handling. He also refused to accept that people could "heal, talk in tongues, drink poison, cast out demons, or handle fire." His wife, Mossie, expected that her husband was going to "chase the Holiness off in time."[11]

In the autumn of 1932, at an area known as Simms Fork, Fancy Brock, George Hensley, and others were handling snakes and fire at the Sunday morning church service when Fancy reached into the small building's potbellied stove and caressed handfuls of hot coals without being burned. The unbelieving James Simpson sat in the crowd refusing to accept what he was seeing as "God's work"; he assumed there was "a trick to it." Knowing of Simpson's skepticism, Fancy Brock walked to a burning kerosene lamp and removed the hot globe. She strolled across the church to James Simpson and placed the globe on his neck. It blistered Simpson's neck badly. Simpson's wife declared that he never again believed there was a trick involved. He became a preacher and a snake handler and remained firm in his convictions until his death.

Another couple that observed Hensley's rituals from the beginning in eastern Kentucky was Henry and Sarah Saylor. The mountaineers who knew Sarah told me that she was a devout Holiness woman who accepted that God gave his followers the power to accomplish miracles. Like James Simpson, Henry Saylor initially reacted skeptically to Hensley's snake-handling doctrine but later came to accept the practice.

Sarah became famous for her ability to handle serpents. On one occasion, shortly after she became a snake handler, she rode in the back of a pickup truck from Harlan to a church service near Berea. After the meeting had started, a man brought a vicious rattlesnake into the church, "daring anyone to handle it." Sarah attempted to handle the reptile but was almost bitten. A member of the church ordered the man who had brought the

First four men from left: Tommy Gambrel, Louis Saylor, Ted Blevins, and Gillis Messer leaving a church meeting in the 1950s (Photo courtesy of Tess Walters)

snake "to get it out before he kills someone." Later in the service Sarah became anointed and said, "Go get that snake and bring it back in here!" Fear spread throughout the church that Sarah would be killed. The rattlesnake was brought back into the church in a fifty-pound lard can. Sarah removed the lid and grasped the snake. She ran around the room twice holding it in her hands, and she reportedly escaped injury.

Wherever George Hensley preached, he gained converts to his snake-handling beliefs. Park Saylor states that "no one had ever handled serpents in Kentucky, in religious services, until Hensley arrived."[12] Hensley found followers of his Holiness and snake-handling doctrines quite easily. He also encountered unbelievers who caused him many problems. One man actually pulled a pistol and shot at Hensley, because he found the contents of Hensley's sermons offensive.[13] However, his snake-handling practices drew large crowds of both believers and unbelievers.

Possibly the most famous snake-handling service in Holiness history was conducted in Tennessee on a hot August Sunday in the summer of 1932.

Many people in the area of Tazewell, Tennessee, drove cars and trucks or rode horses and mules up the dusty road leading to the tiny Free Pentecostal Church at Ferguson Ridge, where a religious service was to be conducted at 11:00.[14] This Sunday morning ceremony was to be the final meeting of a week-long revival. Word had passed throughout the "hills and hollers" that on this day, Little George Hensley would join them for worship.

The Ferguson Ridge Church was a primitive clapboard building, forty feet long and thirty feet wide, with plank floors and one room. Inside were two rows of benches made of rough-sawed lumber, which had been donated to the church by a local man who owned a sawmill. At one side of the structure was a wood stove used for heating in the winter. A rostrum with a lectern stretched across the front of the building. On top of the lectern sat a small bottle of olive oil, a Bible, and a jar of strychnine. At the sides of the lectern and behind it there were additional benches, known as deacon's benches, usually used by musicians and additional preachers during a service. Two outside toilets were situated directly behind the building. The church stood in a field that was usually planted in tobacco. Reverend Thea O. Carter described the church this way: "We had a good church house—not elaborate—but plenty good enough. So, as I said, a revival spirit filled the country in that area. People were praying everywhere; getting saved and baptized with the Holy Ghost. They were speaking in tongues and prophesying."[15]

On this particular occasion, two "sinner men" from the area caught a forty-inch rattlesnake near the church and decided to take it with them to the service in order to watch Hensley handle it.[16] The snake was placed in a fruit jar and put on the lampstand of an old coal oil wall lamp in full view of everyone. One of the men who brought the snake in laughed and said, "I want to see him [Hensley] handle this one." The other man declared, "If that crazy preacher messes with this snake, it will kill him."[17]

Out in the churchyard people had begun to gather in order to socialize and to discuss events of the previous week.[18] Some of the worshipers had come as far away as Alabama, Georgia, and other neighboring states.[19] Park Saylor drove George Hensley and his family to Ferguson Ridge from Pineville, Kentucky, in a 1928 Chevrolet.[20] When they arrived, the church was full and people were backed up to the road. Worshipers crowded around the building's raised windows, trying to look in, and had also massed outside the open doors. The music was in full swing when Hensley arrived. The gathering was singing "There's a Land That Is Fairer than Day":

There's a land that is fairer than day,
And by faith we can see it a-far;
For the Father waits over the way
To prepare us a dwelling place there.

We shall sing on that beautiful shore
The melodious songs of the blest,
And our spirits shall sorrow no more,
Not a-sigh for the blessing of rest.

To our bountiful Father above,
We will offer the tribute of praise
For the glorious gift of his love
And the blessings that hallow our days.

In the sweet by and by,
We shall meet on that beautiful shore;
In the sweet by and by,
We shall meet on that beautiful shore.

The large gathering next sang "When the Roll Is Called up Yonder" and "When the Saints Go Marching In." The music on this Sunday was described as "heavenly singing." Some of the members began to wave their hands in the air during the singing, shouting and talking in unknown tongues. A few jumped up and down, screaming phrases like "Praise the Lord," "Glory," and "Hallelujah precious Jesus." As the music continued, some of the congregation shook and danced uncontrollably. Many communicants focused their attention on the rattlesnake resting in the fruit jar, while others were involved in their own spiritual experience.

After an hour of singing and testifying, the preacher asked for a prayer to be said for the needy. As the prayer began, some members sank to the floor on hands and knees. All of the congregation prayed aloud together. Some members spoke in unknown tongues. The prayer lasted approximately fifteen minutes. At the end one of the male communicants shouted, "Someone sing us a song." An elderly lady rose and began singing "In Heaven We'll Never Grow Old." The instrumentalists joined in, and the song lasted for ten minutes. No one had handled a single serpent.

When the congregation finished singing, a church member announced, "Brothers and Sisters, we have brothers George Hensley and Park Saylor here today." Hensley thanked the congregation for having him there to preach and "thanked the Lord for having a serpent there."[21] He started preaching out of the sixty-first chapter of Isaiah: "The Spirit of the Lord

God is upon me; because the Lord hath anointed me to preach good tidings unto the meek; he hath sent me to bind up the brokenhearted, to proclaim liberty to the captives, and the opening of the prison to them that are bound" (Isaiah 61:1).

During the sermon Hensley began to feel the Spirit. He waved his hand in the air and exclaimed, "Beloved." Hensley then shouted out Luke 10:19: "Behold, I give you authority to tread upon serpents and scorpions, and over all the power of the enemy; and nothing shall hurt you." He danced a few steps and said, "Thank you, Lord."

Hensley then repeated Luke 10:19. When he echoed the verse for the second time, the rattlesnake that had been placed on the lampstand turned over on its back.[22] Hensley paused and then walked to the lamp and picked up the jar that contained the rattlesnake. He removed the lid from the jar and withdrew the serpent. The snake remained "as limp as a towel." Hensley walked back to the pulpit and sat by his wife and baby. He placed the rattlesnake on his thigh in a coiled position. The reptile could not stay in that position and hung to the floor. The worshipers raised their hands in the air and cried out phrases like "Bless him, Lord!," "Thank you, Jesus!," and "God bless our Brother Hensley!" Some of them shouted out expressions in unknown tongues, while others moaned, wept, shook, and jerked uncontrollably.

Hensley rose from his seat and said, "Whoever this snake belongs to, come and get it. The Lord is done with it." The two men who had brought the snake to the church got up from their seats and removed the snake from the building. They took it out behind an old tobacco barn, near the church, and killed it. While doing so they were heard by Park Saylor to say, "You devil you, you won't bite so we'll kill you." The revival lasted for two more days.

In 1931, Park Saylor began his work career with the Pioneer Coal Company. He spent a total of thirty-two years underground in coal mines and now suffers from the effects of black lung. George Hensley and other snake-handling preachers had a substantial impact on him. From birth he had been exposed to Holiness; he claims to have seen levitations, people being raised from the dead, and other miracles. George Hensley's snake handling was only another marvel that could be performed if a person "believed strong enough." When Park Saylor was a child, his mother and uncles had planted the idea that he would be a preacher someday. Saylor sometimes attended church meetings with his family every night of the week. He learned Holiness in the same oral style that had been conveyed to congregations from the time of settlement.

Park Saylor's preaching career began almost simultaneously with his coal mining. He states that God called on him to preach without sending him to seminary school for training. Throughout his career he preached at different churches almost every night. From his home in Path Fork, Kentucky, he commuted to areas such as Ferguson Ridge, Tennessee, and throughout Kentucky, and to the little church on Rural Street in Austin, Indiana, where he preached for nineteen years. Many nights he received only four or five hours of sleep. On May 15, 1933, he married Alma Hollifield, and they have had three children.

From the onset of the snake-handling movement, Park Saylor accepted that God allowed his believers to perform miracles such as "following the signs." In one of the early snake-handling meetings, in 1934, Hensley gave Saylor a rattlesnake, and Saylor handled it willingly. Another snake-handling preacher later placed a rattlesnake around Park Saylor's neck. Again, Saylor fondled the snake without injury.

Four. The Saylors

     The first of Park Saylor's ancestors to settle in Kentucky were Solomon and Sarah Salyer Saylor, who arrived in 1805 from Russell County, Virginia, by way of the Cumberland Gap.[1] During this period, many of the settlers in eastern Kentucky were attracted by the availability of cheap land. Others moved there simply to escape the pressures of civilization. Many pioneers situated themselves in the Kentucky highlands as squatters, planning to purchase their land by accumulating capital through their own labor. Due to an inflation in land values after the initial settlement years, some found themselves unable to raise the required cash and emigrated once again to areas such as Illinois.[2] However, such movement was rare. In eastern Kentucky, residential persistence was the rule. If mountaineers moved, they relocated only a short distance from their initial land tract. As in the system that characterized early America, men stayed in close proximity to their parents, "waiting for their inheritances."[3]

On August 7, 1805, "Solomon received a certificate for 300 acres on the Cumberland River joining the land of Garnet Jackson."[4] The Saylors located among Sarah's relatives, following a pattern among settlers in eastern Kentucky. Voluntary concentrations of settlement in clusters emphasized the importance of communal values.[5] Close friends and relatives could lend assistance when needed. However, these assemblies were small; in most cases, pioneer communities would contain less than twenty people.

In the years that followed, Solomon Saylor and his sons continued to accumulate land in the vicinity of his original tract through grants in court orders and Kentucky land warrants.[6] Their land lay between Saylor's Creek and Forrester's Creek. Although Saylor was prosperous by early pioneer standards, his land was seen among kin as belonging to the family. In the narrow bottoms Solomon and Sarah produced Indian corn, squash, beans, and potatoes. He fattened a few razorback hogs by letting them run wild in the vast woods, where they feasted on an abundance of acorns, hickory nuts, and other foods that the hills provided.[7] This became a common practice for the next century: hogs were allowed to fatten on the mast in the forest until late fall, when they would be brought in and fed on corn for several weeks to harden the flesh.[8] In later years, the owner simply notched the ears of his pigs to distinguish them from neighbors' stock.

Supplementing what the farm provided, the rivers supplied fish, and the forest supplied wild meat such as deer, raccoons, rabbits, squirrels, quail, wild turkey, and bear. Salt came from the many natural licks. Cattle were not normally used as a food source during the early years of settlement. Oxen were employed as work animals to clear land or pull logs. The cows were milked but ordinarily gave only a gallon per day, at most.

During their first year in Harlan County, the Saylors lived in a primitive lean-to that provided some protection from the elements, and Sarah cooked on an open fire while attending to the family's domestic needs. At the time of their arrival at Forrester's Creek, Sarah had already given birth to seven infants (John, Joseph, Rebecca, Martin, Elizabeth, Catharine, and Delila). In 1805 she gave birth to Sally, and in 1807 to Zachariah, bringing to nine the total of children to be fed and cared for in the wilderness.[9]

The year following Solomon's arrival in eastern Kentucky, he built a cabin out of logs notched in the traditional dovetailed fashion. The one-room cabin had dirt floors and stood on the north side of a slope near a spring that bubbled out of the ground. Aley Ledford, who settled close to the Saylor's cabin, described life on the Kentucky frontier during this period: "There was always a lot to do—cut timber, raise corn and a little tobacco, make soap, make most everything we needed. Kill animals for food and hides, for lard and tallow and brushes. Betty was always cooking or preserving food or making clothes or having babies. Nobody was idle."[10]

Forrester's Creek remained distant from commercial centers for over a century. In 1889, local color writer Charles Dudley Warner commented on the area's remoteness: he said it was "nearly eight hundred miles of wilderness road, which was nothing but a bridle-path, from Philadelphia by way of the Cumberland Gap to central Kentucky."[11] Even the tributary system of transportation presented problems. The Kentucky River was navigable only six months of the year, and the region was prone to flooding due to drainage from the steep hillsides.[12] Geographer Mary Beth Pudup notes, "Harlan County straddles the headwaters of the Cumberland River, which did not permit inland navigation, rendering Harlan County largely inaccessible except by overland travel."[13] The most common mode of transportation was by foot and horseback along winding creek beds. Park Saylor informed me that his ancestors traveled by "mountaintops and waterways."

Due to the mountainous terrain and primitive transportation networks, Solomon and Sarah Saylor lived in almost total isolation from the outside world. A few families trickled into the area, but the population remained sparse. There were only a few hundred settlers in eastern Kentucky by 1800. Throughout the Appalachian highlands, a strong reliance on kinships continued. Solomon Saylor acted as a patriarch, and his children remained in close proximity even after they married and started families of their own. A son could give his aging father valuable assistance with farm chores or in time of hardship. A strong feeling of group solidarity developed; especially in times of crisis, families stood together. In such circumstances, family solidarity controlled the actions of the individual. It was rare for an individual to make a decision without the agreement of the entire family. Personal lives were governed by a form of communal legislation that carried on for generations. The community of Beech Creek, which James S. Brown studied during the 1940s,[14] was representative of preindustrial Appalachia: "Within the sphere in which kinship connoted reciprocal obligations the familial mode of cooperation circumscribed many aspects of daily life. Timing of marriage, home leaving, and procreation, in addition to acquisition of an occupation, length of schooling, and other transitions were not solely the individual's decision. Rather, throughout early New England, as in Appalachia, such decisions were in part the outcome of family strategies."[15]

Settlements like that the Saylors established at Forrester's Creek were not a community in modern terms. Homes were separated by a distance of a half mile or more. A community occupied a particular "cove, hollow, or valley and was separated from its neighbors by a rim of mountains or ridges."[16] The geographical boundaries provided by the mountains also served as barriers to outsiders. Secluded locales such as Forrester's Creek were fenced off from each other; virtually no communication existed between these remote neighborhoods. The communities were distinguished by the names of their natural or geographical markings—"Beefhide, Mad Dog, Barefoot, Jamboree, Hogskin Creek, Burning Springs (a well of natural gas discovered in early days), Contrary, Poor Fork, Viper, Traveler's Rest, Hell fur Sartain, Troublesome, Kingdom Come, Disputanta, Fish Trap, Squabble Creek, Quicksand, Cutskin, Feisty or Hazard."[17]

Poor transportation, isolation, and lack of nearby markets resulted in a subsistence economy. The nearest markets were located over five hundred miles from Forrester's Creek, so Solomon Saylor was unable to engage in commercial agriculture. In eastern Kentucky as in early America, "given the absence of an external market there was no alternative to subsistence or semi-subsistence production."[18] Self-sufficiency arose out of necessity. Exchange was calculated by use value, and production was geared toward requirements, not market demands. Solomon and Sarah Saylor were almost totally self-sufficient in raising their food and in making tools, furniture, and other necessities. They were not autonomous, however; the Saylors relied on kin in time of need. A system of barter, reciprocity, and communal labor developed in which people traded surplus items. John Mack Faragher has shown that in pioneer Illinois, "self-sufficiency should be understood as a community experience."[19] The system at Forrester's Creek worked in the same way, principally by ties of kinship rather than by the marketplace.

By common agreement, the mountaineers held that individuals who took more than their share deprived others who might be in need; thus in most cases community members simply satisfied their basic requirements. The settlers at Forresters Creek recognized no class distinctions and viewed themselves as equivalent to their neighbors in all aspects of life.[20] Economic relations at Forrester's Creek were not unlike what Steven Hahn describes in the Georgia upcountry: "The economic relations into which they entered were quite distinct from those characterizing a market society. These petty producers generally owned basic productive resources or were related to those who did; they devoted their energies principally to family subsistence, supplementing it through local exchanges of goods and labor; and the exchanges cast a net that brought producers face-to-face in a market very much governed by local custom."[21]

In their kin-oriented, self-sufficient ways, the Saylors personified tradition. There was no demand for eastern Kentucky coal or timber during this period, so the pioneers remained tied to subsistence farming. In 1899, almost one hundred years after Solomon Saylor settled at Forrester's Creek, William Goodell Frost concluded that the mountaineers had "unconsciously stepped aside from the great avenues of commerce and thought" and gone into a "Rip Van Winkle sleep."[22]

The circumstances prevented Solomon and Sarah's children from obtaining a formal education. There simply were few books and no schools. On rare occasions a Bible or dictionary might be found in a mountaineer's home. By 1850 Harlan County had only two or three schools, and it was virtually impossible for people living in remote areas to attend them. The schools that existed met for only two or three months a year and were taught by local people who were themselves barely literate. Instead of learning from books, the Saylor children became educated in woodlore, farming, hunting, oral tradition (such as folk songs), reading weather signs, and earning small amounts of cash from the local economy and traders. Children were a significant part of the labor force. At an early age they were taught how to perform an assortment of tasks so that the family could labor together as a unit.

Life was particularly hard for women. From the cradle, young girls served a form of apprenticeship under their mother in this male-dominated society. Girls cared for young siblings, along with many other chores associated with the domestic economy. Fertility rates were very high; childbirth was usually an annual event. In addition, women were expected to do agricultural work and attend to their household duties.

Sarah and mothers like her acted as the family nurse, applying remedies that had been passed down from previous generations. When these methods of healing failed, Sarah turned to prayer. Catherine L. Albanese found that it was common for Appalachians to recite a particular Bible verse in healing. For the treatment of a bad cut, for example, a remedy was to quote Ezekiel 16:6: "And when I passed by thee, and saw thee polluted in thine own blood, I said unto thee when thou waste in thy blood, Live; yea, I said unto thee when thou waste in thy blood, Live."[23]

Mountaineers usually felt that it was wrong for men to do "women's work," but women often performed "men's work." Frequently Sarah Saylor assisted her husband in plowing and in reaping the harvest. She helped to clear fields, butcher hogs, and milk the cows. When Solomon was away hunting or "enjoying the fruits of nature," she managed the farm by herself. Like most women on the eastern Kentucky frontier during the period, Sarah never traveled far from home, due to the domestic duties associated with her large household.[24] After working long hours in the fields, Sarah would return to the Saylor cabin and cook, make candles, weave fabrics, or preserve the food that would feed the family during the winter months.

Arguing that there was no religion in eastern Kentucky at the beginning of the nineteenth century, Harry M. Caudill claims that the area was "practically without churches for fifty or seventy-five years after the first white settlers. There simply were no preachers or ministers, few Bibles and little religious knowledge."[25] Bill Surface supports Caudill's position in his study *The Hollow*, emphasizing that the first settlers in eastern Kentucky were suspicious of preachers and the first churches were not constructed for eighty years after settlement.[26]

In fact, though, the mountaineers had retained their religious convictions, although isolation made it difficult for them to worship together. Henry Scalf points out that Baptist churches were organized in eastern Kentucky by Elder Daniel Williams before 1802.[27] Baptist churches were established at sites like Burning Springs, in Magoffin County, in 1814, and Mud Creek, in Floyd County, in 1825. The New Salem Association, a Baptist league, was formed in the 1820s between Letcher, Floyd, Perry, Breathitt, and Pike Counties.[28] There were also Methodist circuit-riding preachers in eastern Kentucky. The seclusion of the Appalachian highlands simply made it difficult to gather crowds for religious meetings in locales such as Forrester's Creek.

Strong Calvinist convictions were evident in the creeds the pioneers brought with them. Solomon and Sarah Saylor were Presbyterians; they believed in predestination, as did many of the other initial settlers in eastern Kentucky. Most of the pioneers who settled near Forrester's Creek were Presbyterian through their Scotch-Irish heritage.

Their Presbyterian faith gave the Saylors a sense of order and comfort in a sequestered world. They were haunted daily by death and danger. Wandering Native Americans were still a menace to pioneers in 1800. People could also freeze to death, suffer from disease or childbirth, or be crushed by falling timber, mauled by farm animals, or attacked by wild animals. If misfortune struck, or Sarah's doctoring skills failed, it was common to attribute the calamity to "the Lord's will."

During the first years of settlement, the only time the Saylors heard any "real preachin'" was when traveling Methodist evangelists penetrated the mountains and stopped at Forrester's Creek to "take the night" and have a meal. The Methodist itinerant would announce the time of his next visit, "perhaps a month or six weeks later, and he was usually there just as he had promised."[29] Wandering preachers and camp meetings were the primary means for religious expansion in eastern Kentucky. At the beginning of the nineteenth century, the religious fervor that was being experienced in the rest of the country had penetrated the Appalachian highlands. The so-called Great Revivals being conducted in the bluegrass section of Kentucky provided a prototype for the smaller meetings that were held in places like Forrester's Creek. By 1820, the Baptist and Methodist denominations in Kentucky had swelled to 21,000 members each, while the Presbyterians claimed only 2,700.[30] The Methodist success in eastern Kentucky can be attributed to the few circuit riders who entered the mountains. The Methodists were better organized than other denominations in gaining converts, and they rejected formalism and other habits traditionally associated with the Presbyterians. The Methodist doctrine of Arminianism, or Free Will, also contributed to their success on the frontier.[31]

The early circuit-riding Methodist preachers and the Baptist farmer-preachers could identify with the problems and lifestyles of the mountain people and thus were more easily accepted. The Presbyterians were more conservative in selecting their ministers: to be ordained as a Presbyterian minister, one had to have a college degree or its equivalent, and many of the early Presbyterian clergymen who entered Kentucky and Tennessee were easterners who had graduated from Princeton.[32] For this reason, Presbyterian sermons contained materials that were highly intellectual in content. This kind of preaching may have suited some of the affluent, scholarly congregations in the bluegrass section of the state, but the poorer folk in mountain communities had no use for it. Presbyterian sermons were generally unrelated to everyday life on the frontier. These conservative Presbyterian practices caused the mountaineers to turn to the Methodists and Baptists, whose "plain and simple" teachings appealed to them.

In mountain locales, a lay religion led by Baptist farmer-preachers emerged. These preachers were largely unlettered men who learned and delivered their messages by oral transmission. People such as the Saylors demanded a ministry directly coupled to folk society, not separated from that society by formal training or starched professionalism. Mountain theology became a blend of simplicity, superstition, and literal interpretation of the Bible. It was a theology that reflected the environment. Albanese remarks, "For those whose lives were sheltered by the rugged beauty of the mountains, nature was a holy place, spiritual power could be found amid the hills. People grew up with a sense that they belonged to the mountains, even more to their particular mountain hollow with its creek bed and its walls rising like boundaries between sacred and profane worlds. . . . Thus, mountain people surrounded themselves with a symbolic system based, for the most part, on nature."[33] The Saylors attributed bad times to "the Devil's work," and scholars have recorded numerous examples of superstitions and evil symbols, including owls:

> The black cat was, of course, an evil symbol, but his repute was only a little blacker than that of the owl. This feathered wanderer of the night was believed to be in the service of the devil, and his approach was viewed with dismay. Some thought he was a spy for the Evil One and he was not infrequently greeted with a charge of shot. Generally though, it was thought best not to offend him. His conduct near a habitation was carefully remarked. If he flew off to the left of the cabin door, bad luck was in store. Perhaps the cabin would burn, or the crops would blight, or the livestock sicken and die. If the owl flew directly over the house, death was coming soon to one of its occupants. But if the bird flapped his great wings and flew off to the right, the household was spared and a run of good luck was sure to ensue.[34]

Poor health and problems associated with childbirth were frequently attributed to the Devil.

Baptist and Methodist preachers did not dress in black garb with white collars, as their counterparts in the East did. In most cases they wore ill-fitting homespun garb, in the style of the mountains. They traveled during every season of the year, fording or swimming the many creeks and rivers and sleeping in the open air when a settler's cabin could not be found for shelter. The frontier evangelist preached in homes, in barns, and in the open air, with a "fire and thunder" style—an emotional, rhythmic chant that was similar to the preaching style in African American churches. Frequently a hickory chair served as a pulpit as listeners sat hypnotized by the preacher's message. Occasionally these protracted frontier meetings lasted for several hours. Mountaineers such as Solomon Saylor respected a preacher who could "mount a stump" and deliver a message they could relate to. They had little use for a man who simply regurgitated a sermon from notes learned in a seminary school. William H. Haney claimed in 1906 that "in the earlier days and sometimes now the minister makes no preparation for the sermon, but preaches from the text that comes to his mind after he faces the audience."[35]

The small congregations, which perhaps included twenty people total, joined in the service by singing hymns by such English composers as Isaac Watts and John Newton.[36] Walter Brownlow Posey contended that these hymns were a powerful device in emphasizing Methodist creed.[37] People would clap hands, jerk, leap, weep uncontrollably, and "fall out under the power." Many would lie motionless and spellbound for hours. At the conclusion of a service the preacher would make an altar call, in which sinners were urged to come forward and repent. Approaching the altar was a symbolic means of rejecting sin and being elevated into the glorified state of the saved. Insistence on an open confession of sins in the form of public testimonials was a means of breaking down personal pride and self-possession. It also reinforced egalitarian bonds of kinship, community, and social solidarity.

At Forrester's Creek, church became a family affair, where religion reflected the social structure. Lay preachers used religion to set rules for disciplining the disorderly. Theology became a method for social control. For the mountain preachers, self-discipline was the key to personal holiness. Living a holy life involved constant struggle; it meant denying "sins of the flesh," such as sexuality or whiskey drinking, and practicing other forms of self-denial as well.

The frontier churches reinforced the dominant male order. Women could not speak from the pulpit or lead services. They had to sit on opposite sides of the church from men and listen to male preachers remind them of their place in the social order. The Baptists and Methodists did provide women with psychological and social space away from the demands of their world. Religion offered a concept of "new birth" that devalued the old life and provided a sense of release from the restraints of pioneer life.[38]

The Methodist circuit riders received modest pay from the Methodist Church, but the Baptist preachers did not receive compensation for their services. To be paid would have meant working on Sunday and thus committing the sin of violating the Sabbath.[39] Receiving a weekly paycheck for preaching would also have indicated a dependence on congregations. On occasion frontier ministers received "love offerings," but generally Baptist preachers in areas such as Forrester's Creek supported themselves and their families by farming.

Shortly after the Saylors established themselves in eastern Kentucky, they abandoned the Presbyterians and joined ranks with the Hardshell or Primitive Baptists. They did so in large part through the persuasion of kin and neighbors who had also converted. The Hardshells subscribed to the predestination beliefs that Solomon and Sally clung to. The Saylors believed that God had a plan and that they were placed on this Earth to carry it out. They never abandoned this conviction.

In 1827, at the annual Kehukee Baptist Association meeting in Halifax County, North Carolina, an issue surfaced that had evoked serious debate among congregations and that caused a deep split between Baptists from the 1820s to the 1840s.[40] The division was known as the "antimission break." Highly Calvinistic Primitive Baptists, such as the Saylors, rejected missions on the premise that man should not intervene in God's plan. Only by God's grace could salvation be gained. The Saylors believed that missionary work was simply "a waste of time." They also rejected Sunday schools, temperance societies, and church conventions, holding that there was no scriptural basis for such organizations. The sects that accepted the opposite view—the "nonscriptural" view, according to the Primitive Baptists—were known as Missionary Baptists. The fight was amplified in eastern Kentucky because the mountaineers distrusted centralized authority and did not feel comfortable receiving dictates from a governing body. The Saylors feared that the postures Missionary Baptists promoted not only threatened their Calvinist creed but also reflected "man's word" and therefore threatened the autonomy of their church.[41]

Although Solomon Saylor and his family rejected the Missionary Baptist position, their own religion was constantly modified to fit the needs of the congregation. Church policy was a matter of communal consensus. Religion at Forrester's Creek was influenced by a variety of beliefs, traditions, and worship practices. Doctrinal issues such as baptism occasionally would almost take complete possession of a man. Solomon Saylor was no exception. He accepted the Baptist creed of immersion and believed that it was not acceptable to baptize infants. Other faiths were not so specific in their convictions. The Methodists accepted all forms of baptism and administered the rite by sprinkling or immersion, whichever their converts preferred. In spite of the variation on doctrinal issues, most mountaineers agreed on the essential points. It was common to find them at each other's services. As Emma Bell Miles commented in 1905,

In a settlement in our mountains one may find missionary Baptists, Hardshell Baptists, Cumberlands, Calvinists, and what not; but at the bottom they are very much the same. Arguments frequently arise and become bitter over questions of immersion, close communication, original sin and the like; but the principles that control their daily habit of mind, the beliefs that are the mainsprings of thought and action, do not differ nearly so much between man and man as the propounders of doctrines would have us suppose. One mountaineer may believe that negroes are descended from some animal resembling a monkey; his neighbor may "see by the scripture" that it is not only improper for a woman to speak in church, but that she must under no circumstances remove her sunbonnet during religious service; another's favorite crotchet may be his conviction that the earth is supported floating on an infinite expanse of water; while yet a fourth declares "once in grace always in grace," and will argue the subject all day Sunday. Each one produces abundance of Scripture texts to fortify his position, and over these matters they frequently disagree; yet although no amount of talking will make them admit it, their attitude toward the supernatural world is really the same.[42]

By 1848, when Solomon Saylor died, eastern Kentucky was still an extremely isolated area. Not only did the Saylors remain secluded from the outside world at their home on Forrester's Creek; they were still separated from other mountain communities as well. Little communication existed between these settlements, and people continued to be oriented toward local community life rather than to the larger society, so each mountain community retained a certain sovereignty and steadiness in politics, economy, and social life.[43] Family households remained scattered, and towns of any size were still rare. The land provided life, space, and shelter; it furnished almost everything people needed.

Since their arrival in 1805, the Saylors had remained traditional in their lifestyles. The distance of markets kept John Saylor, Solomon's son, tied to a self-sufficient, kinship-based agricultural providence of the sort that his father had practiced. Like his father, John allowed his livestock to graze in common herds with his neighbors', using the hillsides for forage. Around 1830, John married his first cousin, Mary "Polly" Hoskins.[44] The couple lived on the north side of the Cumberland River, between Puckett's Creek and Forrester's Creek,[45] in the area known today as Molus.

"Hard cash" or money remained scarce in eastern Kentucky, and barter was still the principle means of exchange. Banking facilities were rare; banks were not established in this area until the beginning of the twentieth century.[46] Some timbering occurred, but not in Harlan County. The subsistence character of the economy, together with the primitive transportation networks and geographical barriers that the mountains presented, restricted commercial logging in most areas, further restricting the Saylors to traditional agricultural methods.

John Saylor and his family remained virtually cut off from the outside world. In such remote areas as Forrester's Creek, societies developed in an egalitarian way. Capitalist practices such as the accumulation of profit remained alien to rural people, prohibiting the growth of a social hierarchy. Ronald D. Eller made the following observation concerning mountain society:

> Status rather than class distinctions . . . were the most important social divisions in traditional mountain society. These status distinctions were functions not of economics (wealth, land, ownership, or access to natural resources) but the value system of the community itself. In remote mountain neighborhoods where economic differences were minimal, measures of social prestige were based on personality characteristics or ascribed traits such as sex, age, and family group. The rural social order was divided not into upper, middle, and lower classes but into respectable and nonrespectable classes, and each local community determined its own criteria for respectability. The status system, of course, tended to break down in the villages and county seat towns where class distinctions (and thus class consciousness) were more noticeable. . . . While status consciousness helped to shape the values and beliefs of mountain neighborhoods, especially at the local level, class distinctions did exist at the larger community.[47]

In 1830 it was still uncommon for the Saylors to hear a "regular preacher." It had become routine for Methodist circuit riders and Baptist farmer-preachers to meet at different locales once a month. In 1905, Emma Bell Miles published this description of Brother Absalom Darney's circuit:

> There is preaching every third Sunday in the month at the Kings Creek log church. Saturday afternoons one sees Brother Absalom Darney's pony amble down the woods-road, its rider's white hair and beard in the wind; one divines the small Bible and brass-rimmed spectacles handkerchief-swathed, and the clean shirt and change of socks in his deerskin saddle-bags; then one tells the neighbors that "no providential hindrance" has prevented the preacher's meeting his appointment, and next morning everybody turns out to go to church. On the first Sunday it is the same at Filmore's Cove; on the second, at a settlement in Sequatchie; and the fourth is claimed by a forsaken little "shack" church

away back in the Cumberland range. This is Brother Absalom's regular circuit.[48]

The only formal institution of significance that gave cohesion to communities was the church. In some locales the Baptist farmer-preachers conducted regular meetings, and small congregations began to gather in various places for worship. The services were still conducted in members' homes, barns, open fields, or wherever was convenient. Occasionally services were held in one-room school houses, but at Forrester's Creek this development did not occur until after the Civil War. The camp-meeting style of worship had firmly taken hold during the 1830s, in the style James S. Dalton described: "Prayers and songs of differing character would be offered up simultaneously. People would be running hither and thither, falling in their tracks, crying out weeping, or rejoicing."[49]

Although Solomon Saylor's estate was settled in the courts, communal legislation usually solved most problems. Many disputes were resolved in church. The Old Regular Baptists still believe that controversy should be settled in that way.[50] The congregation that had emerged at Forrester's Creek frequently settled disputes, but John Saylor refused to turn to them concerning his father's will and then lost his case in the courts. Eller states,

> The mountain church, as an extension of the family, served as an important medium of social control, legitimizing and sustaining the mores of the community. In rural areas where law enforcement was sparse, the family and the church were responsible for policing the wrongdoing of community members. Transgressions against the social mores left a mark not only upon the individual, but upon the larger family unit; consequently, the kin functioned to control such transgressions. Thus, social order was maintained not so much through legal institutions and government agencies as through kinship and primary group relationships.[51]

After Solomon Saylor's death, John and Mary remained in the Baptist fold, but various strains of Arminianism had disturbed the religious consensus at Forrester's Creek. The early Calvinist view that only the elect could gain deliverance had been replaced by the Arminian belief that salvation was open to all. Mountain theology at Forrester's Creek had become a blend of various positions adjusted to fit the needs of the people, and mountain religion was still conveyed orally. The Bible or prepared sermons were rarely brought to religious gatherings, because most preachers were unlettered men. These ministers simply replicated themes that had been "preached on" in previous services. The preachers altered the text in some instances to match the immediate context. The content of the messages was nonintellectual and compelling, and the preachers' major concern was to fight sin. In many instances the early clergymen served a form of apprenticeship to other pastors before embarking on their own preaching careers. Other preachers ascended from the congregations after hearing and mastering replicated sermons and developed their own style of delivery.

For frontier Methodists and Baptists it was not seminary training that qualified a man for the pulpit, but the fact that he had been converted. Conversion was an individual and emotional experience. It meant one had been "born again" and had passed into the glorified state of the saved. Ministers described the experience to the church gathering in order that listeners could share it. Patrick B. Mullen argues that in this way, conversion and religious beliefs in Baptist churches were "internalized from childhood" and that church members "were prepared for the liminal experience when it finally happened."[52] A minister would often tell the congregation how he had once been a sinner and then "saw the light." From that point he was a changed man, fighting sin and preaching the word. Such preachers followed the emotional camp-meeting style that mountaineers sought and identified with. Appalachians such as the Saylors found comfort in this kind of emotionalism.

Five. Industrialization

John and Mary Saylor's son, Josiah Silas, was born on May 27, 1830.[1] Josiah was frequently called "Josh" by his parents and kin, but he regularly used his middle name when conducting legal matters. Josh's lifestyle resembled that of his father and grandfather. He combed the mountains hunting wild game and helped his father with the farming. Josh received little formal education. His mother taught him to read, and he developed a legible handwriting. Since there were few primers at Forrester's Creek, Mary taught him to read from the Bible. Josh cultivated a good knowledge of the Bible, and as a source of entertainment he would often question mountain preachers on matters of Gospel. He usually won his argument, making the preachers mad enough to fight.

At the time of the Civil War, the population of Harlan County totaled 5,494. Forrester's Creek was still remote, but the mountain people were drawn into the conflict from the beginning. During the war Josh sided with the Union and served as an infantryman in Company F of the Forty-ninth Kentucky.

After the Civil War, Jack Weller contends, "religious individualism" had become firmly entrenched in mountain culture:

> This individualism rejects all forms of discipline in religion. If a church does not suit the mountaineer by preaching what he wants to hear in the way he wants to hear it or does not give him enough opportunity to assert himself and be heard, he will quit and go somewhere else. If he is a strong personality, he may even form his own church, where he is the minister and "boss," perhaps erecting a building in his front yard and naming the church after his family.... The mountains hold a great many of these "churches," based on personal desires and feelings of their members, usually split off from a larger group—ingrown little bodies that pamper their people in order to keep them coming and thus confirm them in their favorite prejudices. Up many hollows, churches stand side by side or across the road from each other, seemingly glaring at each other.[2]

Perhaps there is some truth in Weller's argument about individualism and strength of personality. F. Carlene Bryant argues, however, that "Weller's observation leaves much to be desired, for the presence of two churches in this neighborhood appears to have less to do with religious 'individualism,' however defined, than with a strong tendency for each family to act as a group and independently of the others in religious affairs."[3]

The Saylors undoubtedly acted as a group when it came to religious affairs. Josh remained with the Baptists after his father's death in 1870. He had seen many changes in the church during his forty-one years, but from birth Josh Saylor had been immersed in a religion that stressed emotion, spontaneous preaching, and communal spirit. For example, it was customary for early preachers to mingle with congregations before a service to find out their concerns and needs and then to incorporate what they learned in their sermons. This practice strengthened bonds between clergy and lay members.

Baptist spiritual traditions, as the Saylors practiced them, had become a blend of various religious practices. Customs such as the "holy kiss" and the refusal to take an oath had German Dunkers roots.[4] Strains of Methodist Arminianism prevailed in most congregations, but Calvinism was never totally abandoned. In mountain churches it is still common to hear the Calvinist statement "Good works won't get me to heaven, only the grace of God."

Appalachian religion had clearly become distilled into a regional religion where local autonomy ruled. Lay preachers acted as patriarchs, preaching communal spirit and rejecting selfish individualism. The meetings were conducted informally; members frequently passed in and out of the church, and children roamed freely among the congregation. This type of service rarely disturbed preachers, because it was what they expected. The preaching technique itself involved a traditional sort of chanting, in which each phrase was punctuated with an "ah!" or a deep breath. After two or three preachers had delivered messages, the congregation was given a chance to testify. Often testimonies became sermons in their own right, as individuals recounted their conversion experiences and told of dreams and visions. Enlightened women frequently gave "hot" testimonies to a congregation, although women were never recognized as preachers. Near the end of the service an altar call was made to invite people to give up a world of sin and enter into a new relationship with God. If individuals experienced conversion, they were later baptized in a creek or river. Converts at Forrester's Creek were baptized by total immersion in a public ceremony. Baptism was a transformative indication of release from "the old status order" to a "new status order."[5] Through this act one also "committed oneself to the shared ethos of the church community."[6]

At the conclusion of the meeting, everybody joined in a simultaneous group prayer, thunderously giving praise and asking for wishes to be granted. Many screamed at the top of their voices and shed tears while waving their hands in the air. Others simply stood or knelt on bended knee. Occasionally, sometimes annually, the sacraments of communion and foot washing would be performed. Foot washing was a product of the early Baptist revivals in colonial Virginia but spread inland through the Methodists.[7]

By 1900 the Baptists in eastern Kentucky had changed drastically. The service still followed the old patterns of worship, but the sermons were more intellectual; much of the unrehearsed and emotional content that the Saylors had identified with had been eliminated. The primary reason for this change in style was an attempt by both Baptists and Methodists to attract more members into their ranks. It also involved a move by the Methodist church away from the old Wesleyan enthusiasm toward the sober forms of middle-class Protestantism.[8]

The Home Missions personnel who entered eastern Kentucky on a large scale during the 1890s also influenced mountain religion. These missionaries saw highland mountaineers as irreligious or "unchurched." Their goal was to help mountain people "adapt to the new changes in their lives brought on by the industrialization overtaking the Appalachian region."[9] Above all, they hoped to assimilate mountaineers into one homogeneous Christian nation. Josh disliked Home Missions goals and religion. He viewed them as attempting to centralize churches, totally eliminating the Baptist principle of local autonomy in each hollow. People in cities like Middlesboro alluded to Home Missions as "railroad religion"; the services were solemn and exhibited little emotion. Home Missions personnel, in turn, viewed mountain preachers who "relied on the Spirit" for their messages as ignorant. Mountain Calvinist beliefs of conversion by grace differed from the "Victorian Christianity of the home missions," which emphasized education and work toward a state of salvation.[10]

Josiah Saylor disliked the new formal and structured services. Sunday schools had now appeared, along with "fancy" churches, and songbooks were used by most denominations. Josh was heard to say, "If these people would spend more time in church, they would know these songs by heart. Then they wouldn't need these songbooks." Foot washing had become an uncommon ritual. Josh believed that it was necessary to wash feet in church as a symbol of humility. He contended that foot washing was important to remind congregations that "no man was better than the other." Many members began to wear neckties and "fasten-on" shirt collars to worship service. Josh was opposed to elaborate dress in church. "These people are getting too proud," he commented.

Preachers were seen as belonging to the elite, and common farmers could not identify with them. The ministers required members to pay tithes, and failure to honor the obligation would frequently be mentioned from the pulpit. The pastors also insisted on taking up special offerings, in addition to tithes. Josh was not a wealthy man and could not afford to pay the sums that the preachers demanded.

The new preachers were educated men from seminaries and did not deliver their messages in the impulsive, unplanned way made popular by earlier preachers—the method of relying on memory and revelation from the Holy Ghost. One of the few preachers who still delivered messages in the old heart-rending style was "Uncle Nath" Lowe from Jesse's Creek. Josh liked Lowe's old-style sermonizing.

Josh felt that his kind of worship was being threatened by changes in the Baptist and Methodist churches. Around 1900 he left the Baptists and joined the newly emerging Holiness sects. The entire Saylor family went with him. In the Holiness movement they rediscovered the spiritual and emotional enthusiasm that had been lost among the Baptists. Faith healing and other accounts of miracles became widespread where Holiness evangelists preached. Holiness evangelists traveled throughout the South bringing their doctrines of Christian perfection to places like Forrester's Creek. Josiah Saylor's camp-meeting heritage prepared him for the message the Holiness evangelists delivered. Since settlement, religion had been the Saylors' primary outlet for socializing. In 1900 Harlan County was still very secluded, and going to church remained a major means of interacting with other people.

Between 1910 and 1930 many people in Appalachia joined the Saylors in leaving the Baptist and Methodist churches. As a result of cultural conflict and social disorganization, they flocked into such emerging denominations as the Church of God, the Pentecostal and Holiness worshipers, and the Free Will Baptists. Anthropologist Shaunna Lynn Scott found that

Harlan Countians have exhibited a marked distaste for life in the religious mainstream. Some 50 years after the churches of their forebears achieved success and legitimacy, Harlan Countians rebelled against the hierarchy, moral decline and loss of emotionalism that they perceived in their "establishment" denominations. The results of this movement are apparent today, as unaffiliated Baptist churches and, more prominently, charismatic Holiness groups (Pentecostal and Church of God) dot the hillsides and valleys of Harlan County. Some of these churches are so independent that they do not claim sectarian or denominational kinship with any religious organization.[11]

These new fundamentalist churches were "reformist rather than revolutionary or constructive in character."[12] The denominations' practices and beliefs represented an intensification and elaboration of traditional norms, not a drastic aberration from them. John Wesley's position on "worldly things" intensified among them. Holiness preachers stressed the significance of dress and denial of worldly amusements and condemned the improprieties they perceived in Baptist and Methodist churches.[13]

Many of the ministers of these newly emerging sects were fellow workers, friends, and family members. As in the past, mountaineers were more willing to listen to a preacher who could identify with their problems than to a pastor who had little time for them. The new churches and pastors offered participants the freedom to express themselves and gave members the ability to identify with a greater power.

W. J. Cash contends that the Holiness sects established themselves in the villages and poorest sections of town. "It is just in this decade of most rapid expansion of Southern industrialism, of speculation, and of the widening of the physical gulf between the classes that we find such sects as the Holy Rollers and the Church of God (an unorthodox Baptist congregation organized in Tennessee, and sometimes called Holy rollers on their own account) establishing themselves widely and solidly in the South—in the mill villages, in the poorest sections of town and even in the countryside."[14]

County schoolhouses and homes became the first meeting places for the Holiness people. At Livingston, in Rockcastle County, "the old Livingston Coal Company commissary building was used as a place of worship."[15] In areas such as Wallins Creek, Holiness doctrine was delivered by M. G. Disney in 1912. He preached in brush arbors, barns, homes, and tents, in places named Greasy Ridge, Pony Lot, Hazel Green, and Sand Gap. He preached in a thunderous style similar to that the early Methodist circuit riders. Sherman Sizemore also preached Pentecostal doctrine to the mountaineers; his messages focused on the "teaching of the Apostles."[16]

Perhaps the preacher with the greatest impact on the mountaineers was Garrett White of Corbin, Kentucky. White would walk as far as twenty miles to deliver his "hot messages." When people heard him they fell prostrate on the floor for hours. Garrett White was normally uncompromising in his beliefs, and his sermons stressed spiritual activity rather than doctrine. There was an elemental set of truths to be adhered to, according to Pentecostal preacher Alfred Carrier:

> Sanctification came by repentance, confession, and faith in the atoning blood of Jesus. Also, [White preached] that the healing for the physical body was provided for, in the atonement.
>
> Sanctification of body, soul and spirit could be achieved by prayer, faith and dedication. This was essential before the baptism in the spirit could be received. Speaking in tongues was the physical evidence of baptism of the Holy Ghost. The Lord's Supper was to be observed by partaking of the fruit of the vine and eating of broken bread. Those early believers always followed the Lord's Supper with washing of the Saint's feet. The Lord's Supper took on the name of "Foot Washing." The word would go thru the community "We are having a foot washing at Church tonight." Everyone knew it was the Lord's Supper.[17]

Glossolalia, or speaking in tongues, became widespread in mountain Holiness churches in the late 1800s. However, talking in tongues was not

Lewis York, ca. 1925
(Photo courtesy of Park
Saylor)

connected to salvation until that question was raised by Charles F. Parham and a group of Bible students at Bethel College in Topeka, Kansas.[18]

Garrett White, Sherman Sizemore, Lewis York, and others frequently preached to the Saylors at Forrester's Creek, but their blistering sermons offended many unbelievers. The mountain evangelists quickly learned that some unbelievers, such as moonshiners, would retaliate against them for their campaign against sin.

The law would not protect the Holiness people in the early years of the movement. In Jackson County, a preacher named John Blackburn reported that eggs had been thrown at him. Reverend Ralph Mooneyham was shot at.[19] The worshipers were constantly mocked and taunted. Rocks were thrown at the church windows, and snakes and bees were turned loose during services in an attempt to disrupt them. Some buildings were burned or blown up with dynamite. The Saylors did not fear the violence directed at the "Holy Rollers"; they remained among the faithful.

Park Saylor reports that "in Harlan and Bell counties, all of the Holiness evangelists preached on the apostles, and some sermonized on the Holy Ghost." In 1910, Z. B. and Dan Brock began preaching on the Holy Ghost in Harlan County, and people received the message and gave evidence of "obtaining the gift" by talking in tongues. The Brocks equated sanctification with glossolalia in the same way that Charles F. Parham and his Bible students had done a decade earlier in Kansas. The Brocks preached, "You're not going to heaven unless you speak in tongues." Reports of people receiving the Holy Ghost began to spread throughout the mountains. It was seen both in cities like Manchester and in remote areas like Horse Creek.[20]

Many preachers began to preach on the Holy Ghost, but Lewis York was the first evangelist who delivered messages on the signs in Mark 16. "Mark 16 says I can heal, cast out demons, talk in tongues, handle serpents, or drink any deadly thing," exclaimed York to a Path Fork congregation in early 1930. He continued, "No matter how bad things get, the Lord has given us the power to perform these miracles." York organized churches in several places, such as Sand Springs and Sand Gap. He drew large crowds and reportedly performed the act of healing on numerous occasions, but he never handled serpents. Carrier repeated a story told to him about Lewis York by "Brother Willie Roberts" of Clay County:

> Mr. George Sizemore had a daughter that was blind and was very poor in those early times, but showed kindness to the men of God. Rev. Johnny Roberts and Rev. Lewis York, another early Pentecostal preacher, were spending the night with the Sizemores and asked if they might pray for the blind girl. Mr. Sizemore agreed. They had prayer for her then went to their rooms. However, instead of going to bed, they went out back to the hollow and spent the night in prayer. Returning the next morning they found the girl out back picking up coal. This was a notable miracle since the girl was born blind.[21]

Reports of these types of miracles occurred throughout the mountains. One of the greatest acts in Harlan County lore is attributed to the Path Fork evangelist Sherman Lawson, a friend of Josh Saylor's. On a summer morning in 1912, Lawson felt the Spirit come over him and went to the "holler" to pray. When he was down on his knees in deep prayer, "the Lord moved on him" and allegedly told Lawson he had a mission for him. He returned home and told his family, "I have to go to Wallins Creek," which was located fourteen miles from the Lawson home. Lawson walked by the many coal mines in the area and proceeded down the railroad track. He stopped at a branch line and said, "Lord, what way will you have me to go?" Lawson claimed that God "directed him to the right." After walking approximately one mile, he came upon a big white house "with a porch all the way around it."

People were gathered around the house and the yard was full. Some men were making a coffin in the wood-yard. Lawson approached the people and asked, "What is going on?" They responded, "Grover Blanton's daughter Norma is dead." He then walked up to Mrs. Blanton and requested, "Can I pray for your daughter, Mrs. Blanton?" Mrs. Blanton gave her consent. The three-year-old girl was "laid out on a flat board across a sewing machine." She had been "washed, dressed, and prepared for the grave." Nickels had been placed on her eyelids to hold them shut. When Lawson approached the dead girl, who had passed away twenty-five hours earlier, he took her by the hand and got down beside the body in deep prayer. According to the story, life came back into the young girl, she arose from the board, and people came inside to see the miracle that Sherman Lawson had performed. Norma lived a full life and died only recently, at the age of eighty years. Norma gave birth to three children in her lifetime.[22] Commenting on other such reports, Park Saylor stated, "The same power that handles the serpent is the power that raises the dead. . . . I have seen the dead raised four times, but you have to be in a deep anointing for that to happen."

Lawson allegedly raised another woman from the dead at Wallins Creek during the year of 1932. Mary Christian, who had a history of illness, succumbed in the presence of a small church gathering. She had begun to "draw" (a mountain description of rigor mortis), according to bystanders, and had been given up for dead. But witnesses reported that when Sherman Lawson laid hands on her, she arose. Josh Saylor was not shocked by Lawson's feats. He believed that a man of God could accomplish anything.

Following the Civil War, industrialization gradually began to transform eastern Kentucky society. The Home Missions that entered the mountains in the last quarter of the nineteenth century saw the changes resulting from industrial capitalism as proper. Missions assistance in helping capitalism flourish was not unique to Appalachia. Anthropologist Jean Comaroff found that by imposing Wesleyan values on a native population, missionaries played a crucial role in giving the capitalists a hold on central southern Africa. To put it simply, missions laid the groundwork for the process of proletarianization. The missions were an essential medium for reducing confrontation between local systems and the global forces of international capitalism.[23] Mountain people like the Saylor family were seen as static or traditional and as standing in the way of progress. The missionaries and capitalists saw Appalachians as morally weak and lazy because of their indifference to the forced pace of time-clock capitalism. But mountaineers had traditionally performed work in rhythmic seasonal cycles: crops had been planted in the spring and harvested in the late autumn, and other demands were also met at seasonal intervals. In other words, mountaineers were not lazy; they simply worked according to a different ethic.

Since 1805 the Saylors had practiced self-sufficiency. They did not accumulate wealth; they worked only to assure survival. This system was standard throughout Appalachia. The changes that industrial capitalism introduced greatly undermined self-sufficiency and social autonomy.[24] In 1909, H. Paul Douglass of the American Missionary Association of the Congregational Church published a book titled *Christian Reconstruction in the South.* Two chapters, "The Old Men of the Mountains" and "The Passing of the Mountaineer," called for the mountaineers to be evicted from their traditional homelands.[25] The Home Missions endorsed a change in the legal control of land and undermined a self-sufficient mountain society, while making its members into a propertyless wage-earning class. It was the Home Missions goal to convey the culture of the capitalists to the mountaineers.

Harlan County's large timber and coal riches were discovered in the 1750s,[26] but the remoteness of the area kept land speculation casual. By 1850, the "casual" speculation had become significant. Capitalists—mainly absentee owners—held 50 percent of Harlan County land. In adjacent Bell County, 40 percent of the assessed acreage belonged to taxpayers who owned more than one thousand acres. Twenty-one percent of Letcher, 29 percent of Rowan, and 30 percent of Leslie County were retained by these large taxpayers.[27]

Capitalists were befriended not only by the Home Missions but also by politicians. According to sociologist Alan Banks, in 1828 some Kentucky politicians expressed displeasure with the practice of granting land to small settlers at modest prices. Property, they maintained, should be granted to "monopolizing capitalists for the purpose of speculation."[28] Many plans were formulated to assist the capitalists in their attempts at expansion, but not much came of those plans. The shortage of wage labor was a significant problem at the time. The mountaineers who practiced traditional patterns of subsistence farming showed little interest in hiring themselves out for wages. One scheme by the Kentucky government to assist the capitalists in overcoming the inadequate labor pool was instituted by Governor John W. Stevenson in 1868: he attempted to bring in foreign immigrants.[29] The Kentucky house and senate approved the governor's plan and established a "Kentucky Bureau of Immigration aspiring to recruit the needed laborers." A plan was also formulated by the Kentucky government "to finance the passage of immigrants to Kentucky."[30] This plan was largely unsuccessful. In 1930, 90 percent of Harlan County's 64,557 residents were native-born whites; 9 percent were blacks; and 1 percent were foreign-born whites.[31]

For thirty years after the mid-1880s, Harlan and neighboring counties "swarmed with land speculators."[32] As we have already seen, entrepreneurs had bypassed the eastern Kentucky highlands for a century because of its geographical seclusion. But the search for cheap resources caused the Kentucky highlands "to be viewed with a new eye."[33]

Tycoons from the eastern states and Britain now became interested in the region's large virgin forests. The area in which the Saylors had lived since settlement proved particularly attractive. In 1891, Kentucky Coal and Iron bought 6,557 acres in Clay, Leslie, Perry, and Harlan Counties. Other companies purchased similar-sized tracts of land. One of the earliest firms in Harlan County was the Kentenia Corporation, which was formed in 1907 by Warren Delano (uncle of Franklin Delano Roosevelt) of the Louisville and Nashville Railroad, along with other members of the Roosevelt family; Edward Davis and his son Charles, of Philadelphia; and other millionaire speculators. The nucleus of Kentenia had actually been formed thirty-one years prior to the company's founding, when Edward Davis purchased 86,000 acres in Bell and Harlan Counties for $86,000. The mountaineers who sold their lands forfeited all claims to the vast layers of coal that lay just beneath the surface of their farms. Shaunna Lynn Scott explains how it happened:

The agents of major investors used a variety of means to acquire land and mineral rights. Most Appalachian farmers, unaware of the market value of their coal, sold mineral rights and untillable land to these speculators for as little as $.25 to $5.00 per acre. These resources seemed useless to the subsistence farmer; to receive any cash in return for them appeared to be a good deal. Little did they know that the deed they signed, called the "broad form deed," gave the new owner the rights to all mineral wealth, including those which had not been discovered. It also granted them the right to use whatever means they deemed necessary to remove minerals, even building a road through the farmer's fields.[34]

The Saylor family lost their land holdings through another unscrupulous device used by capitalists to rob mountaineers of their property. In 1870 John Saylor died, leaving his estate divided between his wife and children, including a nephew, Nelson Salyer. Josh was appointed administrator of the estate, and he settled it in 1871.[35] However, for a period of ten years the heirs neglected to pay property taxes that they were unaware of. When speculators learned of this oversight, they advised Harlan County officials, and a tax sale was conducted. The Saylors were outbid by the land company and lost their land. Other family members sold their land to speculators.

After the property had been divested, the Saylor family never owned land as they had in the past. Historically, land had always been a safety valve when times got hard. The subsistence nature of the economy made mountaineers immune from the effects of economic downturn. Hillsides that had been used as common pasture by the residents at Forrester's Creek were now owned by the capitalists, who prohibited the practice. Mountaineers could no longer rely on their land for subsistence farming. Their ancestral property had vanished. By losing their land, they also lost control of the means of production.

In a few short years the Saylors had been transformed from yeoman farmers into laborers, and their society had been recast from a consensus system to a complete oligarchy. Josiah Saylor and his son Zachariah were allowed to live on the land that was formerly Saylor property. They were also allowed to grow a garden and raise some livestock, but they had lost control of their ancestral land.

The large virgin forests that still existed also attracted moguls from the eastern states. The uncertainty of business and the seclusion presented by the mountains kept most railroads out until the eve of World War I, and lack of transportation, in turn, made any serious logging operations impractical. But when large-scale conveyance of the timber became a reality, the speculators sent their agents into the mountains to acquire timber rights by any means necessary. Thousands of trees were purchased for less than one dollar apiece. Harlan County was covered with huge popular, oak, walnut, hickory, beech, and maple trees, and many other varieties of native timber that were worth fortunes. The logging operations and lack of conservation have left the mountains with culls and second-growth timber that barely endure today.

The majority of the land buyers and coal mine owners in eastern Kentucky were not of indigenous stock.[36] The same applied throughout Appalachia. Over 77 percent of the coal producers in the southern mountains between 1880 and 1930 were born outside the region.[37] Regarding these capitalists, Scott wrote, "They allied themselves with the local elite who used kin ties and their status in the community to lend legitimacy to the investors' efforts. In cash-poor, subsistence-oriented Harlan County, investors bought land and mineral rights at low prices, from $.25 to $5 per acre."[38]

Between 1911 and 1930, the number of coal miners employed in Harlan County grew from 169 to 11,920.[39] The rapid population increase associated with industrialization tended to break down the mountain society and disintegrate traditions. The most immediate consequence of industrialization was the disordering of economic customs that took place as the money-based economy replaced an economy grounded largely on barter and subsistence farming. The societal change with the greatest impact was the crumbling of community and family organization. Appalachian sociologist John Photiadis commented,

> People who had always lived in stable primary groups were thrown together with masses of other uprooted individuals. The restraints of family clan and neighborhood ceased to be effective. The social values of the frontier society lost their meaning in these new communities. Competition and exploitation replaced friendly mutual aid as social relations became casual and impersonal. . . . The destruction of the older social order was almost complete. . . . The ties of the family clan tended to disintegrate under the impact of this new way of life.[40]

In an attempt to locate the large labor pool near the work sites, coal operators built housing for miners and their families. By 1930, four out of five residents of Harlan County lived in company-owned coal camps. According to Mack H. Gillenwater, "Often this construction resulted in new settlements, but occasionally houses were merely added to an existing community."[41] These neighborhoods were known as "mining camps" or "company towns." Most of the dwellings were built out of native lumber.

The coal operator would choose a site for the camp and then would cut enough lumber (usually either hemlock, poplar, or oak) to build the necessary housing.[42] Inside bathrooms were rare in the company houses. Outside privies were constructed and situated parallel to streams in an attempt to transport human waste away from the mining towns. Communal washhouses were provided so that miners could wash the coal dust off after a day in the mines. As a result of these practices, wells and water supplies that provided drinking water for miners and their families became polluted and generated health problems.

The water supply for the city of Harlan, where mine bosses lived, was inspected and found to be excellent. The wells and sources of water in rural areas and coal camps, however, were largely uncontrolled. High rates of mobility between company towns fragmented the traditional kinship networks and further alienated mountaineers. Exploitative conditions were so bad for mountain families that voices of protest were soon heard. As James W. Raine wrote in 1924, "The mountain people are suffering from the ruthless exploitation of large financial interests. These foreign juggernauts may have secured the coal and timber lands for a song, but taking money from those that have no special use for it is not a fatal damage. The deadly sin is the thrusting of a ferocious and devouring social system upon an unprepared and defenseless people."[43]

The capitalists used every means possible to gain a total grip on mountain society. Toward that end, missionaries and educators played a particularly important role. Their function was "to make legitimate the exploitation, to eliminate some of the worst abuses, and to educate and change values so that the people would accept the new ways."[44] Schools, churches, movie theaters, ballparks, and other recreational facilities were built by the mine owners as disguised means of achieving these ends. They were critical in restructuring local communities and the lives of mountaineers. Company preachers and teachers were used to harness any destabilizing factors that threatened the interests of the mine owners and to mediate the process of proletarianization. J. Wayne Flynt writes, "Churches and schools taught the values of organization and planning. Such denial of traditions by institutions that mountain children respected made many of them ashamed of their heritage. Teachers and missionaries helped legitimize economic exploitation by blaming Appalachian ills entirely on the mountaineer and his ways. Few of them recognized that the economic system shared the blame."[45] For capitalists to attempt to change professions of faith was nothing new. Eighty years earlier, in the 1840s, the papermaking industry in Massachusetts had done the same to prevent religious groups from speaking out against abuse.[46]

Mountaineers in eastern Kentucky could not relate to the methods of school teaching in the mining camps simply because they were "instruments of the 'big bosses,' reflecting exactly their philosophy of management and business."[47] In most mining camps two schoolhouses were usually built, one for whites and a smaller one for blacks. For both races, the education received was less than ample.

The coal companies brought with them the "nefarious scrip system" and introduced it into the commissaries.[48] At the end of each month, miners were paid not with U.S. currency but with coal scrip that the company had printed.[49] Some mining camps coined aluminum or brass scrip embossed with their corporate logos. Because the company had printed the scrip, only company commissaries honored it; miners were thus forced to buy all of their goods at the company store, which usually sold low-quality food, clothing, shoes, and tools at inflated prices.[50] They also had to supply their own tools for extracting coal. If a shovel or pick broke, the miner had to buy a replacement at the company store. As a result of low pay and infrequent paydays, miners frequently received credit from the company store. At the end the month, once his debts were subtracted, the miner received little or no pay, and the cycle started again. The stores encouraged buying on credit and charged miners high rates of interest.[51] The miners referred to the company stores as "pluck-me" stores. "Many went from paycheck to paycheck without ever pocketing a nickel in cash or scrip."[52] This system placed miners in total dependency on mine owners. Miners who were caught buying goods outside the company commissaries were dismissed, beaten, or killed. According to Harry Caudill,

> the miner came to be almost totally insulated against the world outside his coal camp. In return for his labor his employers clothed his back, filled his belly, sheltered and lighted his household, and provided his family with medical treatment, fuel and water. The thoughtful operators even organized burial associations, withholding a couple of dollars each month from the workman's wages for payment to a favorite undertaker, so that when death came the mortician's bill had been paid in advance. Needless to say, the company realized a profit from each of these endeavors. The miner found himself on a treadmill from which he lacked the knowledge and self-discipline to escape.[53]

Coal mining states adjacent to Kentucky also used company scrip. West Virginia had laws prohibiting the use of coal scrip, but nearly all of the mines in southern West Virginia, "including the mines owned by U.S. Secretary of the Treasury, Mellon, openly used it."[54] If miners complained about the scrip system, the company made examples of them and silenced their grievance.[55] Those coal miners who objected to conditions at the camps could be harassed, or in some instances even killed, by armed company thugs.[56] In 1925, "the U.S. Coal Commission found that, on the whole, living conditions in the mining camps of the southern mountains were among the worst in the nation."[57]

On July 26, 1915, Park Saylor was born on Forrester's Creek to Zachariah Saylor's son, John Austen Saylor, and Kate Eads Saylor. Kate stated

Park and Carroll Saylor
with their mother,
Kate, in Harlan County,
Kentucky, ca. 1920
(Photo courtesy of Park
Saylor)

that at the time of delivery she heard a voice say, "A child for Jesus." Park Saylor grew up spending time with his brothers, hunting and working on the family farm. He learned to read and write from the old Blue Back Speller, but he only completed four years of formal education.

As a child Park Saylor was exposed to much of the violence that had begun to spread throughout eastern Kentucky. In the summer of 1919 his grandfather, Zack, rode off on a "big blue mule" to a baseball game being played between Forrester's Creek and Puckett's Creek at Path Fork. The two teams disliked each other. As the game progressed, the Forrester's Creek team came to believe that they were being cheated by the umpire, who was making calls in Puckett's Creek's favor. Zack became terribly inflamed during the course of the game and proclaimed loudly, "If that Howard boy, from Path Fork, hits this next ball, I'll shoot his shoe heel off before he gets to first base." Howard hit the ball, and Zack delivered on his promise. As the young man hobbled toward first base, his relatives pulled pistols, and the ball game broke up into an volley of gunfire. Zack's son, Austen, joined in the shooting.

Zachariah Saylor in Harlan County, Kentucky, ca. 1915 (Photo courtesy of Park Saylor)

Since Zack and Austen were outnumbered, they retreated into an old barn and relentlessly continued to inflict casualties on the Howards. Then a member of the Howard family left and returned with a high-powered German Mauser rifle. Shortly, a marksman used that gun to shoot Zack through the chest. As Zack lay on the barn floor dying, he told his son, "Run, Austen, they will kill you." Later in the evening, Austen arrived home with twenty-two bullet holes in his clothes and a finger shot off.[58]

Journalists have long argued that such outbursts were a result of Kentucky's tradition of feuding. On the other hand, John Hevener disputes this "feud theory" and argues that Harlan County's violence surfaced as a result of the "rapid two-decade transformation from a rural, agrarian county to a semiurban, industrial society."[59] Harlan County's society certainly suffered from social disorganization as a result of the rapid industrialization and population increase between the later decades of the nineteenth century and the Great Depression. During the first three years of the depression, several meningitis epidemics swept the county and killed 231 children. Malnutrition killed 56 children in 1929, 91 in 1930, and 84 in 1931. In 1930, one of every four local marriages ended in divorce—a situation almost unknown in the preindustrial era. Forty-two taverns appeared that fostered many types of crime, along with dancing, gambling, prostitution, and brawling. By 1942 one-third of the adult male population suffered from venereal disease. Along with other problems, Harlan County's homicide rate jumped to 77.6 murders per 100,000 in the 1920s.[60] Hevener adds that Harlan County's homicide rate "was twice as high as that of the most violent state, Florida, and seven times as high as in Al Capone's Chicago. . . . Harlan's homicide rate had been far lower in its pastoral past and peaked in its first decade as a semiurban society."[61]

The conditions that industrialization brought were deplorable. "Low wages, irregular employment, and unemployment quickly brought poverty, hunger and disease in their wake."[62] Miners could do nothing about the horrible circumstances in which their families lived. Iva B. Miller, who was employed by the Save the Children Fund of America to investigate children's health in Harlan County, filed this report: "As an indication of the unfavorable conditions which we found among the first 400 children, all of pre-school age, which we examined, I may mention that we discovered that 93 per cent of them needed immunization against diphtheria, 84 per cent needed cod liver oil, 68 per cent were receiving less than their necessary quota of milk, 37 per cent needed treatment for worms not to mention several other items."[63] Providing an adequate milk supply for children posed formidable problems. In 1920 Harlan County had no dairies. Thirteen years later only twenty-four existed—still not enough to produce the amount necessary for a healthy diet for Harlan County's children. Miller summarized the situation this way: "There are 12,000 children under six years of age in the county and 23,000 under twenty-one, that is, still in the growing period. To supply adults with their needed one pint a day and each child with a quart would require some 50,000 quarts— and the supply is fully 30,000 quarts short of that."[64] Moreover, the milk available was not "prepared or administered according to the best ideas of hygiene and sanitation."[65]

As a result of the grave conditions in the coal camps, the Saylors became all the more ardent in their religious conviction, attempting to avoid the sin and malady that they saw everywhere around them. Holiness religion flourished in the coal camps. Arnold Saylor informed me, "My people just prayed harder. There wasn't anything else to help them." Similarly, Park Saylor recalled, "Many people who had hard times turned to the church

John Austen Saylor, ca. 1940. Note the fingers missing on his right hand from the gun battle discussed in Chapter 5. The woman seated on Austen's right is Park Saylor's wife, Alma. (Photo courtesy of Park Saylor)

during those times. That's all we had." Gambling, prostitution, and murder were commonplace. Divorce—another act that Holiness people saw as sinful—had become common, too. As they were exposed to the "wickedness" that had surfaced, the Holiness people began to believe that the world was close to ending, and they turned to their religion in an attempt to reject the "evil world." Within the Holiness faith it was believed that the millennium predicted in the book of Revelation—Christ's thousand-year reign on Earth—could happen at any moment. They thought that God would strike out at wickedness in the near future and that they must be ready. Their religious values and belief in the millennium gave a sense of order and security in a world that appeared to be collapsing. Religion was not the only means mountain people used to maintain their cultural values. Many turned their interests to a revival of Appalachian music or handicrafts.[66]

Shortly after the death of his father, John Austen Saylor, who was living in extreme poverty, moved his family into one of the Pioneer Coal Company mining camps. The mining camps now contained nearly two-thirds of Harlan County's population. John Austen became a brakeman for the company railroad. Park Saylor recalled, "He was a brakeman for ol' number 909. I wish I had a picture of it to show you. . . . We lived in a mining camp 1 1/2 miles long. The company was owned by ol' man Frost of New York. We had three sets of three-room houses, three sets of four-room houses, and three sets of six-room houses. We moved into the first house."

By 1922 John Austen was working underground, in the mines. Over the years he moved to many work sites, but he always eventually returned to the Path Fork area in order to be with family and friends. After moving into the coal camps, Park Saylor's mother, Kate, began conducting prayer meetings in her home out of fear of the "evil world." On several occasions her house and yard were filled with people who had gathered for services. Kate's religious fervor had a lasting effect on her son. He was saved at the age of fifteen, when his family lived in the area of Ferguson Ridge, Tennessee. Park states that his mother's influence kept him from indulging in sinful behavior, such as using tobacco or alcoholic beverages. His lifelong friend, Thea O. Carter, described his and Park Saylor's baptism:

> At Molus (Kentucky) is where I was baptized in 1931 by Rev. George Eads down below the swinging bridge. Rev. Park Saylor and I was at Forresters Creek attending a revival in the old schoolhouse. Rev. Z. B. Brock was preaching. We were welcomed and stayed in the home of Uncle John Daugherty. We left there on Sunday morning. We came across the mountain and down to the old schoolhouse at Molus. Rev. Harve Eads and Kitt Brock were having meeting there on that Sunday. It was good, warm weather. Brother George Eads was there. He baptized me. We both (Carter and Saylor) went on in our wet clothes and dried out. That night Park and I stayed with Brother Ephie Blanton. We were about the same age; boys together. At that time Park and I lived in Tennessee.[67]

The Holiness people associated the rapid changes that were occurring in eastern Kentucky with evil. The new system of capitalism was seen as unnatural. "Capitalist domination of the mountains changed the very structure of how the human beings there dealt with one another and even dealt with themselves."[68] Their society had become market-organized, market-dominated, and geared to the accumulation of goods. Profit-seeking took precedence over people. In a short period of two decades, many families like the Saylors had totally lost their property and become a landless, wage-earning class. Autonomy, or "each man for himself," was now the rule. Mountaineers at places such as Forrester's Creek had been historically conditioned to believe that life should be lived for the welfare of the community, and their religious beliefs expressed those values. The Saylors' Holiness religion reflected a society's attempts to restore a lost era. The intensity of their religious practice was a response to the social anomie that had resulted from the emerging industrial capitalism.

Six. Industry and Snake Handling

The Devil received credit for many of the misfortunes the Saylors and Holiness people suffered. Adherents of the folk religion that had been shaped largely through the use of symbols and had seen signs and omens around every corner were primed to believe George Hensley when he preached that the snake was the Devil. The snake became a symbolic intermediary in the contest with the evil capitalists, who operated coal mines and had destroyed mountain society with their worldly ways.

From the Holiness perspective, the serpent is, according to Steven M. Kane, "man's worst enemy in the animal kingdom, a creature governed by a more or less unremitting urge to hurt and kill." There had been a natural animosity between mankind and the snake since the legendary Fall, when

Satan took the form of a snake and persuaded Eve to eat of the forbidden fruit. To punish them, God put a lasting enmity between serpents and humans. Kane adds, "A great many Holiness people believe that serpents of the present day are animated by the spirit of the Devil, or as some would have it, by a 'mean' spirit akin to that of the Devil. They do not, however, consider snakes to be unique in this regard. All harmful creatures of nature are endowed with such a spirit. And human beings may willfully harbor one or more bad spirits."[1]

The serpent became the intermediary between the conflicting economies not only because it represented evil and death but also because victims of the capitalist system still viewed the mountain economy in personal rather than commodity terms; that is, they saw capitalism as exploitative. The capitalist system that coal mining introduced was a frightful distortion of the mountain social and economic order, and snake handling represented a form of supernatural retaliation.

In late July of 1934, after his nineteenth birthday, Park Saylor accompanied George Hensley and a few other Free Pentecostal ministers to a church gathering in Leslie County. The group made the journey in a Model A Ford and occasionally had to remove chickens and hogs from the road along the way. Finally they arrived at their destination on Bath Creek. Three hundred people, many of whom had gotten there by horseback, were at the church.

Hensley, Sherman Lawson, John Bolen, and Everett Jackson spoke at the service. Worshipers at the gathering handled serpents, including seven or eight timber rattlesnakes and one Rocky Mountain rattlesnake that was only fifteen inches long. Hensley was so anointed that he placed the small snake on the bald spot of his head. the rattlesnake just sat in a coiled position for a long time, while Hensley delivered his message. Finally the serpent reached down and struck Hensley on his earlobe. Hensley said, "Thank you, Lord, I forgot about him being on my head," then placed the snake in a box. He reportedly suffered no ill effects from the bite. Hensley preached until four o'clock that morning.[2] Later, at an area known as Bad Creek, Hensley was bitten in the "side of the head" by a twenty-inch "ground rattler." Hensley was so involved in delivering his sermon that he did not acknowledge the bite. Again, he suffered no ill effects.

Shortly after Hensley's arrival in the mountains of eastern Kentucky, another evangelical preacher named Bradley Shell began to draw much attention by performing miracles and "following the signs." When Hensley

Bradley Shell, 1988
(Photo by the author)

learned that Shell was outside a schoolhouse gathering, he instructed some of his members to bring Shell inside so they could be introduced. "We want to see that man Shell," said Hensley. After Shell and Hensley were introduced, Hensley asked, "Where did you get into this at?" Shell replied, "I prayed fourteen days and nights and never had my shoes off. I said, Lord, I want everything you got. As I was coming out of the mountains, the Lord said, 'Get your Bible.' Well, I did, and it fell open to Mark 16. The Bible says there is five signs that follow those who believe. The Lord said, 'I'm going to give you that [snake handling and drinking poison]. The most dangerous part of the Bible.' The Devil said to me, 'Now that will kill you.' Then the Lord said, 'When I give you something, it won't bother you.'"

Hensley was impressed with Shell, and eventually they became good friends. During the service that first day, George Eads told Shell they had a rattlesnake in the church that no one could handle. Shell asked, "How mean is it?" Eads replied, "It strikes everything that moves." Shell claims that

God told him at that point to handle the snake. He told Eads that "he would do it." Eads announced to the congregation, "We have a man with us tonight that works at Black Star [Coal Company], who drinks strychnine and handles serpents. We have a rattlesnake that no one can handle. We have Brother Shell and we are going to turn him loose and turn him over to the Lord." Shell went to the snake box and removed the vicious serpent. He handled the snake and was not bitten. After that event, people throughout the mountains brought Shell the snakes that no one could handle.[3]

In Letcher County, Kentucky, there was another Free Pentecostal preacher named General Washington Hensley. He was a freight conductor for the Louisville and Nashville Railroad and was known as General George.[4] He and his congregation actively performed the ritual of fire handling. One Sunday evening in the early 1930s, church members were handling fire during a service. A "sinner man" and "moonshiner" named Rowe Collins sat among the crowd, not in the least impressed with the spectacle. Collins said to the gathering, "I've seen all of this I want to see." Collins then got up from his seat and left the church. He returned shortly with a "big blowtorch." The torch was "roaring and shooting out a blaze twenty inches long." Collins set it on the Bible stand and dared the congregation to handle that fire.

The church members arose from their seats and started to leave the church, arguing that Collins was asking them to "tempt God." But all of a sudden a woman named Cory Sexton, who had long black hair, began to scream and dance. She went to the Bible stand and placed her face in the flame that was coming from the blowtorch. The fire allegedly blew her hair back, but Sexton kept her head in the flame and continued to dance. She suffered no injuries. George Eads then put his hands into the fire and also suffered no ill effects. Mrs. Rowe Collins recalled, "They made my husband get the blowtorch out of the church because they were afraid someone would get hurt. Some boys took it around to the side of the church and stuck it through the window. Those people came up to that fire and stuck their faces in it and everything. No one got hurt."

In 1934, shortly after Bradley Shell began "following the signs," he took a red-hot log out of a fire during a worship service and carried it in his arms for a long time. He then placed the log on his shoulder and danced in front of the congregation with it. The audience was astonished and inspected him to see if he had been injured in any way. Shell showed not so much as a blister. The next day a large group of people from Harlan visited Shell to see if he had suffered any ill effects from carrying the hot log around. After close inspection, they could not find a singed hair on him.[5]

Bradley Shell's "hot preaching" may have impressed some mountaineers, but it offended others. Park Saylor says, "Shell stepped on the sinners' toes." Shell has been threatened, attacked and, on one occasion, actually shot at because of the vehemence of his Holiness beliefs. While he was preaching a sermon on the eighth chapter of Romans about walking "not after the flesh but after the Spirit," one mountaineer became offended, stood up in the church, and shouted out to Shell, "What did you say?" Shell repeated his statement. At that point the mountaineer pulled a gun and fired several shots at Shell. They all missed Shell, but a man in the congregation was struck and suffered severe lung damage.

When the mountaineer started shooting at Bradley Shell he screamed, "Are you going to stop preaching now?" Shell replied, "No, I'm still going to preach Holiness more than ever." When the police arrived at the scene of the shooting, the mountaineer was asked why he "shot up the church." He replied, "I didn't have the Spirit on me, so I tried to blow Bradley Shell's brains out." The policeman said, "I know you didn't have the Spirit on you if you tried to kill someone."[6]

During the summer of 1934, one of Little George Hensley's best friends and a co-establisher of the East Pineville Church of God, Sill Eads, went on a twenty-six day evangelical trip in the eastern Kentucky mountains. In the vicinity of Hyden, he was sitting one day with Sherman Lawson on the porch of a man named Barney Stubblefield, singing and playing his guitar. The two men were waiting for the evening church service to begin. Two WPA workers who were aware of Eads's snake-handling abilities brought him a rattlesnake in a box, hoping to see him get bitten. The men said, "Preacher, we have you something." Eads walked down the stairs of the porch and opened the container. Immediately, the snake struck him on the neck. Eads bled on his shirt, but he refused to wipe off the blood or change shirts. The bite never fazed him, and he showed no ill effects.[7]

Some of those who witnessed the episode reported it to people in the area. Many mountaineers went to church that evening to see Eads and hear his religious message. Reportedly a large number of people were saved that night. Some moonshiners actually went home and cut up their stills after listening to Eads at that service. Even the famous moonshiner Rowe Collins "mended his ways that particular evening." Collins got the blowtorch that Cory Sexton, George Eads, and others had handled in Letcher County and used it to destroy his moonshine-making equipment. Collins was convinced that surviving a rattlesnake bite to the neck made Sill Eads a man of God.[8]

After Park Saylor's "Uncle Sill" had received a snakebite and lived to

Sill Eads, ca. 1940
(Photo courtesy of Park
Saylor)

preach about it, another preacher named Ernest Brown performed a similar feat at a church in Bluefield, West Virginia. Park Saylor attended this
service. It was a "divine gathering," according to Saylor, with some of the
best music he ever heard. Great mountain musicians such as Claude Ely
and John and Burley Parks participated. Park Saylor recounts, "Burley
Parks would sing and you could see his wisdom teeth." When the service
was about to conclude, Ernest Brown stood and delivered a beautiful
rendition of "Sinner Man, Sinner Man, Where You Gonna Run." After the
hymn, Brown grabbed his hair and said, "When I feel like all these hairs
are one, I don't care to handle a serpent." He then reached into a snake box
and removed a fifty-inch-long rattlesnake that was as big around as a
man's arm. Almost immediately, the serpent struck Brown in the palm of
his hand with such force that a fang broke off in Brown's hand. The bite
never fazed Brown; he kept handling the snake. Finally Brown put the
snake back in the box and sat down by Park Saylor. He said, "Brother

Sill Eads in his coffin, 1946 (Photo courtesy of Park Saylor)

Saylor, God bless, he did all he could do, didn't he?" Brown then pulled the broken fang out of his hand and laid it in a church window. Park Saylor says, "It left a red hole in his hand, but he showed no ill effects. Now that's serpent handling, David."

Shortly after the Ferguson Ridge meeting, George Hensley and Doyal Marsee of Bean Station, Tennessee, went to a church revival at Hazzard, Kentucky. The regular preacher of the church had been bitten by a rattlesnake a few nights earlier and was sick. Many of the church members had lost faith in their pastor, and church membership had dwindled to nine people. Hensley's revival built the congregation back up to seventy-nine members. On the final night of the service, Hensley went to a snake box that contained a copperhead and handled it. Marsee then took the snake from Hensley and was bitten on the palm of the hand, but he was not injured. When Hensley and Marsee were returning to Pineville from the revival they were approached by a coal mine operator that had caught a large, vicious rattlesnake. The miner said, "Let's see you handle this one, George." Hensley reached in the container and handled the snake. The snake never attempted to bite him.

In the summer of 1935, Holiness preacher Oscar Hutton was preaching on "following the signs" to his congregation in Kentucky when someone brought a large rattlesnake into the church. Hutton opened the container and was bitten on the right hand. His arm became swollen and turned blue.

Oscar Hutton at the Kentucky / Virginia line meetings (Photo courtesy of Richard Golden)

Reverend Jimmy Morrow of Del Rio, Tennessee, wrote about what transpired after the bite: "A few days later, as Oscar was recovering at his house, a doctor from the hills who had heard that Oscar had gotten bitten came to the house and asked to see Oscar. He asked Oscar if he wanted treatment and Oscar refused. The doctor then asked Oscar what he would do if someone brought him another snake and he told the doctor that he would handle it with his good hand. Shaking his head, the doctor left."[9]

At a religious gathering of five hundred people, in Ramsey, Virginia, on August 18, 1935, George Hensley shouted, "All sinners and children stand back." Hensley then took a three-foot mountain rattler and passed it among the believers. When "tension reached its peak" during the meeting, a twelve-year-old mountain boy, Clifford Greear, grabbed the snake. The *New York Times* described the scene this way: "Seizing the squirming snake in one hand, Greear, unbitten, tore the head from its body with the other."[10] The faithful pressed close around the boy, shouting and screaming, until a near riot erupted. State and county officials stormed the meet-

Oscar Hutton at the Kentucky / Virginia line meetings (Photo courtesy of
Richard Golden)

ing at this point in an attempt to restore order. In the confusion, Greear
was knocked down, still clenching the headless snake.

In May of 1939, a five-foot rattlesnake struck twenty-year-old Lose Duff
in the right temple at a weekend service near Verda, Kentucky. Duff refused to receive medical attention, even though his head reportedly swelled
to twice its normal size. A few days following the bite Duff was seen
walking around in his mine camp house but was forced to rest because of
dizziness.[11] Duff later recovered fully.

Not all snake handlers escaped death. On March 1, 1936, Hensley was
evangelizing in central Florida, drawing large crowds of spectators. At a
vacant store in Tampa, Hensley handled a five-foot rattlesnake in front of a
congregation of 125 people. In response to the recent heckling from nonbelievers who claimed Hensley had extracted the venom from snakes he
handled, Hensley responded, "If you don't believe this . . . come down here
and stick your finger in its mouth. . . . Some fellows don't believe it. . . .
They're old fellows with bald heads that can't keep out of the picture
shows. They say, 'Aw, that feller's done something to the snake.' Well then
let 'em handle the snake. They won't do it."[12]

Hensley then began waving his arms. "He went up and down the aisles in an Indian dance with head bent low and knees moving high." Without warning, Hensley then grabbed a snake and began to handle it. Two women and a man then took the snake, but one of the women let it escape. As the snake crawled through the crowd, people ran pell mell into the street, screaming and shrieking. Hensley recaptured the snake and put it in its box.[13]

After the store meeting in Tampa, Hensley conducted a service at the Bloomingdale Crossroads Country Church, where he preached to a congregation of three hundred.[14] Hensley did not advertise his meetings to attract large crowds, because some cities attempted to charge him "a license for running a snake show." It was during this meeting that Hensley was bitten twice by a rattlesnake that had been caught at a canning plant near Arcadia, Florida. Before he was bitten, Hensley shouted, "This is a deadly viper . . . and you have to have a holiness that makes your bones shake to handle him. Get your hand in that box and it will show you how close you are to glory."[15] Hensley then took the snake from its box and waved it above his head, and the snake struck him twice on his arm. In response, Hensley shouted "loud hallelujahs." As perspiration poured from his face and tears streamed from his eyes, he pulled off his coat and showed the gathering where he had been bitten. He exhibited "two swelling marks to his forearm and drops of blood on his shirt sleeve." Hensley told the gathering that he would not need medical treatment.[16]

Following Hensley's bite, the *Tampa Morning Tribune* published an article titled "Snake Expert Warns People Preacher's Rattlers Poisonous." George End, a man who actually canned rattlesnakes, alerted reporters that Hensley's snakes were extremely dangerous and were "apt to kill somebody sometime and warned religious worshipers and others not to handle" them. He expressed regret that he "had anything to do with supplying this gentleman with a rattlesnake," as he was in a "most advantageous position to know with certainty the potency of our diamondback rattlesnake's venom."[17]

After Hensley was bitten, he left Florida and went to Georgia to continue his evangelizing. However, he returned to Florida after a brief stay in Georgia.

It was during this trip that Hensley witnessed his first death from snakebite. On the evening of May 4, over seven hundred people gathered at a tent meeting in Bartow, about fifty miles east of Tampa. As the service progressed and reached an emotional height, a twenty-seven-year-

George Hensley at a Florida meeting at the time of Alfred Weaver's death
(Photo courtesy of the *Tampa Tribune*)

old strawberry picker and itinerant shoe peddler named Alfred Weaver
opened a snake box containing a five-foot rattlesnake and was bitten on the
hand. When the snake struck, Weaver "threw off the snake and it landed
across a lady's legs on the front row" of the gathering. The woman kicked
the snake, and as Weaver picked it up, he was bitten again.[18] This time he
was struck on the wrist. Weaver soon fell unconscious and was taken to the
home of Mrs. J. R. King, a fellow worshiper, who had also handled the killer
snake. Weaver's arm was badly swollen and had turned black. Medical
treatment was offered but Weaver refused, claiming that his faith was
strong enough to get him through the crisis.

George Hensley told reporters that Weaver "was bitten because he was
not quite ready for the demonstrations of the power. . . . He will get all
right. I have seen people bitten twice as worse."[19] But the following afternoon Alfred Weaver died.[20] A coroner's jury was impaneled following the
death, but after deliberating for only ten minutes they returned a verdict
that Weaver was killed because "of his own carelessness."[21] Polk County
officials paid burial expenses for Weaver, because he was impoverished, but
the death caused considerable unrest.[22] A *Tampa Morning Tribune* commentary titled " 'Faith' Failed" stated that Hensley's snake-handling demonstrations should be banned:

The authorities should put a prompt stop to the dangerous performances of Hensley, the self-styled evangelist, and his snake-handling "revivals."

One over-zealous devotee of this new brand of "religion" is dead, the result of taking one of Hensley's rattlers to his bosom. The snake didn't appreciate the "faith" of the "evangelist" and, true to nature, bit the "worshiper" twice with fatal effect. Hensley and the victim waited for the alleged Biblical charm to assert itself as an antidote to the rattler's venom. It didn't. The "apostle" died. Hensley explained: "He was not quite ready for the demonstration of the power."

These spurious purveyors of sensational evangelistic methods usually are harmless. When they employ agencies dangerous to life they should be stopped, silenced and de-snaked.[23]

As a result of Weaver's death, the city commission of Bartow passed an ordinance "making it unlawful for any person to have in his possession any poisonous snake not confined to a pen."[24]

In the summer of 1938, Johnny Day of Harlan visited General Washington Hensley's church on Greasy Creek in Harlan County, Kentucky.[25] Day's wife and others handled serpents at an evening service. Day instructed his wife to stop handling serpents. A few days later the Days attended a snake-handling meeting at K. D. Browning's church on Pine Mountain. Mrs. Day joined in the snake handling, and as a result Johnny Day filed a lawsuit against Bradley Shell, Jim Couch, and General Washington Hensley for "breach of peace." Shell, Couch, and Hensley were all arrested but were acquitted at the trial in Harlan. Judge C. E. Ball ruled "that the church had a constitutional right to indulge in snake handling if such acts were part of the belief."[26] This was the first known attempt by state authorities to prohibit serpent handling.

Although there was no legislation against snake handling in church services, the snake handlers began to experience problems with authorities. In 1938, Perry County judge Billy Jones "locked his Court House against the snake religion cultists after they left a box of rattlers in the courtroom where they had been holding a meeting."[27] At Louisville, Kentucky, in the spring of 1940, two itinerant preachers from Middlesboro—Reverend Leonard Green and Reverend Willie Winston—were conducting snake-handling services in the yard of Reverend J. S. Guess's house at 832 East Market Street. Crowds of three hundred gathered to view the snake-handling exhibitions. Later the meetings were convened in "in an old saloon building at Eighteenth and Main."[28] After a church member was bitten, city officials began to look for ways to "control the meetings without subjecting themselves to a charge of religious persecution."[29] During a gathering at the old saloon, Leonard Green showed people scars on his hand from two snakebites he had received. In response, Willie Winston gave his opinions of snakebites: "If you live, you live with faith, if you die, you die with faith." Winston then offered to let viewers handle the snakes, but "there were no takers."[30] City building inspector Fred Erhart provided a simple solution to the problem: he determined that the building was unsafe and condemned it. The services died down following Erhart's actions.

In the spring of 1940, Senator D. C. "Baby" Jones of Harlan County introduced a bill in the Kentucky General Assembly which made it unlawful to handle serpents in religious services. The bill was soon approved and went into effect immediately.[31] It declared: "Any person who displays, handles or uses any kind of reptile in connection with any religious services or gathering shall be fined not less than fifty dollars nor more than one hundred dollars."

However, the snake handlers were determined that the new anti-snake-handling legislation would not interfere with their practices. General Washington Hensley said that members of the Pine Mountain Church of God would substitute poison for snakes. He added that Bradley Shell had taken a "large dose of poison about 6 o'clock last night in services. We stayed with him until 11:30 and there was no bad effects on him because of his faith." Hensley added, "The constitution isn't like it used to be, giving a man the right to worship as he pleases but at the same time letting legislatures pass laws against it. . . . When Paul went to jail, he appealed to Caesar and we're going to appeal to the courts to uphold the Constitution and let us worship as we please."[32] In response to the arrests and fines of three snake handlers at Barbourville, Kentucky, General Washington Hensley petitioned the Harlan Circuit Court for an injunction against application of the snake-handling laws.[33] His requests were denied.

In September of 1941, Tom Lawson and four other snake handlers (Romer Bowling, Mrs. Romer Bowling, Ruth Jeffers, and Temus Head) in Whitley County were fined fifty dollars for serpent handling by Judge Flem D. Sampson. Lawson appealed the decision in the Kentucky Court of Appeals but lost. The opinion, written by Judge Henry J. Tilford, stated,

Laws enacted for the purpose of restraining and punishing acts which have a tendency to disturb the public peace or to corrupt the public morals are not repugnant to the constitutional guaranties of religious liberty and freedom of conscience, although such acts may have been done pursuant to, and in conformity with, what was believed at the time to be a religious duty. Without violating the constitutional guaranties, the state, under the police power, may enact laws in order to promote the general welfare, public health, public safety and order, public morals, and to prevent fraud.[34]

The legislation was passed in response to the snakebite deaths that had already occurred. Between the summer of 1932 and the time Kentucky's anti-snake-handling legislation was passed, six people had been killed. People had also been killed in adjacent states. The first death was that of a man from Alabama named Jim Wiley Reece, which occurred sometime before 1920. Another Alabama man died in 1934.[35] At a Jonesville, Virginia gathering on September 27, 1936, George Hensley handed Reverend H. T. C. Anderson a rattlesnake. Anderson—a former schoolteacher, a farmer, and an unsuccessful candidate for the state legislature—shouted, "The Lord works in mysterious ways. This time last year I was bitten by a rattlesnake. That bite cured my arthritis." Shortly later, the snake that Hensley handed Anderson sunk its fangs into his hand. Two other snakes that Anderson grabbed, a rattlesnake and a copperhead, also struck him. He died from the bites three days later.[36] Initially Anderson refused medical attention, but his daughter later appealed for medical intervention from Dr. T. B. Ely. The doctor said he could not help the dying man "because too much time had passed since the bite." Church members on the scene remarked that Anderson "would hold out faithful to the end," and he did.[37] Following Anderson's death Sheriff R. F. Giles condemned snake handling as "out of reason for enlightened Christians . . . harking back to the dark ages."[38]

A Kentuckian, Birchel Arnett of Clay County, was killed sometime after Anderson, and Mrs. Jeffie Smith, a Georgia woman, was fatally bitten in 1938. Two other Kentuckians died in 1940 as a result of snakebites. On August 21, Martha Napier, a forty-year-old mother of seven children, died after receiving four rattlesnake bites at approximately 11:00 P.M. at a little country church on Bull Creek in Leslie County. Mrs. Napier was admitted to the hospital at Hyden three and a half hours later. Following her death, the hospital's medical director, Dr. John H. Kooser, released this medical report:

Mrs. Napier received six doses (10cc each) of antivenin serum. Mrs. Napier was given sedatives, including morphine, and intravenous fluid

(3,500cc in all) and stimulants. Mrs. Napier died at 6:45 P.M. August 22, 1940.

The effects are either hematoxins or neurotoxins, and of course they may be combined. Locally there was severe extravasation of blood up to the wrist (for the first nine hours). After this time this process extended rapidly up to within one inch of the shoulder. This extravasation was visible in the hand, and one could almost see it in the arm and forearm. The general reaction of the patient otherwise was that of intermittent shock which was progressive.[39]

Less than a week after Martha Napier's death, Jim Cochran, a thirty-nine-year-old mechanic, met his fate in Hazard, Kentucky, in Perry County. After the death of Cochran, Lige Bowling, pastor of the church, was fined fifty dollars for violation of the state's anti-snake-handling law. Along with twelve other members of the church, Bowling was also "held for the grand jury on a murder charge."[40] John F. Day described the defense Bowling offered at his trial: "He defended himself; he defended his cult; he declared, 'I ain't never suffered from a snakebite because I've got the faith.' He told of fasting for a week to 'get the power.' He asserted that through the power and the laying on of hands a paralyzed child had been cured."[41] The grand jury rejected Bowling's plea, and he was held over for trial and later jailed. The initial charges were filed by Jim Cochran's brother, Fred. Cochran told magistrate Sam Campbell that his brother "had begged for a physician after he was bitten while handling snakes during religious services, but that he was kept in the church while services continued for another two hours."[42] Cochran added that his brother was told to "trust in the Lord."[43]

Eleven other members of the church, including five women, were offered their freedom by Perry County judge Billie Baker "if they would stop handling snakes at their religious services."[44] They refused and as a result were incarcerated at the Hazard, Kentucky jail. Judge Baker told the believers, "If you are going to stay in the snake business, you had better get some snake hunters out, for I'm going to kill every snake in this county."[45] According to a newspaper report, "Mrs. Viola Tharp, one of the defendants, carried her 16-month-old baby in her arms. Mrs. Bessie Collins, another defendant took her 2-year-old girl and her 4-year-old boy into the cell with her." Outside the courthouse, members sympathetic to the defendants danced and talked in tongues. Reverend James Stidham—one of the defendants who had been released on bond pending an appeal—declared, "God Almighty will act to release these men and women from jail shortly."[46] The believers conducted an all-night service at their church in Duane. Reverend Stidham told the gathering to "pray for the deliverance of their brothers and sisters from the jail in Hazard town."[47] The convicted snake handlers were later released, and they continued with their snake-handling practices.[48]

The anti-snake-handling laws did not stop snake handling and certainly did not halt the deaths. In 1942, Bradley Shell saw a large rattlesnake crawling across the road about one-half mile from the Pine Mountain Church of God. Some women whom Shell believed to be witches also saw the snake and challenged Shell to take it up. Shell caught the snake and placed it inside his shirt. He then walked to the Pine Mountain Church with the large rattlesnake still inside his clothes. Shell went inside the church and joined the service. When the snake stuck its head out of Shell's shirt, a man named Jim Couch asked Shell, "What's that sticking out of your shirt?" Shell responded, "It's a rattlesnake that will kill you." Couch reached for the snake in an attempt to handle it. The snake struck Couch on the hand. Couch became seriously ill, and his hand became badly swollen. He lost every fingernail, and the hand turned black. After a week of suffering, Couch died.

Some Kentucky snake handlers from the Pineville area went with Johnny Hensley to a snake-handling meeting at La Follette, Tennessee, in the summer of 1944. Johnny Hensley, a distant cousin of George Hensley, had a tremendous reputation as a snake handler. He never backed down from the most vicious snakes; he would say, "Why handle the tame ones? You have got to handle the mean ones to prove anything." On this occasion, from the time Hensley entered the church, one rattlesnake began buzzing and staring at him from its box. As Hensley walked around the church socializing, the snake continued to focus on him. One church member noticed the snake watching Hensley and said, "Brother John, I believe that snake would like to bite you." The church member turned the box around hoping to "get the snake's attention off of Hensley," but to no avail. The snake remained focused on Hensley. Another church brother cautioned Hensley, "John, you stay away from that snake. He will kill you." Hensley remarked, "I hope the Lord moves on me to handle him." Others in the church were fascinated by the snake's relentless staring at Hensley. They begged him to "stay away from that snake." When the church service started, Hensley went to the box that housed the snake and attempted to pick it up. He was bitten with such force that the snake had to be "pried off of him."[49] Hensley died from the bite. Shortly after Hensley's death, Maudie Lankford, a twenty-eight-year-old Harlan County housewife, was killed at the Harlan River Street Church of God. Mrs. Lankford was bitten three times by a rattlesnake. Immediately after Mrs. Lankford's death, Oddie Vieu Shoupe, General Washington Hensley, and Willard Cress were arrested for violating Kentucky's snake-handling laws.[50] The men were later fined and released.

Perhaps the most dramatic deaths occurred in 1944 and 1945 in Harlan County, Kentucky. Jesse Coker was handling a rattlesnake in a church service at Ages in late 1944. As he attempted to put the reptile back in its box, he received a severe bite on his arm. He died as a result. His father, George Coker, grieved over his son's death but refused to "stop taking 'em up." Approximately one year later, on September 19, 1945, at a small church in Verda, Kentucky, the sixty-four-year-old Coker shouted, "Some people said I ought to stop handling serpents. When I die I want to go just like my son did." Coker got his wish. He was bitten by a rattlesnake on his right arm, and the bite killed him. An eyewitness named Sweet Ball from Harlan, Kentucky, recalled, "Coker shouted, 'I want to die just like my son did.' As soon as he did, I saw the sleeve of his shirt pull out. I knew the snake had hit him, but it happened so fast you could hardly see it. He died the next day."[51]

George Went Hensley was bitten many times before his death in 1955. Hensley told a 1950 church gathering near Chattanooga, Tennessee, "Been bit four hundred times 'till I'm speckled all over like a guinea-hen."[52] The *Louisville Courier-Journal* had run an article on June 3, 1935, that told of Hensley's recovery from a snakebite in Virginia:

Three big rattlesnakes refused to bite the Rev. George Hensley, Holiness revivalist who says his "faith cure" is healing a previously bitten arm, as an excited throng shouted and prayed at open air services today.

Hensley and five other persons handled the snakes at a revival at Ramsey, near here, but neither the preacher nor his followers was harmed. This the revivalist attributed to his prayers, citing Biblical passages to support his faith.

A crowd estimated at 1,000 was present as Hensley took the three large snakes in his right hand, and after he made his demonstration, the Rev. Oscar Hutton of Wise County, the Rev. Connelly White and Bill Edmonds of Evarts, Ky.[, and] Told Lawson and Loyd Scott of St. Charles took rattlers in their hands and ran through the crowd, shouting and praying for such "miracles of faith."

The shouting became tremendous after the rattlers refused to bite. They had seemed vicious while in the cage.

One of the snakes was four and one-half feet long with eleven rattles and the other two were three feet long with five rattles each. They had been caught recently in the mountains of Kentucky.[53]

In the autumn of 1938 Hensley stated that God had told him to go on an evangelical mission to Alabama, but he refused to go. Shortly afterward, Hensley walked out on his front porch early one morning and saw an apple hanging from a tree, and it aroused his appetite. But in reaching for the fruit he slipped and fell off the porch, breaking both of his arms. Hensley felt that it was God's way of punishing him for disobedience, so he cried and prayed, asking for forgiveness. He then went to Alabama, though he was unable to feed or care for himself. In Alabama a woman who was regarded as a prophet approached Hensley and told him that there would be a snake at the church meeting and that someone would get bitten. Hensley acknowledged her statement and went out to pray on a little hill. Hensley recalled that when he started to pray, "The Lord directed him around the hill." Suddenly a copperhead crawled up to him. Hensley asked, "Lord, how can I handle it?" According to Hensley, God replied, "Your servant prophesied that there would be a serpent here." Hensley bent over, and the serpent crawled around his suspenders. He then hurried down to a house, where the serpent was put in a box. During the church service Hensley reached into the box containing the copperhead and received a bite. Hensley displayed no serious effects from the bite, however. When he returned to Kentucky, he showed Park Saylor the fang marks on his thumb where the copperhead had struck him. Hensley said, "Brother Saylor, when the woman prophesied that someone would get bit down there, I didn't think about it being me."

On another occasion, which Park Saylor witnessed, some "sinner men" rubbed an ointment called snake oil on a Stone Mountain copperhead in attempt to make the snake mean. The ointment burned the snake and made it strike constantly. It "struck a total of five people nine times," including Sherman Lawson and George Hensley. Polly Ann Long of Rose Hill, Virginia, was the only person who handled the snake and escaped injury. All of the people who suffered bites spent the night at Park Saylor's home. During the night the snakebitten people "moaned and groaned," except for Hensley; Saylor said that Hensley slept peacefully through the night.

Polly Ann Long, who was eighty-eight years old when I interviewed her in 1989, indicated that she saw Hensley receive a bite on his finger during a church service in the early 1930s. After the service, Hensley joined Ms. Long and other members of the congregation for Sunday dinner. When the meal was served, Hensley remained on her front porch in a chair. He would not eat or drink water and appeared to be in deep thought. He remained in the chair for several hours, then finally went into Ms. Long's house and ate, showing no ill effects from the snakebite.

On other occasions Hensley did suffer some very serious bites. His daughter Jean Hensley Potts remembered several such episodes: "Three or four times I saw my father's head swollen and turned black from snakebites. He almost died several times."[54] His son Loyal Hensley said, "By the time my father died his hands were all deformed from all of the bites he received. A few times he was so sick from the bites we figured that he was going to die at any time."[55] Shortly after Hensley received the bite in Virginia, he was placing mole traps in his yard in a rural area near Harlan. According to Denver Short, the preacher of a Holiness church in Ages, "George heard God speak to him saying, 'Pray.'" Hensley answered, "I will, Lord, when I put this last trap under this rock." When Hensley placed the mole trap under the big rock located in his front yard, he was bitten by a large rattlesnake. He became ill immediately and almost died as a result of the bite.[56]

During the summer of 1940, Hensley was bitten in the face by a "large yellow rattlesnake." The snake broke one of its fangs in Hensley's nose. As blood ran down his face, he told the church gathering that the Lord spoke to him and told him he was not going to die. Hensley became ill as a result of the bite and suffered for three days. His head swelled to twice its normal size, and "he had to hold his hands to both sides of his neck so he could breathe."[57] But at the next service he attended, Hensley handled a rattlesnake.

In 1939 George Hensley was evangelizing in Florida. During one service a doctor from New York approached Hensley and asked him if he would handle his serpent. Hensley replied, "If the Lord moves on me, I will." The physician returned later that evening accompanied by seventeen doctors and thirty-five nurses. In his possession was a seven-foot snake, which some believe to have been a cobra. The people in attendance stated that anyone bitten by the serpent would perish in thirty seconds.

As the service progressed, Hensley finally went to the snake box and started handling the giant serpent. The snake struck Hensley in the palm of his hand. The congregation believed that he would perish at any moment. Hensley started to dance almost frantically and to talk in tongues. The physician who owned the serpent examined Hensley, because he felt that the great evangelist was in danger of losing his life. The doctor allegedly reported, "His pulse is actually getting stronger." The doctor also spoke many languages. When he listened to Hensley speaking in tongues, he began to cry and said, "I don't know any of this." Park Saylor says, "When Hensley was full of the spirit he would handle any snake put in front of him. . . . If you are living right, like God would have you to live, and walk like God, live holy and honest before God, that snake might as well bite on a dogwood stick. God is not going to put you in jeopardy. A few years ago there was a man who said he had the faith of 'blue steel.' He was killed by a rattlesnake. Faith isn't enough. You have to be anointed to handle snakes."

Hensley traveled throughout the South preaching his snake-handling beliefs. He also evangelized in some northern states. In the summer of 1939, he and Doyal Marsee traveled into Canada preaching their Holiness beliefs. Upon their return, Hensley received national attention one day when he preached at the McGhee Street Church of God in Knoxville, Tennessee. The event was covered by the *Knoxville News-Sentinel.* Two hundred people watched Hensley as he walked toward a box of deadly snakes on the floor. Hensley said, "Now you little children stand back out of the way. . . . Now let's have a little song, brothers, maybe that will get the power up." Instantly the entire congregation rose and began singing a gospel tune. "Blessed Jesus, hold my hand!," screamed a woman. The tempo picked up as musicians began to play their guitars, banjo, fiddle, and tambourine. A chorus of shouts greeted Hensley as he lifted "two coiled, vicious-looking snakes high in the air." One of the snakes was a copperhead, the other a rattlesnake; they flicked their forked tongues and writhed in the preacher's hands. The two snakes were then handled by a "sea of groping, twitching hands." Some believers wrapped the snakes around their necks, "others put them in their hair or stuck them in their shirts—but the coiling snakes never appeared to offer to bite." Unknown tongues could be heard over the noise. The snakes were then placed back in their box, and the excitement died down.[58]

The services continued through the week. On the final night of the meetings, a disagreement surfaced between the "snake custodian," Jesse L. Pack, and the pastor, Reverend J. L. Batts. Pack told the congregation that he had carried snakes in his shirt throughout the services. Reverend Batts told Pack to put the snakes away. "Put them snakes in the box, Brother Pack, and leave them there. You're not supposed to handle snakes unless the power of the Lord is on you," said the preacher. Pack told reporters what happened next: "The more he talked the worse I got. . . . I just picked up that old copperhead and run his head about halfway down my throat. Them women there just like to had spasms—they thought I was going to eat him—oh, they nearly had convulsions. You ought to had a picture of that snake hanging out of my mouth. I stuck him about six or eight inches down my throat and he commenced wriggling and whipping his tail around—they threatened to call the law."[59] After this event, Hensley went back to Pineville "to rest up a spell." He was supposed to return the following day and preach a revival at the John Sevier church. Pack claimed that Hensley was expecting someone to bring him a diamondback rattler for the services.[60]

Hensley was constantly away from his home on his evangelical trips. He spent very little time with his family, although he did take his son Loyal with him on snake-hunting trips. Loyal told me that his father would make him carry the sacks that contained the captured snakes. When he complained to his father that he was "afraid that he might be bitten," George laughed and said, "They won't bite you through the sack, son."

During his Kentucky years, Hensley did very little work other than his ministry. He told Archie Robertson that an accident in a Kentucky coal mine had crippled him for a year. Robertson reported what Hensley had said in one of his sermons: "They sent for the machine that pumped life into me. And for a year I lay in the bed, this arm and that leg paralyzed. They said I'd never walk again. But they carried me to a tent where I was prayed for, and right then I began to move—little by little."[61] I have found no period in Hensley's Kentucky years when he was actually laid up for a year; he was constantly on the move with his preaching.

In 1941, the Hensleys lived on a farm near Duff, Tennessee.[62] It was while they were living at Duff that Hensley received a near-fatal bite. Loyal Hensley claimed that the family believed George would die: "Dad had the death rattle on him. If we had been Catholics we would have called for a priest to give him his last rites." But George survived the bite. George and Irene fought bitterly during this period, because George would not support the family. Thomas Burton claims that in the early 1940s, Hensley moved to Evansville, Indiana, after being separated from Irene. Irene and George reunited when he "promised to get work,"[63] but he always failed to deliver on his promise. He subjected his family to terrible conditions, sometimes forcing them to live in houses with dirt floors. Loyal Hensley claimed that many times the only thing the children had to eat was biscuits with cooking grease poured over them. Irene was periodically left at home for weeks at a time with four children to care for. Loyal Hensley reported that Irene had to do the child rearing almost on her own: "My father never gave any of us kids much attention. He was very indifferent. He really never pushed religion on us at home. My mother gave us our religious training." Hensley finally became so tired of Irene's complaining about his failure to provide for the family that he tried to put the children in an orphanage, according to his daughter Emma Jean. Hensley wanted to get rid of his children so that he and Irene would be free to evangelize. This caused a further division in the marriage, and in 1943 Hensley finally decided to obtain a divorce.

Seven. Back to Tennessee

When his divorce from Irene became final, George Hensley moved back to the Chattanooga area, staying mainly with his sister Rosa. Irene was left to care for their four children. Because she was extremely ill at the time and unable to work in order to provide for her children, she contacted Hensley's first family in Chattanooga and was invited to join them. Irene relocated to Chattanooga but died of a heart attack in early 1944 following goiter surgery. George went to the funeral home and viewed the body but had little contact with his second family after Irene's death. Esther, Hensley's eldest daughter by his first marriage, raised his second family. Emma Jean Hensley Potts remembers that "Esther was a saint. I can't talk about her without getting all choked up. She had children of her own but treated us all the same."[1]

After he returned to Chattanooga, Hensley was constantly exposed to trouble because of his snake-handling practices. In Hensley's absence, people in the Dolly Pond area had begun following a young Jesus' Name preacher named Tom Harden, who had been influenced by Oscar Hutton. Hutton was making trips to Tennessee from his home in St. Charles, Virginia. In eastern Kentucky, Hutton was referred to as a Newlight preacher, and believers that followed the Trinity belief were called Oldlight. Harden was a powerful leader whom members followed readily. He never preached for material gain. On one occasion in the 1930s, when he conducted a service at Daisy, the congregation took up an offering of six dollars and twenty-four cents out of appreciation for his message. Harden refused to accept the money, even though he only had sixty-five cents in his possession. "I'm after their souls, not their money," he reportedly stated.[2]

During the summer of 1945, Harden's Dolly Pond church was receiving much national attention. Between July 20 and July 23, the *New York Times* featured several pictures of the church's religious services. Raymond "Buck" Hayes was driving from Cumberland, Kentucky, to Dolly Pond on the weekends to serve as an evangelist. Many people were performing phenomenal feats in the church. Hayes's daughter, a "pretty girl in her early twenties or late teens, took a rattlesnake with ten rattles and a button and put its head in her mouth."[3] She was not bitten. J. B. Collins's *Tennessee Snake Handlers* shows minister Tom Harden's sister, Ida, performing the "kiss of death" with a large rattlesnake.[4] She too escaped unscathed. Members such as Luther Morrow held blowtorches to their skin, while others drank various poisons. These types of activities attracted news reporters from everywhere. Some members were being bitten by the snakes but dodged serious injury. Flora Roberts, Ella Rowe, and Luther Morrow were bitten during the second week of July but suffered only minor injury.[5]

It was not long before tragedy struck. On September 3, 1945, a two-hundred-pound, thirty-two-year-old Dolly Pond man named Lewis Ford was bitten and killed by a rattlesnake during a church service. Lewis was the son of Walter Ford, a deacon at the Dolly Pond church, and had only been a believer since June, when he was saved at a meeting in Evarts, Kentucky. Ford had been turned down from serving in the military because he suffered from a weak heart. During the summer of 1945 he was employed as a truck driver for a munitions plant near Grasshopper.[6] Lewis was constantly ridiculed by coworkers and nonbelievers. "One of those big rattlers will get you some day," they predicted. Ford's reply was, "If that's

George Hensley with a crown of rattlesnakes. The man to the right is Lewis Ford. He died shortly after this photo was taken. (Photo courtesy of J. B. Collins)

God's will then I'm ready to go. . . . I may be bitten some day to prove to the unbelievers that the serpents will kill and that we can handle them only when God anoints us to handle them."[7]

Lewis and Tom Harden attended a brush arbor meeting at Daisy, where they had been invited to hold a service. They took several snakes with them to be used in the meeting. Shortly after the service began Lewis was struck on the second finger of his right hand. His father gave this account of Ford's death:

> He took out three snakes and laid them over his arm before he was bit. When he reached in his second box to take out either the rattler or the copperhead that was in it, the rattler struck him. The snake, a four-foot black rattler he caught himself up on a ridge around here, bit him on the finger when he reached in. He brought his arm up and the snake was hanging by his fangs buried in Lewis' finger. . . . Lewis went on preaching for 10 minutes or so after he had got a good victory over the serpent. The snake was lying over the pulpit like it was dead before Lewis stepped down and said he had been bit and felt sick. . . . They took him over to my niece's house near there and laid him on the grass outside. He said he wanted to be taken inside. When they got him inside on the bed he couldn't talk any more, but he signed them he wanted them to pray

for him. Some of the saints gathered around and prayed for him, but I guess the Lord called him home.[8]

Later that evening his body was taken from Daisy to the Physicians and Surgeons Hospital in Chattanooga. Ford was pronounced dead of the snakebite by Dr. Tom Curry about 2 A.M.[9]

Lewis had been bitten three times prior to his fatal bite, with only minor injury, and had told believers about a week before his death to "be sure to have the snake-handling ceremony at his funeral." Raymond "Buck" Hayes stated that the church would give Ford the service that he wanted. Hayes added that the snake that killed Lewis had also bitten four other people at the same service. His daughter Alice had been struck and was still in bed suffering from the attack; Luther Morrow, Tom Harden, and Mrs. Oscar Hutton were also bitten, but like Alice, they survived.[10] The believers were convinced that Lewis Ford's death was simply a "steppingstone across into heaven." His death was one of God's ways of testing their faith and showing the world that the snakes used in religious services were not "doctored up" through milking or defanging. It was predicted that others would die a similar death at certain intervals to reinforce the faith. As Perry Bettis put it, "The Lord said take up serpents. He didn't say they wouldn't bite."

On September 8, Lewis was buried in the Dolly Pond Church of God cemetery. As he requested, poisonous snakes were handled at his three-hour funeral. A crowd of 2,500 attended his last rites. More would have attended but were turned back due to the large traffic jam along the route to the church. State police were on hand to help direct traffic along the narrow backroads leading to the church. People came from Alabama, Kentucky, and Georgia, and many brought snakes with them. Sheriff Grady Hand and two other officers were on hand to "protect the crowd from the snakes."[11]

The church members had originally planned to conduct the funeral outside, but a rainstorm forced much of the gathering inside the church. Buck Hayes, who was to preach the funeral, agreed to conduct the service behind a roped-off section of the church in attempt to keep the snakes away from the five hundred spectators that had squeezed into the building. The remainder of the large assembly stayed outside, hoping to get a glimpse of the activities.[12]

Ford's body rested in a "open gray casket . . . in front of the pulpit and immediately behind the rope." Hayes warned the unfaithful to remain behind the ropes, then opened the service with a prayer. The believers joined in the benediction, shouting aloud in unknown tongues. As the devotees prayed, they "shook and moaned and weaved about on their

Believers handling snakes over Lewis Ford's coffin (Photo courtesy of J. B. Collins)

knees." In six screen-topped boxes were five rattlesnakes and a copperhead. The rattlers could be heard buzzing above the praying.[13]

After the prayer, on Hayes's request, several of the believers began to play "guitars, tambourines and cymbals." As the music increased in tempo, the church members "began to sway and jerk with the rhythm of the music." Within a few minutes one of them approached a snake box and began to slap it. He then yanked the box open and grabbed a four-foot rattlesnake. He shouted in unknown tongues and waved the snake above his head. The believer then placed the snake on his shoulders. The rattler "stiffened its body and weaved its flat, darting head about. Its rattles kept up a constant buzzing." Within a minute other church members were handling the snakes also. A few of the members lighted cans of gasoline and held the flames to their chins and faces. Charles Pennington of the *Chattanooga Times* described what happened next: "Seizing a long black rattler, Brother Hayes shouted to the crowd that 'this is the one that killed our brother.' He took it to the open casket, and, lifting back the veil, he thrust the snake in beside the body of Ford, which lay with the hands clasping a small open Bible. Other reptiles were passed to Hayes and he placed them all in the casket, and then finally removed them all."[14]

Dolly Pond Church (Photo by the author)

Walter Ford handled three of the snakes and rubbed them in his face as he stood at the head of his son's coffin. Lewis's widow, Ressie, "stood by the casket dry-eyed but haggard, clutching the snakes as they were passed to her. Her eldest daughter, 9 years old, watched without emotion, but her little face was stained with tears she had shed earlier."[15]

Hayes placed one of the snakes on the floor, and as it tried to escape he placed his foot on it and was bitten on the ankle. Two hours later his ankle was swollen, but he claimed that he suffered "no ill effects." Hayes told reporters that he had been bitten by rattlesnakes twenty-three times before but had escaped injury. As he made his claim, Charles Pennington noticed that Hayes's right index finger was still swollen and its tip mutilated from the bite of a large rattler about three weeks earlier.[16]

After the snakes were handled, they were placed back in their boxes. Hayes, Tom Harden, and Oscar Hutton then took turns preaching the funeral service. After the service, Lewis Ford's body was buried in the newly established graveyard at the church. Ford's death was the first at the Dolly Pond church. The attention generated by the press caused authorities to attempt terminating snake-handling services in the Chattanooga area.

On the afternoon of September 23, 1945, two weeks after Lewis Ford's funeral, George Hensley and Tom Harden conducted a faith healing service at the home of a believer, W. L. Wright, in East Chattanooga. Wright had invited the preachers to conduct the meeting for his blind wife. Hensley and Harden brought a three-foot rattlesnake to the service, which drew a large crowd of spectators; as a result, streets were blocked and a traffic jam developed. When Police Chief H. D. Edmonson learned of the activity, he ordered Captain C. R. Hartness to investigate and determine whether the snake was a threat to bystanders. Hartness was accompanied to the scene by Detective A. C. Smith and Patrolman A. C. Floyd. When the officers arrived they found Hensley and Harden preaching to a crowd of roughly one hundred people. Harden was holding a Bible in his hand, and the snake was draped across his forearm. Captain Hartness approached Hensley and ordered him to put the snake back in its box. Hensley agreed to the captain's demands and relayed them to Harden, but Harden refused to return the snake to its container. Hensley then went back to Hartness and told him that they could not put the snake away. He added that "the Lord wanted them to preach with the snake out."[17]

In response to Harden's refusal to put the snake back in its box, Hartness told Harden to "throw the snake on the ground" and declared that both men were under arrest. At that point Harden dropped the snake. The preachers were then seized, and Officer A. C. Smith "blasted the head from the snake" with a shotgun. Police Chief Edmonson said that he ordered the arrest of Hensley and Harden because the police department was responsible for the citizens of Chattanooga. He added that handling a rattlesnake within the city limits "could easily result in the death of someone not associated with such rites." One bystander who was sympathetic to the beliefs of Hensley and Harden offered to post bond but was "rebuffed by the reply 'They did the same thing to Paul.'"[18]

About a dozen other believers were arrested along with Hensley and Harden but were freed under bond. Once released, the believers gathered outside the jail that contained the preachers and prayed for the policemen who arrested them. They prayed, sang, and shouted "long into the night."[19] Inside the jail Hensley and Harden also prayed and sang, "beseeching the Lord to open the doors of the prison as He had done for Saint Paul."[20] The following morning at the preliminary hearing before Judge Martin A. Fleming, the preachers were fined fifty dollars each "on a charge of disorderly conduct." Both men refused to pay the fine or allow anyone else that was sympathetic to their beliefs to settle with the court. Paying such a fine, they declared, was a violation of their religious principles. They chose instead to work off the fines in the county workhouse at a rate of one dollar per day. After working several days on the road crew in the hot sun, though, Hensley began to become weak. His friends acquired an attorney to appeal the case. The preachers were brought before Criminal Judge Frank Darwin, and the judge dismissed the charges. Hensley and Harden were joined by their followers, who shouted and praised God for their preachers' deliverance from jail. J. B. Collins claims that "They felt that the judge's decision was a modern miracle, a new method God had of opening the doors of the prison."[21]

On July 13, 1946, at a meeting in Clyde Leffew's home in Daisy, a fifty-one-year-old Ooltewah man was killed by a four-foot rattlesnake that had been purchased for $1.50 from a "sinner man" on Signal Mountain. Joe "Clint" Jackson died forty-five minutes after the snake sank its fangs into his left hand. After the bite, Jackson uttered a few understandable words and then lapsed into speaking in unknown tongues. No medical aid was requested. Church members gathered around Jackson and prayed for his recovery, but to no avail.[22]

Jackson had come to the Leffew home around eight o'clock, where twenty-five people were gathered for the service. As the meeting began, Reverend Reece Ramsey retrieved the snake from a box and placed it on a small table next to a Bible. The *Chattanooga Times* reported, "Mrs. Annie Harden handled the snake for a few moments . . . and was followed in the rites by the 'minister' and three other persons . . . Mrs. Inez Hutcheson, Mrs. Sally Leffew (Leffew's mother) and Jackson. . . . Jackson was standing just a little ways from the table when he walked over and picked up the serpent. . . . It bit him on the hand between his thumb and forefinger and he dropped it on the table." Jackson told Ramsey, "It bit me," then said, "Lord, I can't let you down." Ramsey put his hand on the snake, then laid his head on it. He then put the snake back in its box. At that point Jackson was helped outside, put in a truck, and taken to the nearby home of another worshiper, where he died.[23]

On August 17, 1946, eighteen-year-old Harry Skelton was bitten by a rattlesnake at the Blythe Avenue Mission in Cleveland, Tennessee, and died after suffering for six days in a hospital. According to the preacher, William Henry, the meeting was over, but Henry, Skelton, and Henry's fifty-one-year-old father, Walter, were still handling snakes in a roped-off area behind the altar. The preacher attempted to put the snake back in its box, but it was "stubborn and did not go all the way in." Skelton removed the snake, and it struck him "between the thumb and forefinger on the right hand." After the bite, Skelton was taken to Henry's apartment, which adjoined the church, and members attempted to "pray away the effects of the venom." His throat and arm became badly swollen. He endured severe pain and finally asked to be taken to a doctor. Skelton was taken to the Physicians and Surgeons Hospital and treated by Dr. Claude Taylor.[24]

After Skelton's death, Walter Henry sought to handle the snake that had killed Skelton. He announced that the power and anointing would protect him from "the serpent's fangs," then reached for the killer snake and was bitten. He refused medical attention and, like Skelton, was taken to his son's home. Walter Henry's wife told newspaper reporters that her husband would not see a doctor. She said, "It was those doctors that killed Brother Harry. . . . Walter will live because he won't see a doctor."[25] However, Walter Henry did not survive the bite; he left behind a wife and nine children.[26]

At Henry's funeral on September 2, yet another man was killed—Hobart Wilford, a forty-six-year-old brother-in-law of Henry's. Shortly after the funeral began, Wilford was bitten by a rattlesnake that was brought to the services by Tom Harden of Dolly Pond, and he died "in paroxysms an hour and a half later at his home on Blythe Street."[27] This death, the fourth snakebite death in two months, increased efforts by legal authorities to prohibit snake handling in the city limits of Cleveland; however, they did not succeed.[28] The *Chattanooga News-Free Press* highlighted an article that was run on September 4 by the *Cleveland Daily Banner:*

> The Cleveland Daily Banner in a Page 1 editorial today called on the next session of the legislature to enact laws which would prohibit the handling of dangerous reptiles, wild animals, etc., in public places.
>
> The Daily Banner editorial said that officials, under present laws, cannot stop snake handling, which caused three deaths here last week as the result of religious ceremonies by members of a snake handling cult.
>
> "Religious liberty must be protected," the editorial said, "but public safety also must be considered and the public must be protected."[29]

Near Newport, at the Indian Creek Church, funeral services were conducted for Hobart Wilford after funeral director John Holder received a promise that no snakes would be handled.[30]

The authorities could not stop George Hensley's snake handling and evangelizing, though. During a brush arbor meeting at Daisy he met his third wife, Inez Riggs Hutcheson, who had witnessed Clint Jackson's death at Clyde Leffew's home meeting on July 13. Inez had been married before; her previous husband had died and left her with ten children. George and Inez were married on September 23, 1946, and Hensley moved to Inez's farm near Soddy.[31] The marriage was short-lived. Hensley's daughter Jean informed me that Inez's children and George could not get along.

In response to the five snakebite deaths that took place in church services within one year, the Tennessee legislators introduced a bill on February 4, 1947, that would have outlawed snake-handling demonstrations in the state. Similar laws had been passed in surrounding states. The legislation was introduced simultaneously by Senator Willard Hagan of Lebanon and Representative I. D. Beasley of Carthage. They called for the passage of the following law: "That it be unlawful for any person or persons to display, exhibit, handle or use any poisonous or dangerous snake or reptile in such a manner as to endanger the life or health of any person."[32] The sponsors of the legislation asked that penalties for violations of the proposed law be a fine of "$50 to $150 or a jail sentence of six months or both."[33] On February 28 the bill was approved.

The believers were concerned about the new law. Their religious convictions now placed them in direct conflict with the authorities. A newspaper article in the *Chattanooga News-Free Press* on March 31, 1947, began, "Doors of the Dolly Pond Church of God With Signs Following After Those That Believe were locked tight Sunday, and the hills that usually echo the chants of the congregation were strangely silent."[34] Church member Luther Morrow announced that he would continue to handle snakes "come spring even if they cut my head off." However, much division was expressed in the church, and believers gathered at the home of their preacher, Tom Harden, to discuss the issue. Some members favored abandoning snake handling, while others suggested hiding out and holding services in caves or mountain thickets.[35] Morrow claimed the new law gave many of the weaker members of the church a chance to leave. He added, "They are eager to obey the law. . . . They are afraid to handle snakes anyway, and want the law for an excuse."[36] Harden sought advice from the church's eldest member, Mark Braddam, who was dying of cancer. From his sickbed Braddam listened to all the opinions, then made this statement: "We will not give up our serpents, nor will we hide out in caves like lawbreakers. . . . Turn to the sixteenth chapter of Mark and read the eighteenth verse."[37] The church members began to shout and speak in unknown tongues. As they left Braddam's house, they announced to the world that they would "obey God's law not man's law."[38] In an interview, Lewis Ford's father, Walter, commented that the last time snakes had been brought to Dolly Pond was December 8, for the funeral of B. A. "Boots" Parker. He said that because it was winter, the snakes were hard to get, but "Warm weather'll be here some of these days, and the snakes will be crawling—and we'll be catching 'em."[39]

When the spring came, the Dolly Pond church members began handling snakes again. The authorities were intent on stopping the services, and on Wednesday night, July 23, Hamilton County sheriff Grady Head took all the available law enforcement officers he could find to the church. Head found a large gathering of spectators and a few church members, but no services were being conducted. The sheriff walked into the church chewing a cigar and kept his hat on, showing no respect for the church. In front of the Associated Press reporters and newsmen from Chattanooga, Head barked out to Harden, "You in charge?" Harden replied "Well, now, I guess I am." The sheriff then inquired, "Where's your snakes?" Harden responded, "We ain't got none here. As a matter of fact, I didn't know there was to be any services tonight. I just came down here to see what the trouble was." A news reporter then interrupted, saying, "You might as well go ahead and get your snakes and handle them tonight. You're going to have to be arrested sooner or later, and you might as well get it over with." Collins states that the reporter was "disappointed with the prospect of travelling all the way from Chattanooga without seeing snakes handled and the first arrests to test the new state law."[40] The reporter then said, "Look, there are a lot of us reporters here and we're all set for the big show. Get out the snakes and let's get it over with." Harden looked at the man and answered "Well now, I reckon I sure do appreciate all that, mister, but before I handle those snakes I believe I'll still wait on the Lord." The sheriff and his officers had searched the church and were preparing to leave when one of the church members shouted, "You folks be back on Sunday. We'll have some serpents if it's God's will."[41]

The snake handlers did not wait until Sunday. That Saturday night, two snakes—a three-and-a-half-foot rattler and a copperhead—were handled after a believer slipped them into the building through a back window. As the snakes were passed among the crowd, one of the members shouted, "Now where's the sheriff?"[42] The following night, police officers returned to the church "by the carloads. When they arrived the service was being conducted but no snakes were found. One of the deacons told them, 'We had them a while ago . . . but we put 'em away when the Lord moved us to.'"[43]

After being thwarted by the snake handlers and failing to make any arrests, Sheriff Head became the object of public ridicule. As a result he became even more determined to apprehend violators of the anti-snake-handling ordinance. On August 9, instead of sending the usual uniformed policemen to the services, he sent two plainclothes officers, George Ely and Hughie Baker. The men sat at the back of the building, where over one hundred people had gathered for the service. When the meeting began, a believer named Cecil Denkins took a rattlesnake and a copperhead out of their boxes and passed them among church members.[44] The officers waited through the rite, offering no interference until the snakes were placed back in their boxes. Once the reptiles were properly secured, the officers stood and displayed their badges and declared, "All of you who handled a snake tonight are under arrest for violating a state law and we'll take the snakes over."[45] One snake handler, J. W. Posey, hid a snake inside his shirt to prevent the police from capturing it.

In response to their arrests, the believers shouted, "Hallelujah . . . We are going to jail for our Lord." Tom Harden actually hugged one of the officers and thanked him for giving the snake handlers a chance to suffer for their convictions. The officers arrested nine of the church members and allowed three others to escort their small children home and turn themselves in the following day. As the believers were being processed into the jail, they never quit singing and praising the Lord.[46]

The snake handlers obtained attorney George W. Chamlee to represent them. Chamlee had each defendant released on a $250 bond "pending their appearance in general sessions court the following afternoon for a preliminary hearing before Judge Joe Goodson."[47] As the believers left the jail, one of them told some policeman and spectators, "Come up Sunday. We may have another rattlesnake by then."[48] The following day, a trial was set for October 15, but it was postponed later by Criminal Judge Thomas S. Myers. The judge claimed that he "had not had time in which to look over these cases and that he wanted to review the law against snake handling before trying the cases."[49]

On November 13, the case was finally tried by Hamilton County judge L. D. Miller. The courthouse was filled with local observers and Dolly Pond church members "who had come down to give their brethren moral and spiritual support." The trial also drew church delegations from Georgia and Kentucky, including Reverend Gordon Miller of Cartersville, Georgia, who had been recently acquitted by a jury on a charge of involuntary manslaughter: a member of his church had died from drinking strychnine.[50] Another Georgia preacher, E. L. Flowers of Waleska, had a three-year-old child who according to Defense Attorney Chamlee had recently been raised from the dead through prayer. George W. Hensley also attended the hearing. Chamlee instructed the believers not to bring snakes to the trial and told them their defense was based on the ground that the state law against snake handling was a violation of state and federal "constitutions and violated the rights of freedom of worship." He disclosed to the *Chattanooga Times*, "I've told these people that they can't bring their

George Hensley preaching outside the courthouse, 1947 (Photo courtesy of J. B. Collins)

snakes to the courtroom. . . . There may be some singing and maybe some preaching. . . . If we don't win in Judge Miller's court, we are going on to the supreme court of Tennessee, and if we don't win there we are going on up to the Supreme court of the United States in Washington. We are prepared to take this case all the way to the top if necessary."[51]

The state's case was presented by Attorney General W. Correy Smith and Assistant Attorney General Cardinal Woolsey.[52] The believers were honest about their activities and did not dispute the charges. Tom Harden admitted to handling serpents and said that nonbelievers were warned not to come to the area of the church where the reptiles were being handled. Chamlee used Harden's statement as part of the defense and also alleged "that the state had failed to prove the snakes were poisonous at the time they were used in the ceremony."[53] To Judge Miller's disgust, members told of miracles that had been performed in the church.[54] They also stated that they believed the state was violating their constitutional rights. Miller "pointed out the trial would not be decided on the constitutionality of the law, but whether the law as it stood had been violated."[55] The judge also cut

George Hensley (front row, second from left) and Tom Harden (front row, third from left) at their court hearing (Photo courtesy of J. B. Collins)

short the church members' testimony about details of their religious creed, again emphasizing that the court was only trying to determine if the anti-snake-handling law had been breached. The case ended in a mistrial when the twelve-member jury became deadlocked at six for a conviction, six for acquittal. The frustrated judge gave the jurors more time, but finally he was forced to declare a mistrial. After the court decision the believers left the courthouse in order, but when they reached the courthouse steps, they began "singing, shouting and praying." The celebration was joined by four guitar players and a fiddler. When the Spirit moved on the members, they began passing a coal oil lamp among themselves. Luther Morrow grabbed the lamp "and danced back and forth with his hand held over the flames." Others also held their hands in the flames for "a minute or so."[56]

The victory was short-lived, however. On February 10, 1948, J. D. Miller retried the case. The new jury was first deadlocked, with eight for a conviction and four against, but after being kept overnight they all voted the following afternoon for a conviction.[57] The jury also recommended "extreme leniency." Judge Miller fined each of the defendants $50 and allowed their attorney fifteen days to appeal the verdict.[58] Tom Harden was optimistic about the court decision and expressed his opinion: "Maybe this is a good thing. If we were acquitted here, they'd just have to come out and arrest us again. If this case is taken to the United States Supreme Court, we'll beat it."[59]

As it turned out, Harden's hopefulness was misguided: the Tennessee Supreme Court upheld the guilty decision on December 11, 1948, and the law thus remained on the books.[60] A rehearing was denied on January 27, 1949.[61] The supreme court decision may have been influenced by the snake-handling activities that followed the first trial. Five of the Dolly Pond group were arrested for handling serpents on June 13, 1948, at an East Chattanooga brush arbor.[62] On August 9, thirty-two-year-old Harvey Bell of Lindale, Georgia, was killed by a rattlesnake bite during a Dolly Pond church service. Bell, a crippled man, had visited his friends to attend the Sunday night meeting. Shortly after the service began, Bell "removed one of the largest rattlers ever captured in the Birchwood area from a box without the knowledge of the snake handlers conducting the service." The snake struck him several times on the left hand. Bell died before he could be carried to a church member's home.[63] Bell's death caused several members to leave the Dolly Pond church. W. L. Ford was one of those who quit the church, according to his daughter, Mrs. Pauline Clark. She claimed that her father did not have "faith enough" to handle snakes and was "going to quit it."[64]

The Dolly Pond church members kept on with their practices and made national news again on August 23, when fourteen-year-old Pauline Barbee was bitten on the right wrist by a rattlesnake that had been passed to her by Reverend Reece Ramsey. Ramsey was arrested after the bite, but the girl absolved him of the blame, stating that she reached for the snake while "shouting under the power." Pauline added that she felt no ill effects from the attack and would not seek medical attention "in the event of illness from the bite."[65]

All of the arrests and media coverage did not discourage George Hensley from his evangelizing or snake handling. on December 13, 1947, the *Chattanooga Times* ran an article titled "Snake Cult Opens Church on Sunday." The church, located in South Chattanooga, was described as being "established in a tent on West Nineteenth Street between Long and William streets." Reverend W. A. Leffew was listed as pastor, with Hensley as assistant pastor.[66]

Writer Archie Robertson attended one of Hensley's meetings at Dolly Pond during the late 1940s and described the event in his book *That Old-Time Religion*. He characterized Hensley as "an able old man with a keen brown face and blue eyes which had seen much suffering."[67] Robertson went on to describe Hensley's sermon on the "rulers":

George Hensley
shortly before his death
in Florida. (Photo
courtesy of Jean Potts
Hensley; retouched by
Anthony Feyer)

"Hit's the rulers ever' time," he was shouting, while a woman stand-ing at the oil-drum read the story of Christ and Nicodemus. "Hit's the rulers that persecutes the people." An old-fashioned, vigorous mountain preacher, Brother George slapped his knee and danced vigorously about. Serpents had already been handled and he was preaching now for converts.

"Now brethering, I'm an ignorant man. I can't read nor sign my name. When they arrested me, the judge was a-feared to let the serpents come in the courtroom. But I've handled 'em all my life—been bit four hundred times 'till I'm speckled all over like a guinea hen. But the judge wouldn't look at 'em!

"And he was a learnt man," he concluded triumphantly. "Now read over there in Hosy. Wait a minute 'til I fix this telephone. I'm a leetle bit deef." He paused to adjust his hearing aid.[68]

Later in his sermon, Hensley made another reference to the authorities' interfering with his snake-handling practices: "I'll handle 'em even if they put me on the road-gang again! Just you wait! Now hit's handlin' serpents that's agin' the law, but after a while hit'll be against the law to talk in tongues, and then they'll go after the Bible itself!"[69]

In Chattanooga during the early 1950s Hensley met his fourth wife, Sally Moore Norman, who was originally from Jackson, Mississippi. Hensley called her "Peg" in reference to her false leg; one of her legs had been amputated due to a childhood injury.[70] When Sally when to bed at night, she removed her wooden leg and placed it under the bed. Hensley told his granddaughter La Creta Simmons, "I bet I have got the only wife in the world that sleeps both on top of the bed and under it at the same time."

George W. Hensley continued to evangelize throughout the South for the next few years. He and Sally moved to various places before settling in Albany, Georgia. On Sunday July 24, 1955, he was leading a meeting at Lester's Shed, near the community of Altha, which lies in northwestern Florida twenty-five miles from the Georgia state line. Hensley was now seventy-five years old but had lost none of his ability to preach the gospel. When the Spirit moved him, he went to a lard can that held a large eastern diamondback rattlesnake. Hensley opened the container and removed the snake. For fifteen minutes he handled the serpent in various ways, placing it on his head, rubbing it in his face, and wrapping it around his neck. When Hensley began to put the snake back in the can, it suddenly turned and struck him on the wrist. His arm became swollen and turned black. He began to vomit blood.[71] Many of the spectators tried to persuade Hensley to seek medical attention, but he refused. Calhoun County sheriff George Guilford asked Hensley to visit a hospital, but he responded, "I'll be saved by my faith. I won't go to the hospital for anything." Early Monday morning, George Hensley died. His wife said that his final words were "I know I'm going. It is God's will."

On Wednesday afternoon, July 26, George Hensley was buried in a simple service at the Mount Olive Cemetery, only two miles from the site of his death. After the funeral, several people met at Lester's Shed and pledged that they would continue to practice the style of worship that George Went Hensley was so instrumental in spreading throughout Appalachia and the rural South. Since snake handling was prohibited in the state of Florida, county authorities offered to hold an inquest into the death, but Hensley's widow refused. The death was listed as a suicide.[72]

Eight. Fights with the Law

In 1945, the Shrine of Divine Healing in Lee County, Virginia,
drew two thousand people a week for ten weeks; a crowd of five thousand
attended the congregation's "national snake handling demonstration,"
which took place in July at Stone Creek Cove.[1] *Life* magazine had profiled
these Virginia meetings in 1944 in a three-page article that included
pictures of snake handling and fire handling. One photo showed a man
with a bandage on the lower part of his face, covering a snakebite received
at a recent gathering.[2] In response to the many deaths and injuries associated with snake handling, the states began to attempt to pass and enforce
legislation prohibiting the act. On July 29, 1945, Virginia state policemen
acting on the orders of Governor Darden broke up the Stone Creek Cove

snake-handling meeting mentioned above. When Captain H. W. Lawrence and eight troopers arrived at the scene, Lawrence read the believers a proclamation from the governor "forbidding such a dangerous practice."[3] The officers then sat for two hours "fidgeting uncomfortably as the service opened with prayers and singing." Two ailing women "limped up" to the altar requesting prayer, and Reverend William Parsons and twenty fellow pastors anointed the women's faces with olive oil while praying over them. The faithful women left the gathering healed, according to *New York Times* correspondents.[4]

Captain Lawrence then told Reverend Parsons that he was ordered to "confiscate the snakes and arrest anyone who brings poisonous reptiles into the gathering. It's my orders. Guess I'll carry them out if anybody starts something." Paul Dotson, one of the worshipers attending the meeting, went to his car and pulled out a large box containing eight big rattlesnakes. "In a twinkling the faithful were around him, praising the Lord and reaching for snakes." Before the police could get organized to stop the snake handling, "eight big reptiles were twirling about the heads of the hysterical worshipers." The police then went into the crowd waving nightsticks and shouting. One of the believers responded by yelling, "Come and get me! Praise the Lord!" He then touched his lips to the flicking tongue of a large snake. Four men were arrested and pushed into patrol cars. The policemen then killed three of the snakes with clubs. One of the men pushed into the car was Bradley Shell, who had "slipped a big rattler under his shirt, hiding it close to his chest." While putting Shell into the patrol car, an officer discovered that snake and killed it too. During the confusion, the faithful saved the remaining four rattlers.[5]

On September 4, 1945, Captain Lawrence attempted to break up another meeting for Governor Darden. The service ran smoothly for two hours, then Reverend Oddie Vieu Shoupe got up to preach. When Shoupe reached the pulpit, he shouted, "Now friends, the time has come for the snakes."[6] An unidentified worshiper produced a large copperhead. Fifteen people handled the snake before four state troopers interrupted their activities. Captain Lawrence instructed his men not to kill the snake but to take it alive. The snake was delivered to Governor Darden, who handed it over to authorities for examination. The tests revealed that the snake had its venom sacs and fangs intact.

A few days before Captain Lawrence captured the copperhead, a woman had been bitten by a rattlesnake at another Virginia meeting in Wise County on September 1. Anna Kirk, the twenty-six-year-old wife of Reverend Harvey O. Kirk, was struck three times on the wrist after "patting the head" of a snake that her husband was handling and waving her arms over it.[7] Anna became ill immediately but refused medical attention. She stated, "I promised the Lord if I was ever bitten, I would trust in Him. Precious God! Glory to His name!"[8] Mrs. Kirk's hand became swollen and turned black. *Time* magazine reported that in an attempt to save Anna from death, "Harve prayed as never before and every available Faith Holiness member hurried up to pray, too."[9] Three days later, Anna gave birth to a child that died a few moments after delivery. About one hour after the childbirth, which was not attended by a physician, Anna died also. Her family reported that she died singing hymns.[10] John Roberts, Virginia's attorney, ordered samples of Kirk's blood sent to the state laboratory to determine whether she had died from snakebite or from childbirth complications. It was determined that Anna died from snakebite. Three men from Stone Creek, Virginia—Paul Dotson, Leander Ely, and John Wilson—had brought the killer snake to church, along with a box of other poisonous reptiles.[11] After Anna Kirk died, her husband Harvey and the three Stone Creek men were arrested and placed in the Wise County jail.[12] Charges were dismissed against the Stone Creek men, but Harvey Kirk was indicted for murder. He was later convicted of voluntary manslaughter "on evidence that he gave his wife the snake."[13] The Virginia Supreme Court later reversed the decision, "citing improper jury instructions at the trial's outset."[14] Reverend Kirk was given a new trial in circuit court. "He pleaded guilty to manslaughter and accepted a sentence of three months in jail."[15]

Following Anna Kirk's death, Governor Darden's successor, William Tuck, continued to instruct Virginia police "to seize and destroy all snakes brought into [religious] gatherings."[16] Governor Tuck told reporters, "If they want to demonstrate the greatness of their faith, they can heal the sick, raise the dead or cast out demons if they want to, but handling poisonous snakes in public will not be tolerated."[17]

In 1947 Virginia became the third state to outlaw snake handling in religious services. Georgia, the second state to ban snake handling in church services, had passed its law in 1941 following the snakebite of Leitha Ann Rowan and fatal snakebite of Mrs. Jeffie Smith. Georgia's law was by far the most severe. Section 3 of the legislation stated, "In the event, however, that death is caused to a person on account of the violation of this Act by some other person, the prisoner shall be sentenced to death, unless the jury trying the case shall recommend mercy."[18] As in Kentucky, strict anti-snake-handling legislation failed to stop Holiness activity in Georgia. One death in Georgia that attracted national attention was the strychnine death of farmer Ernest Davis at Summerville, Georgia, in 1947. *Time* magazine covered the death in detail: "Then Preacher Miller brought out the 'salvation cocktail.' He shouted: 'Brother Davis, do you believe in the power of the Lord great enough to take what's in this bottle?' Farmer Ernest Davis, 34, grabbed the glass, took several gulps. Five days later, Farmer Davis died of strychnine poisoning. As he was buried last week, his wife standing beside the grave said: 'Ernest just had too much faith.'"[19]

The legal sanctions did cause the snake handlers to conceal many of their meetings in order to avoid being arrested, but the anti-snake-handling laws did not stop the handling of snakes. In fact, the believers became more determined after police harassment. In 1947 several members of snake-handling churches were arrested, but most of the trials dragged out inconclusively. Reverend Oddie Shoupe of Cumberland, Kentucky, was arrested fifty times and jailed on nine occasions for handling serpents. Another snake handler was sentenced to thirty-five days in jail. Joe Creason of the *Louisville Courier-Journal* told how steadily this man practiced his religion, even after he was jailed: "Every night he would hold a one man preaching service in his cell. He'd pray, sing and shout for hours. Finally, the strain became too much for the other prisoners and the jailer. The man was told bluntly to get out of jail and go off somewhere. But he refused to leave. The jailer compromised finally by leaving his cell unlocked at night as he could go out and do his singing and regular Holiness meetings and then return."[20]

Near Harlan, Kentucky, on October 12, 1947, an estimated three thousand "unbelievers gathered to watch "fifty snake-handling members of the Holiness Faith Healers" as they conducted a public church demonstration.[21] The event was held to honor twelve-year-old Faye Nolan of Cawood, who had recently recovered from a snakebite to the hand without medical attention, though gangrene had allegedly set in. She was said to have been on the brink of death for a week or more.[22] Shortly after the meeting began, Faye took the snake that had bitten her and shouted, "God be praised." She then "allowed the snake to coil like a necklace around her, and cried until tears rolled down her cheeks." With her hand still swollen from the previous bite, "Faye testified before the crowd that she had never been in pain and that all she wanted was 'to continue to do the Lord's work.'"[23] The believers then spoke in tongues and "powdered their lips" with strychnine. One man described as a "raw-boned miner in a dark gray suit opened his coat, tucked three or four copperheads under his armpit and closed the coat over the crawling reptiles."[24] Buck Hayes handled fire during the meeting: the *Louisville Courier-Journal* reported, "Raymond Hayes, 47, Cumberland, who said he had been bitten by snakes 31 times

Lee Valentine (left) is showing reporters the snake's fangs. Note the bloody snakebite at the top of his forehead. (Photo courtesy of Richard Golden)

with no ill effects, allowed another cultist to hold a blow torch within a foot of his arm. He held a piece of paper in front of his arm, and the paper was burned, but he apparently was unharmed."[25] Both Kentucky and Virginia police were on hand to stop the meeting, because it was held near the Kentucky-Virginia state line. The Kentucky police claimed that they were on hand simply to "keep order and keep the highway clear of cars." The Virginia police could not stop the meeting, since it was being conducted on the Kentucky side of the line. The Virginia authorities did have a "Joe Doe warrant for the arrest of anyone who might handle snakes on the Virginia side of the line,"[26] but no one crossed the line.

When the preaching began, Oscar Hutton of St. Charles, Virginia, blasted critics and unbelievers who condemned the snake handlers' beliefs. George Helton, a Harlan garage mechanic who had received five battle stars in World War II, told the gathering, "I didn't, and my buddies didn't fight in that awful war so we could come home and be persecuted for worshiping as we please." Oddie Vieu Shoupe told the gathering that he had been arrested fifty times for snake handling and bitten fifty times as well. He discussed his upcoming appeal in Harlan County Court: "We'll

Brother Collins (Photo
courtesy of Richard
Golden)

take an appeal all the way to the Supreme Court in Washington . . . and I
want to go to Washington and handle snakes on the White House steps."[27]

Shoupe and three other defendants—Cinda Mays, Buck Hayes, and
Gladys Sturgill—had been convicted of snake handling at Cumberland,
Kentucky, on August 14, 1947, and fined fifty dollars each in county court.
They appealed to the circuit court, though, and Circuit Judge James S.
Forester dismissed charges against the defendants. Forester said that he
had dismissed the charges at the request of Commonwealth Attorney
Daniel Boone Smith. Smith declined to say why he had had the charges
dismissed, but Judge Forester stated, "We were afraid of a storm. . . . If they
want to kill themselves with those snakes, that's their business.[28]

Even though charges were dismissed against Shoupe and the other defendants, he was arrested again following his initial hearing for handling
snakes at the Harlan County Courthouse. About four hundred or five hundred spectators watched the arrest, but Shoupe took the copperhead that

Lee Valentine (Photo courtesy of Richard Golden)

he had been handling and stuck it in his pants pocket. He then asked the police to search him. After twenty minutes of negotiations, Officer Felix Belcher "fortified himself with a heavy canvas glove and removed the reptile, described as a 3-foot copperhead." Belcher then killed the snake on the street. A person in the crowd shouted, "Let 'em kill it. We've got plenty of them. They ain't rationed." Following Shoupe's arrest, a believer named W. H. Edmonds was arrested when he too started handling a snake. Both men were fined a hundred dollars. Again, the defendants planned to appeal the decision. Police Chief Harmon Noe told Shoupe and Edmonds after their trial that he "would not tolerate future demonstrations of snake-handling on City streets." Chief Noe said, "Now you might as well get this straight. . . . You are not going to handle snakes on the streets in Harlan. . . . If you want to do this thing, I suggest you go to a church or find a vacant lot."[29]

Arrests continued to be made in an attempt to stop snake handling, but to no avail. On October 26, 1947, Harlan judge Lige Howard fined six snake handlers one hundred dollars each for handling a copperhead on the courthouse steps. Those fined were listed as O. V. Shoupe, Mrs. Flora Nolan (Faye's mother), Mrs. Cinda Mays, Roscoe Long, Ed Miller, and Paul Watkins, all of Cumberland. Mrs. Nolan had taken the copperhead to the courthouse in a paper bag. As the arrests were being made by Harlan

Sister Capps (Photo
courtesy of Richard
Golden)

police, an unidentified worshiper stuck the snake in his shirt and escaped
into the crowd that had gathered.[30]

Oscar Hutton continued to use snakes in his religious services three
times a week.[31] Senator R. F. Jasper of Somerset, a Baptist minister, spon-
sored a bill that would have repealed the Kentucky snake-handling law.
"There is no semblance of enforcing the law," he said, "and repeal would
prevent handlers from becoming martyrs to others."[32] Senator Jasper
expressed similar sentiments in another interview: "They go singing to
jail . . . martyrs in the eyes of their fellow cultists, in the rare cases when
authority, prodded or taunted, bothers to enforce the law which says
snakes shall not be handled in public."[33] The bill passed the senate twenty-
two to five, but died in committee in the house.[34]

The believers continued to gather on the Kentucky-Virginia state line to
conduct their services. Joe Creason of the *Louisville Courier-Journal* wrote
an excellent article called "Snake Handlers: A Dying Cult," which included

Charlie Hall (Photo
courtesy of Richard
Golden)

pictures of Oscar Hutton, John Wilson, and Buck Hayes handling snakes
and fire.[35] Although these "miracles" were spotlighted by the news media,
twenty-nine believers had lost their lives by August of 1955.

On August 14, 1955, fifty-two-year-old Kentucky preacher Lee Valentine was killed at Fort Payne, Alabama, when he was struck behind the ear
by a four-foot diamondback rattlesnake. Valentine's bite was allegedly
foreseen in various ways by several church members. On a previous visit to
Alabama, a church member known as "Sister Cooper," who was characterized as a prophet, approached Valentine and said, "I have seen a vision of
you being killed by a serpent. If you go back to Kentucky and never return
to Alabama, you will live to be an old man. If you return you will surely be
killed."[36] Shilo Collins claims that when he was told of George Hensley's
death, which occurred one month before Valentine's bite, he involuntarily
said, "Brother Lee will be next."[37] Preachers Tommy Coots of Middlesboro, Kentucky, and Doyal Marsee of Bean Station, Tennessee, warned

Lee Valentine places a rattlesnake around Louis Saylor's neck (Photo courtesy of Richard Golden)

Valentine of visions that they had of his death. Another man, Ed Hopkins, cautioned Valentine not to go to Alabama. Valentine himself predicted his death. Shortly before his trip to Fort Payne, he told some believers in Leslie County, Kentucky, "You know, brothers, I believe I will be killed for the cause of God." One man asked, "What do you mean, Brother Lee?" Valentine declared, "I believe I will get serpent-bit and die."[38]

On the last night of his life, Valentine howled at the crowd at Fort Payne, "We have champions in football. We have champions in basketball, but we are champions in the Lord."[39] During his sermon Valentine was holding a large rattlesnake. The snake began getting rowdy, so Valentine threw it across his shoulder to calm it down. At that moment the fatal bite occurred. Valentine looked puzzled and remarked, "That thing bit me." Members of the congregation who knew Valentine and had seen him receive bites on previous occasions were shocked. When he was bitten in the past he had continued to preach, but this time he stopped preaching and asked worshipers to pray for him. They fell to their knees and prayed.[40] Valentine then handed the serpent to his friend Harve Fee, who had accompanied him on the trip from Kentucky. Fee placed the reptile in its container. Lee

Overhandled rattlesnakes simply died. (Photo courtesy of Richard Golden)

Valentine lived for approximately ten hours after the bite. He refused medical attention. His final request was "that his snakes be used at his funeral and passed over his grave."[41] Valentine had received approximately one hundred bites previously. He described copperhead bites as bee stings. Rattlesnakes had failed to severely injure him in the past. He had handled twenty-five snakes at a time on occasion. Usually, before he began to handle snakes, he would start singing "Go Down Moses, Down to Egypt Land." At that point there was not a snake he would not handle.

Valentine was a large, friendly man, known throughout the mountains. During his sermons he related that he had been a "sinner." "The Lord took one of my children and I still ignored him," stated Valentine. "He took seven of my children, but I didn't see the light." In 1945, a slate fall at a coal mine where he worked severely injured Valentine and convinced him that "the Lord wanted me to do right and I said if I got over the fall, I would turn to Him."[42] Valentine's conversion is a legendary tale in eastern Kentucky. After he was crushed in the slate fall, his friends took him to the hospital at Pineville. Dr. William Shafer and other medical personnel gave Valentine up for dead. However, the physician decided to do surgery to repair broken bones and other internal injuries in a last effort to save him. When Holiness preacher Willie Napier heard of Valentine's condition, he went to the hospital and prayed for the injured man. Napier told Valentine that he had had a vision of him "lying in a gray-colored coffin" and said that if the doctor performed the operation, Valentine would die. The next morning, as Valentine was being prepared for surgery, he told Dr. Shafer to leave him alone, because he was putting the situation "in God's hands." It is said that when Valentine made his request to the doctor, a "mist came down over the operating room and the doctors and nurses fled in fear." At that point, according to the story, you could hear Valentine's bones begin "snapping back into place," and he was healed.[43]

Valentine then joined the Holiness church and began preaching. Shortly after he became a minister, he started attending church with Shilo Collins and became a snake handler. He loved everyone, including rival mountain preachers who spoke against his snake-handling convictions. Valentine was also free of contempt, disrespect, or jealousy toward other denominations. Shilo Collins recalled, "Lee Valentine was the friendliest and happiest man that I ever saw. He was always the same. The only sins that I know of him committing was smoking cigarettes. At the time of his death he had quit smoking. He only drank milk and water and fasted a lot of the time. That is what puzzled me about his death. I'll tell you one thing, if you go to heaven, you will meet Lee Valentine."[44]

Lee Valentine's funeral was originally set to be held at the little Pentecostal Church of God at Rella (Potterstown), which is located on Straight Creek about five miles from Pineville, Kentucky. But the large crowd that attended made it necessary to hold the event at Red Hill Cemetery in the open air. Two thousand people attended the ceremony. More than a dozen mountain preachers from Alabama, Tennessee, Virginia, Georgia, and Kentucky delivered eulogies to Valentine.

Funeral services opened with a song telling the story of Daniel and the lion's den.[45] Later a woman serenaded the crowd with a beautiful solo, which is unusual at such services; usually the entire congregation sings. Later all of the people at the service joined in the singing. The songs included a recorded solo by Valentine himself. His voice echoed across the valley as he lay in the flower-decked coffin. When the tempo of the music increased, the congregation began to handle two large copperheads. The funeral was a lengthy affair, with much preaching, singing, and snake handling.

A few days later, on August 21, 1955, four thousand people gathered in a remote mountain clearing in Harlan County, only fifty yards from the Virginia state line. The news media announced that the "faith-healing snake-handlers of the Pentecostal Church" would conquer the snake that had killed Valentine.[46] Due to the publicity, it was estimated that ten thousand people might attend the meeting. The police planned to halt the service. Sergeant Roy W. Cundiff of the Kentucky state police stated that the police would "be up there to handle it just like any other violation of the law." The believers planned to simply step across the state line to avoid arrest if they were harassed by Kentucky authorities.[47] However, snake handling is also a violation of the law in Virginia, and Virginia state police waited on the Virginia line to arrest anyone who practiced snake handling on their side.

The snake handlers were not intimidated by the police and brought several snakes to the gathering. The snakes were kept in a brush arbor that had been constructed for the event. They also concealed some snakes in case the police attempted to confiscate them. Valentine's killer was among them. Correspondent Richard D. Golden of Pineville, Kentucky, attended the meeting and made the following observation: "On this day the center attraction was a large box in the shade of a sourwood tree. It was covered with heavy screening behind which could be seen a wriggling swarm of 50 rattlesnakes and copperheads. A smaller box, heavily padlocked, contained two exceptionally dangerous snakes: a six-foot eastern diamond-back and a cottonmouth of extraordinary size."[48]

The meeting began with the usual formalities of group praying, singing, and Bible reading; Oscar Hutton served as the preacher. Hutton told the crowd that he was glad he "did not have to be in a position of having to enforce a law that is against the will of God." About two hours after the service started, sixty-nine-year-old William Vernon of Keokee, Virginia, father of thirteen children, pulled the snake boxes out of the shelter in front of the spectators. He then shouted that the snakes could not be handled until God had "made His will known." He then started dancing and talking in unknown tongues. Vernon then opened the boxes and picked up two snakes in each hand. When he returned the snakes to their boxes, Cundiff arrested him. The state police also confiscated the snakes and held them as evidence. As Vernon was being led away by police, he declared, "I don't want any bond! I prefer to stay in jail, carrying on services and singing." Reverend Hutton said, "I would rather die now of the salvation I have than be in the place of the state police." He also expressed sympathy for the arresting officer, Sergeant Cundiff, "hinting that he expected God to punish the policeman."[49] Hutton added, "They won't stop us, the time I'll stop is when I'm six feet under." Buck Hayes shouted that the police "weren't here to protect the people but to fight God." Hayes recalled the August day in 1918 when he left Harlan to serve in the army: "Congressman Robison stood there at the train station and told us we had to go off and fight and protect our country. He said the Germans wouldn't let us worship. Now our own country wouldn't let us worship the way we want to." Hayes also stated that he had been arrested fourteen times and convicted three times. "It only cost me 30 days in jail, I had my snakes in jail with me and handled them anytime I wanted. And I ate chicken three times a day."[50]

Later in the afternoon Hayes picked up a flaming blowtorch, "plunged his hands into the flames shooting out more than a foot and waved it slowly up and down the length of his outstretched arm, apparently without feeling the heat. His shirtsleeves was [*sic*] not even scorched." It was after Hayes handled the blowtorch that the police found and impounded the hidden box of snakes. In disgust Oscar Hutton declared, "They didn't get 'em all," as he watched the police walk away.[51] Hutton later told reporters, "Vernon got in too big a hurry." Hutton felt that with a little more patience they might have handled Valentine's killer, which had been named Alabama by the serpent handlers.

On July 19, 1959, fifty-one-year-old James Estep of Arjay, Kentucky, received national media attention when a four-foot rattlesnake struck him on the finger at his home.[52] Estep was bitten as he and Shilo Collins were moving the snake from a box to a cage. Following the bite, Estep refused to see a doctor. He stated, "I'm letting the Lord do my doctoring." In response to Estep's bite, Collins told the press, "Brother Estep is having severe pain, his arm is badly swollen, but he's trusting in the Lord. He ate a hearty dinner."[53] Estep's finger became swollen "to twice its size and covered with large black blisters"; however, after he prayed and anointed the finger with olive oil, he began to improve.[54]

Estep had been bitten thirty-one times in the past three years. On July 6—two weeks prior to this bite—he attended a church meeting at Blue Hole, Kentucky (near Manchester, in Clay County), where one hundred people had gathered at a small house. Shilo Collins was the meeting's preacher. Collins had received seven snakebites in previous services but had not become ill. While delivering his message at Blue Hole, Collins "wrapped a 4-foot rattlesnake around his arm, stroked its head, and exhorted his audience: 'Have faith and ye can take up serpents.'"[55] Estep then grabbed two rattlesnakes out of a box. He wrapped them around his arm, "then suddenly lifted two others from the box. One curled about his neck." Collins and Estep then demonstrated to the crowd that the snakes had not been tampered with "by pressing open their mouths with matchsticks [and] showing their fangs."[56] One year prior to the July 6, 1959 service, authorities had stopped the snake-handling meetings at Blue Hole, but

Collins had soon revived the meetings, which now gathered in private homes or wherever he find a meeting place.

The same evening that James Estep was bitten, Earl Adkins of Stanfil was bitten on his left arm by a diamondback rattler as he was putting some snakes in a box that he intended to take to a Harlan County church meeting. Following the first bite, Adkins was also struck by a second snake—a timber rattler. Atkins waited eight hours before receiving medical treatment, only when the pain from the bites became unbearable.[57] When Adkins was later questioned about why he wanted medical attention for the bites, he answered, "I've got no fight against medicine. If you can't get hold of the power of God, medicine is a wonderful thing."[58]

Some judges preferred not to preside over snake-handling trials. In regard to a snake-handling trial at Louisville, Kentucky, the *Louisville Times* published an article about the judge, Gordon B. Winburn, titled "Judge Confesses He's Rattled by Rattlesnakes." When Kelly Clemons was arrested and put on trial for handling snakes at a church in Jefferson County, Judge Winburn said that he did not want to see the evidence, which was a three-foot rattlesnake: "The evidence is a rattlesnake. . . . You can put me down as a coward."[59] The trial was continued until August 25 in Special Judge Overstreet's court. Overstreet fined Clemons fifty dollars and gave him a lecture. Overstreet stated that the police should not have brought the snake in the courthouse. He added, "They could just as well have got one corroborating witness at the scene and then killed the reptile." Overstreet then turned the snake over to the University of Louisville.[60]

Between Lee Valentine's death in 1955 and February 1967, eleven other snake handlers died as a result of snakebite. On February 19, 1967, twenty-five-year-old James Saylor was bitten by a rattlesnake at his uncle William D. Saylor's church in Covington, Kentucky. The following day James was taken to a hospital, where he died as a result of the bite. Three church members were arrested as a result of Saylor's death: Reverend William D. Saylor, pastor of the Free Holiness Church; Mrs. Dorothy Saylor, James's wife; and Jesse Brock.[61] The three were arrested for violating Kentucky's snake-handling laws. On March 8, 1967, Defense Attorney Howell Vincent requested that Police Judge William B. O'Neal dismiss the charges on the grounds that the law violated a person's freedom of worship.[62] Vincent stated, "A real serious question is involved here. . . . I don't think the state legislature can pass a law which abrogates the federal Constitution which says a man can worship according to the dictates of his conscience." Judge O'Neal responded, "I agree that a man's religion is a very deep and personal thing . . . but I also believe that there are certain safeguards a state can impose to protect the health and welfare of its citizens."[63] The judge continued the case until April 5 so that briefs could be filed on the constitutional issue. On April 5, Judge O'Neal granted the snake handlers a trial by jury at the request of their attorney.[64] The trial was set for April 15.[65]

At the April 15 trial the defendants were acquitted: Judge O'Neal directed the jury to return a verdict of not guilty after Reverend William Saylor testified that he did not know that a rattlesnake had been brought to the church until James had been bitten. When William was asked if he would handle snake again, he commented, "I'm not prepared to answer that. . . . I have nothing against handling snakes if the Lord so wills."[66]

That year ended very sadly for Kale Saylor and his children. At 2:30 P.M. on December 9, 1967, Kale's wife, Jean, was bitten by a rattlesnake on her arm at Kettle Island, located in Harlan County. When relatives and friends asked if she wanted to be taken to a doctor, she refused. She said that she would rather be taken home with her children. Many people visited the Saylor home that evening, asking God to heal Mrs. Saylor. Gospel songs were sung, and much of the same activity that occurs in a church was performed at the Saylor home. At approximately nine the next morning, Jean Helton Saylor died. She passed away practicing the religion she believed in so strongly.

On August 18, 1968, in Big Stone Gap, Virginia, sixty-nine-year-old retired coal miner Oscar Franklin Pelfrey was bitten on the forehead, near his left eye, by one of two rattlesnakes he was handling at the Church of God in Jesus' Name. The snake that struck him was a four-foot yellow timber rattler. Pelfrey had been bitten seven times before and had "recovered without medical aid, each time strengthened in his creed."[67] After this bite occurred, church members asked Pelfrey if he wanted medical aid. He refused to be treated and requested to be taken home, where he died six hours later.[68] Over five hundred people attended Pelfrey's funeral, which was preached by Ed Arwood.

During the 1940s, Pelfrey was going to a church service in Kentucky from his home in Virginia. He was bringing along a rattlesnake that he had handled at various times for the past year. As he approached a wooded area, he decided to turn the snake loose. "He took the snake box out of the car, walked over to a bank and set the snake free."[69] Pelfrey then returned to his car to find that the snake had followed him. He picked up the snake and put it back in its box and continued his journey. When Pelfrey arrived at the church in Kentucky, a woman handled the snake and was bitten. She was not injured.

Fourteen years before his death, Pelfrey had been arrested for handling serpents, but he continued to practice his beliefs. Arrests were also made after Pelfrey was killed. Officials attempted to prosecute the minister of the church, Reverend Kenneth Short of Harlan, Kentucky, who had supplied the snake that killed Pelfrey. The Wise, Virginia circuit court jury freed Short but fined Roscoe Mullins, assistant pastor of the church, fifty dollars and a thirty-day jail sentence for handing Pelfrey the snake a few minutes before it struck.[70]

Ten more believers died of snakebite from the time Oscar Pelfrey was killed to the summer of 1976. Even the famous Buck Hayes was bitten and killed by a rattlesnake at Crockett, Kentucky, in 1968. The same snake that struck Hayes had killed another Kentuckian, Johnny Newton, only a few days earlier.

At Austin Long's church in Rose Hill, Virginia, thirty-one-year-old Frank H. Wagner was bitten on his right hand on August 16, 1976. Immediately after the attack, Wagner was taken to the home of Clifford Moore, where he died approximately twenty-five hours later. A church member described the bite to Jon Greer of the *Kingsport Times-News*: "I saw how it happened. . . . He came in during the preaching and sat down in front. Then after the sermon he went to the altar. . . . He was down praying then he raised up and went to shouting. And he reached down and pulled the snake box out from under the pew. When he went to open it, the big yellow rattler nabbed him."[71] The church member added that Wagner "wiped the blood off with a hanky . . . then continued shouting . . . but he set back down all of a sudden, and his color went pale, and he bent over and they carried him to the car."[72]

In June of 1978, a forty-two-year-old Harlan County man—Aaron Long, a building contractor and preacher—was killed by a rattlesnake that struck him three times on his right hand at the Martins Fork Church of God in Cawood, Kentucky.[73] Long refused to be taken to a doctor and died at his home in Baxter.[74] Harlan County coroner Phillip J. Begley reported that Long received the bites around noon and died at 5:45 P.M.[75] Three preachers extolled Long's life at his funeral, where over a hundred mourners gathered.[76] Reverend Denver Short said, "He's been down and out, like us all, but he sought the help of God and was saved."[77] Aaron Long's death attracted much publicity. A commentary in the *Richmond Register* claimed that snake handling is a temptation. The writer cited 1 Corinthians 10:9 as evidence of his position: "Neither let us tempt Christ, as some of them also tempted and were destroyed by serpents."[78] Even *Hustler* magazine featured an article largely on Long's death.[79] Almost a year after Long's death,

Oscar Davidson, a church member who lives near London, Kentucky, explained why men such as Long can die from snakebites: "The Lord just got through with him and didn't need him on earth any longer. . . . There was also the chance the man might have misread the urging of the Holy Spirit or the faith of the congregation might have slackened."[80]

Shortly after Aaron Long's death, thirty-seven-year-old Roy Leon Johnson was killed by a rattlesnake bite in a church service near Lebanon, Virginia.[81] Later that year, a Georgia man named Wayne Thornton also died from a rattlesnake bite. At the Jim Sizemore Pentecostal Church on Couch's Fork, ten miles east of Hyden, Kentucky, thirty-two-year-old coal miner Claude Amos died from the bite of a fifty-nine-inch rattlesnake.[82] After Amos's hand was bitten—on Friday night, September 12, 1980—he went into shock and was taken to the Mary Breckinridge Hospital at Hyden, then transferred to the Albert B. Chandler Medical Center at the University of Kentucky in Lexington. He died three days later, on Monday, at 4:30 P.M.[83] Amos had handled snakes hundreds of times before and had been bitten at least twice before.[84] His wife, Laverne, said the most recent bite had happened "about a year ago."[85] Eighty-two-year-old snake handler Will Holland gave his assessment of Amos's death: "Just because somebody got bit and died doesn't bluff us a bit. . . . Amos was a good man, a strong family man but he just didn't have enough faith." Amos's sister stated, "[We were] angry at first, but now we have no regrets. We have no doubt he has gone to a better place."[86] Amos left two children—Anna, ten years old, and Sarah, eleven.

Only ten days before Amos's bite, Kale Saylor had received multiple rattlesnake bites at a church in Bell County. After Kale passed out from the bites, he was taken to the Pineville Community Hospital. A sixteen-year-old Bell County boy was also bitten shortly before Claude Amos was killed. The young man refused to be taken to the doctor, and his family supported his decision. It was not until Bell County health officials obtained a court order against his family that he received medical attention. He was treated at the University of Kentucky medical center.[87]

Thirty-eight-year-old John Holbrook was killed by a rattlesnake bite at the Lord Jesus Church in Jesus' Name near Oceana, West Virginia, on August 24, 1982.[88] Newspaper and magazine articles that were unsympathetic to Holbrook's family and church members appeared around the nation. One article called snake handling a "barbarous practice" and a "savage ritual."[89]

At Mt. Sterling, Kentucky, a forty-six-year-old woman, Mary Vice, was bitten by a rattlesnake at a home service and taken to the University of

Kentucky hospital for treatment.[90] She survived the bite. A thirty-nine-year-old Phelps, Kentucky man, Mack Wolford, did not survive. He was killed by a rattlesnake at a McDowell, West Virginia church meeting in August 1983. Wolford lived for approximately eight hours after the bite.[91] Even in the face of such snakebite deaths, and even though the snake handlers were attacked by the authorities and occasionally by the press, they refused to abandon their beliefs.

Nine. Relying on Prayer

Holiness snake handlers believe that God's power manifests itself through them as a result of their prayers, making them able not only to handle poisonous serpents but to perform other miracles as well—to cast out demons, heal sick people, and so forth. They see such actions as affirmations of James 5:13–16: "Is any among you afflicted? Let him pray. Is any merry? Let him sing Psalms. Is any sick among you? Let him call for the elders of the church; and let them pray over him, anointing him with oil in the name of the Lord: And the prayer of faith shall save the sick, and the Lord shall raise him up; and if he had committed sins, they shall be forgiven him. Confess your faults to one another, and pray for one another, that he may be healed. The effectual fervent prayer of a righteous man availeth much."

During the 1930s Oscar Hutton's wife was stricken with typhoid fever. She became deathly ill. After she had remained in bed for five days as a result of the sickness, Hutton's neighbors threatened to have him arrested for not calling a doctor. He still refused and gave the sick woman ice water to drink and prayed constantly. For twenty days the woman was on the verge of death. On the twenty-first day, the "fever left her suddenly and she got out of bed and cooked breakfast."[1] Park Saylor relates,

> Prayer is all we had to rely on years ago. There wasn't any doctors like there is today. We had to turn to God. There was a lady that slipped into one of our churches and took a bottle of oil that we rub on people during prayer. The Bible says "anoint with oils." Well, she had seen us fall out under the power after oil was rubbed on us, and believed the oil made us have fits. Well, she took that bottle of oil home and rubbed it on a sick cow that was down. She believed that the cow would start dancing. But the cure did not work because the woman was not under the power of God.

Saylor said he saw animals healed on several occasions. "Some people healed a cow at Straight Creek, and my Uncle Harve Eads healed a cow for Jim Jackson. Jackson had a family of nine children. He raised them by praying. Jackson went to Uncle Harve Eads one day and said, 'Brother Eads, I have nine children and no way to feed them. My cow is down.' Uncle Harve said, 'Let's go look at it, Brother.' They went down to Jackson's house, where the cow was lying in a pasture. Uncle Harve and Jackson laid hands on the cow and prayed. She raised up and pitched about ten feet before they were done praying."[2] Another account of a cow being healed was told to me by Kale Saylor.

In the summer of 1961, Park Saylor was forty-six years old. The old leaders such as Hensley and Valentine were gone. Saylor was recognized as a leader among the Holiness people at this time and was respected as a true man of God. He performed miracles such as healing, snake handling, and raising the dead. Hospitals and adequate medical personnel were still rare in eastern Kentucky at this time, and the Saylors still dealt with their problems by turning to prayer and by receiving assistance from kin. The few doctors, police, and other professionals who did exist were viewed as outsiders and not trusted. It was to men like Park Saylor that mountaineers looked for guidance when tragedy struck.

Shortly after his forty-sixth birthday, he conducted a seven-week revival in Clay County. During the event thirty-five people were saved and were baptized in the Red Bird River. While Saylor was conducting a baptism, a twenty-year-old woman with long black hair walked out into the river toward him. When she got close, he noticed that she was spitting up blood severely. The woman was in an advanced stage of tuberculosis and wanted to be baptized. After Saylor submerged her in the water and said, "I baptize you in the name of the Father, Son, and Holy Ghost," the bleeding stopped. She turned to the people standing on the riverbank, began crying, and shouted, "I'm healed! I'm healed! I'm not sick anymore!" Saylor says, "I've seen cancer healed, broke backs, ankles and the blind cured. People just don't ask God for help anymore. God wants to be praised. To be capable of His good will, you must walk, talk, act, and believe like God." Shortly after this incident, Park Saylor undertook another act of healing, this time at Tess Walters's church in Blackmont, Kentucky. Bill Stewart had been bitten by a rattlesnake on the right arm and almost immediately became very ill. Bags the size of eggs had formed on Stewart's arm. His hand was swollen to three times its normal size and had turned black. Stewart's mother asked Saylor to pray for her son. "I knew death was close," says Saylor, "but when we prayed those bags went away like pouring water out of a boot."

In one service, Tess Walters was bitten by a seven-foot rattlesnake and passed out within minutes. The congregation took him to Harve Eads's house, which was near the church. Park Saylor called for prayer: "Everyone come and pray. It's time to meditate upon God." Reverend Saylor asked two of the church sisters to follow him to Eads house to pray for Walters.

Eads's porch was full of people, and it was impossible to find room to pray inside the house due to the large gathering. Reverend Saylor told the women, "Just find a place to pray." At that point, the Lord moved on one woman and through her said to Tess, "I have counseled you many times and you failed to take my instructions." Reverend Saylor states that "the death look was on Tess at this time." The woman then uttered the words, "I'll have you to look up and I'll help you." When the woman spoke that time, she fell over and almost tore the curtains down. Reverend Saylor recalls, "The power of the Lord was on her heavy." After the woman spoke the second time, Walters got up from the bed and went to the toilet. As he began to urinate, blood passed through his kidneys, and he was "all right from that point on."[3]

At Pottertown, in Lee Valentine's church, Tommy Gambrel was bitten by a big rattlesnake and became ill. Saylor says, "Serpent bite is hard to pray over. I went over and took him by the hand, stood him on his feet, and

Tess Walters, ca. 1950 (Photo courtesy of Tess Walters)

the Lord healed him instantly." He is careful not to take credit for his healing ability, however: "I have never healed anyone. The Lord has used me as the clay to do the job."

Everett Jackson of Leslie County injured himself severely while in the process of lifting a log that was too heavy for a single man to handle. He showed signs of serious internal bleeding. After he "bled two quart peach cans full, besides towels and newspapers," he was moved to the church to receive prayer. When Park Saylor arrived at the church, he was met by Dewey Hensley, who informed him of Jackson's condition. Reverend Saylor claims that God told him to go inside the church and lay hands on Jackson in order to heal him. As he walked up the aisle toward the injured man, though, the Devil reportedly told him, "You are showing out." Reverend Saylor says he was stunned by the Devil's comment and "just sat on the altar. . . . I felt like a man who had never had God. I broke down and began to cry. I then said, 'Lord, if you will put that back on me, I'll obey you in spite of every devil in hell.'" Saylor claims that God "then jumped me four or five feet in the air." God then moved on Jackson and he "moved in the air" toward Park Saylor. Saylor laid hands on Jackson, and he was said to be instantly healed of his injuries.[4]

Brothers Frey and
Meadows, ca. 1960s
(Photo courtesy of Tess
Walters)

Saylor is also credited with healing Ernest Brown. Described as a good-hearted man who was very poor, Brown had seven or eight children and lived in a shack on his father-in-law's place. While working as a coal miner at Benton, Kentucky, he suffered a broken back. Saylor, who was working in the coal mines at Lynch during this time, gave Brown a substantial sum of money and a freezer. Saylor prayed and said, "Lord, there has to be a better way to help this man." Saylor recalls, "Well, the Lord showed me how to heal him. I had enough faith to do it. At the Path Fork Church, I got a knife and started to cut the cast off. The Devil spoke to me and said it would be shameful to cut that cast off with him wearing no shirt. I let the Devil defeat me." Later, Saylor returned and healed Brown. After Brown's back healed, he was visiting another local church and received a serious snakebite. At the moment Brown was struck, he turned around and saw some members of the congregation grinning and winking at each other. As Park Saylor said, "That wasn't a great comfort to him." Brown then went to Saylor's church and asked some of the members to have Park meet him outside. When Saylor got the message, he went outside and asked Brown what was the matter. Brown answered, "I just wanted to talk with you. I was just serpent-bit by a big black rattler." Saylor replied, "Hold your faith,

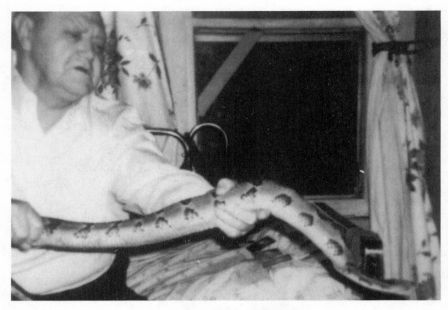

Mark Daniels, late 1970s (Photo courtesy of Tess Walters)

brother. Nothing has happened to you yet." Park Saylor recalls, "Well, you see, those people grinning and winking weakened his faith. I just told him to look to the Lord."

Around eleven that evening Saylor received a telephone call requesting him to pray for Ernest Brown. "Come and pray for Ernest Brown," said the caller. "He is dying." Saylor asked his uncles, George and Harve Eads, to go with him to Brown's shack to assist him in prayer. When Saylor arrived, Ernest Brown was actually "flipping in his bed" in agony. Saylor recalls, "The Lord moved me to lay hands on him, and he was instantly healed." Brown later told him, "Brother Saylor, I saw a light come down about four or five feet from me. I'd like to swap this ol' barn off for a real mansion." Saylor says, "The Lord healed him, but he was a rack of misery."

In the summer of 1955 at Sister Nicely's church in Mount Vernon, Kentucky, a man allegedly died during a large Sunday morning worship service. Forty people reportedly stood outside the church and listened to the meeting through raised windows. When the man died, George Eads informed Park Saylor what had happened. Saylor claims that almost immediately he felt the "power of the Lord. . . . It felt like cold rippling water was poured over my body and my heart quivered."

Saylor was asked to pray for the dead man, but he says the "Spirit was on him so heavy" he could not see or hear the people making the request. He

Judy Brock, early 1950s (Photo courtesy of Tess Walters)

walked around the altar and heard a church brother yell and put oil in Saylor's left hand. Saylor yelled out, "If this brother shouted a good shout and danced a good dance, he has met his reward." He then heard a church sister scream. She fell down in deep prayer at the feet of the dead man and placed her hands on him. Park Saylor kept on preaching. He recalled, "When God moved me to the dead man, I laid my left hand on him, which contained the oil." He states that God then spoke through him, saying, "In the name of the son of God sit up." Saylor recounts, "He was dancing like a sparrow on a limb before I could get my hand away." The man said to the congregation, "People, I died and left this life and God brought me back." At that point people in the crowd rushed Park Saylor, asking him to pray for them. He prayed for over forty people that afternoon.

Although Park Saylor and the early church leaders were given credit for performing "miracles," some tragedies could not be avoided. On January 18, 1960, five Holiness church members were killed in one of Bell County's worst automobile accidents. Eighty-one-year-old Anthony Collett; his nineteen-year-old wife; Mrs. Troy Miller and her sixteen-month-old son, Paul; and Mrs. Nettie Helton were fatally injured when Collett pulled his 1951 Chevrolet in front of a tractor-trailer truck a few miles north of

Pineville on US 25E. The truck completely destroyed Collett's vehicle. Kale Saylor preached the funeral for the people killed in the accident.

The group was returning from a church meeting at Manchester, Kentucky. In the trunk of Collett's car was a box containing a rattlesnake that had been used in the service. The impact of the wreck freed the snake from its container. Bell County coroner Billy Durham and State Trooper Paul Cassidy crawled under the vehicle getting bodies out, unaware of the snake's presence. Luckily, neither man was bitten. The following day, several hundred people viewed the vehicle without encountering the rattlesnake, which was still free in the wreckage. Sim Collett, Anthony's son, visited the wrecked car at the Gamble Wrecking Yard on Harlan Road in Pineville and retrieved Mrs. Collett's shoes and coat from the car, not realizing the snake was near. Two days after the wreck, as wrecking yard employee Sewell Wilson was walking by the demolished automobile, he noticed the snake lying on what was left of the trunk. Wilson swung at the rattler with a wood plank, but missed it. On the second swing he hit the snake with such force he broke the board and mutilated the reptile. Later Ernest "Troy" Miller picked up the dead snake and the container.[5]

The Devil surfaced frequently among Holiness congregations. In Solomon Saylor's time, demons permeated everyday life and were likely to be given credit for a bucket of spoiled milk, a strange dream, or an untimely death. With the problems that had emerged with industrial capitalism, demons and spirits played a larger part in explaining everyday troubles. Community anxiety and social interrelationships fed belief and fear, and accusations of demon possession grew more common, as they had in early America.[6] Each community explained demons and witchcraft by the local standards, and belief in demons took distinct forms. For example, some saw witchcraft and the Devil as one being. Others, such as Park Saylor, believed in suicide demons, murder demons, and diverse spirits. The Holiness people saw society as a war between agents of the Devil and servants of God. When I asked Park Saylor whether he had demons cast out, he answered, "I have seen many things happen concerning evil spirits."

Saylor alleges that he has seen people "beating themselves in the face, foaming at the mouth, and changing complexion" due to possession by an "evil spirit." I inquired about the possibility that these people were having epileptic seizures. Park Saylor replied, "No, you can take medicine for that. It takes God to get an evil spirit off of you."

Many reports of demon possession exist in the Appalachian highlands. Bruce Helton, George Hensley, Bradley Shell, George Eads, and other old-timers, including Park Saylor, are said to have cast out demons in their pastoral careers. It is commonly believed that a person with a weak spirit, or one who does not believe in God or demons, is a particularly good candidate for demon possession. Mrs. Doyal Marsee of Bean Station, Tennessee, claims that she saw her father cast out demons throughout rural Appalachia. She believes that demons are floating about looking for a "weak soul" to enter and that they cannot enter the soul of a strong Christian. I have been ordered out of churches, for my personal protection, if a person displayed signs of possession. I was informed that a demon could enter me after it was cast out of a devil-controlled individual.

Perhaps the most famous minister who performed exorcisms of evil spirits was a Jesus Only preacher, the late Reverend Tommy Coots of Middlesboro, Kentucky. In an interview, his wife stated that it is difficult to identify a possessed person unless they enter a church. She claimed that "the Word stirs them up." When the demons are in this condition, it is possible that the physical features of a possessed person might change. Mrs. Coots recalled, "One time when we were living at Nicholasville, a woman grew tushes hanging out of her mouth and a young boy's eyes turned over in his head." I asked her whether she had ever seen one of these demons. Mrs. Coots answered, "No, but you can feel their presence. They will talk to you through the person they have entered." I asked, "How do you know that they are not just putting you on?," and she replied, "Because they talk in different voices. They talk like men sometimes, or maybe in the voice of a child." Mrs. Coots then described the event that alarmed her the most in her husband's pastoral career. At a church in Nicholasville, Kentucky, a man approached her husband and declared, "If you have got the power to cast out a devil, I want to see you do it." Reverend Coots touched the allegedly possessed man, and the man fell to the floor. Mrs. Coots said, "He hit the floor and swelled like a balloon and said, 'I'm here, and I'm going to stay here.'" When I asked whether her husband cast the demon out, Mrs. Coots responded, "No, because the man did not want delivery strong enough."[7]

In the 1980s, at a small Pentecostal church near Manchester, Kentucky, a preacher allegedly cast out several demons from a woman that exhibited evil spirit possession during a church service. However, the woman ran out the back door of the church before the preacher had completed the exorcism. The preacher felt that the woman was still possessed, so he told her to come back to the evening service, and she agreed to return. Before the woman reappeared at the church, the preacher anointed the rear door of the building with oil. Once the woman entered the church for the evening service, the preacher slipped to the front door of the church and anointed it with oil as well. When the meeting began, the preacher started preaching on "casting out demons." The woman became uneasy, according to the preacher, and then took off running toward the rear door of the building. When she approached the opening, she could not pass through it because of the anointing. The woman then turned and attempted to run through the front door, but she could not go through it either, and she fell to the floor. Knowing that the woman was trapped in the church, the preacher then completed the exorcism. The woman is still living in the Manchester area and remains free of evil spirits, according to the serpent handlers.

It is common for snake handlers to attribute problems they suffer to the Devil, or "the enemy," as he is commonly called. The ministers feel that the Devil torments a person in many ways. In an interview with Reverend Floyd McCall of Greenville, South Carolina, Karen W. Carden and Robert W. Pelton asked questions regarding possession by the Devil. McCall said, "The devil is over their life, in control of it. I do know, just about every time, what specific devil has got the person bound. Either it's a sexual devil, or it's a suicide devil. There are lots of ways a devil can bind people. The Lord always lets me know exactly how to pray for them. He tells me what direction to go in. He leads me to the correct way of beating the devil spirit in the person."[8]

In August of 1986, Reverend Liston Pack performed an exorcism at his church in Carson Springs, Tennessee, on a woman from Cincinnati, Ohio. During his sermon, Pack indicated Satan's presence when he pointed his finger at the woman and screamed, "Get out, Satan!" The woman raised out of her seat in the second row of the tiny church and talked in three voices. One voice was of a small child. The second was the sound of a man. Finally the woman used her own voice, making slanderous and obscene remarks at the pastor and congregation. Pack then repeated his demand, "Get out, Satan!" At that point the woman vomited on Pack. Liston Pack recalled, "That woman threw up the most foul stuff you have ever seen. You can ask my wife. We never got the smell off of me for three weeks. As soon as that happened a little creature of some sort came out of her and passed out the back door. After that she was all right."[9]

Preachers have informed me that one can sometimes tell a person is possessed: they may begin to show signs of a changing personality, such as depression. Physical signs of diabolical control are also displayed on occasion. Bradley Shell states that he has seen people suck the blood out of their bodies, bite their tongues, and slobber. During church service women have stood and literally torn off their clothes. Shell says on such occasions he would cover them with a blanket and then "cast out the demon in the name of Jesus." When I asked Shell whether he had heard possessed people talk in multiple voices, he replied, "Lord yes. I have seen them talk in many different ways."[10]

During World War II, Bradley Shell heard of a soldier being held in jail at Harlan for beating people to death with his fists. When the authorities tried to feed the incarcerated man, he would attack them. He assaulted his family or anyone else who tried to give him attention. Shell decided that he would visit the soldier and try to help him. The prisoner was totally nude, unshaven, and filthy when Shell first saw him. Shell claims that he was convinced the man was possessed by "evil spirits." Shell told the jailer to open the cell because he wanted to help the prisoner. The jailer said, "Shell, are you crazy? If you go in that cell that man will kill you." But Shell displayed no fear of the prisoner. When the cell door was opened, Shell laid his hands on the man's back and prayed. The prisoner said to Shell, "Do that again, that is the best feeling that I have ever had." When Shell placed his hands on the soldier again, he informed Shell that he would like to have a "pair of overalls, a shirt, and something to eat." The man never showed any signs of violence again. I asked Shell, "So you feel that man was possessed by the Devil?" He replied, "I know he was. I have cast devils out of others too. In some cases I would actually jump in bed and stay with a man possessed until the devil was gone." I pointed out, "You know your critics will say those people were just having seizures or suffering from an epileptic fit, don't you?" Shell responded, "Yes, but there is a big difference in the two. If a man is sick with epilepsy you can tell it. If he is possessed everything about him changes."[11]

Although Park Saylor has been given acclaim for his pastoral works, he has witnessed the snakebite death of two fellow Kentuckians. Saylor watched Robert Ely receive a fatal rattlesnake bite in 1965, and on October 28, 1973, he observed the snakebite death of Shirley Wagers, a seventy-two-year-old coal miner and father of ten children. Another man, twenty-eight-year-old Luster Johnson, was also bitten on the left hand at that church service, but Johnson was not injured.[12]

The fatal rattlesnake bite was not Wagers's first snakebite. He had been bitten by a copperhead just a few weeks prior to his death and survived.[13] Wagers was a well-liked man. Eight months before his death, Wagers, "his wife Mandie, and relatives were in the Wagers' East Bernstadt home on a March night, huddled around a tape recorder and telling the spinning, silent machine about their religious faith." "Bless His good name. He's coming after people who have made themselves ready. . . . Before I really got saved they brought the good gospel in there to Clay County where I was living and began to preach the five Bible signs. . . . I began to see the signs carried out, and I began to believe."[14] Wagers was devout in his beliefs and had seen many miracles worked through prayer. His son, Fred, had been badly injured in a car wreck and was reportedly made well through Shirley's prayers. Shirley broke both of his legs in a mining accident "and was healed in a church service." He witnessed several other miracles worked at Holiness churches in eastern Kentucky and expressed his feelings about them on his tape recorder: "If they could all be one, how great the Lord could do through all his people and how many good miracles he could work and the sick could get healed." Shortly after noon at the Sunday meeting on October 28, Wagers took up a rattlesnake that struck him on the left hand. "Seven hours and 10 minutes later at his son's home in London . . . and without medical attention, which he refused . . . Shirley Wagers was dead."[15]

Oscar Davidson, who helped found the church on KY 80 near London, believed that Wagers "moved ahead of the Spirit." Wagers's son, Fred, said he too felt that his father had not waited for a full "movement of God."[16] Gene Carter, a friend of the family, spoke at the funeral and gave his opinion of Wagers's death: "If the Lord didn't want Brother Shirley Wagers to go, he could have stuck his head in a barrel of rattlesnakes . . . and nothing would have happened to him."[17] Park Saylor gave this account of the death:

> There was this man named Shirley Wagers from over around Bullskin. He was at London one Sunday morning on Route 80. He always greeted everyone with a kiss, but this particular Sunday. The Bible says greet ye one another with a holy kiss of charity. He handled a serpent and it bit him. We went on with the service, but Wagers got up and went home. After the service was over I ate dinner with Oscar Davidson, Preacher Henry Swiney, and Brother Oaks. After we had eaten, some of the members got up and started home. Well, I stopped them and said, no we can't go home. We have to go out there and pray for this man that got snakebit. When we got out there he was in bed and some people were praying for him. His body was already turning colors and he was terribly sick. He lived to around 7:30 that evening and he died.

A large number of people, including many of the founders of the serpent-handling movement, attended Shirley Wagers's funeral. Tess Walters, Henry Swiney, George Eads, Johnny Saylor, Park Saylor, and Jimmy Long were just a few of those who gathered to pay their respects. George Eads started the service by reprimanding the church: "Me and this brother have been together for years, but this death is uncalled for." Eads added, "I've been handling serpents for forty years and I don't have a crooked finger or scar on me. Now this is uncalled for." One gentleman remarked to Park Saylor, "I would have given fifty dollars for him not to be here." Saylor replied, "I only have forty dollars, but I would give it all for him to be here." Park Saylor recalls, "He was telling the truth. He was one of our old leaders. I've seen him handle snakes and they would die. He would throw them in the creek after he was done. The power of God would get on him. God protected him, Brother. They just couldn't get the job done when they bit him."

After George Eads opened the proceedings, the congregation started to dance and shout. Jimmy Long took a snake box containing four rattlesnakes and stuck his head in it. He ran around the Bible stand with the snake box over his head without being bitten.[18] Park Saylor next preached the funeral sermon. Several people had informed him, he declared, that Wagers was killed because of confusion and disorder in the congregation.[19]

Death and injury from snakebite still haunt the snake handlers. At Baxter, Kentucky, on February 13, 1986, a five-foot-long eastern diamondback rattlesnake struck and killed thirty-eight-year-old Shirley McLeary of Toledo, Ohio, who was attending a wake for her uncle. McLeary did not seek medical attention after she was bitten on her left wrist. She was taken to a house next to the church, where she died.[20] County attorney Alan Wagers said that he would not prosecute the case. He also commented, "I'm leery of prosecuting anyone for exercising their religious beliefs, no matter how different those beliefs are."[21] In July 1987, another believer—a Bell County, Kentucky woman—was bitten and refused medical treatment.[22]

On the final weekend of January 1989, forty-one-year-old Ernest Wayne Short of Teetersville, Kentucky, was killed by a two-and-a-half to three-foot rattlesnake at his church in Harlan County.[23] The son of legendary preacher Denver Short, Wayne Short was bitten near his right elbow and died refusing medical treatment.[24] He left three children and two stepchildren. His wife, Dorothy, was pregnant at the time of Wayne's death. She had also lost her first husband, James Saylor, to a rattlesnake bite.[25]

Only two months before Short was killed—on November 20, 1988—a Tennessee man, twenty-nine-year-old Gerald Fleenor, had been bitten by a four-foot rattlesnake at Wayne Short's church.[26] After Fleenor was bitten, he was taken to his home in Sneedville, Tennessee, by Reverend Austin Long of Rose Hill, Virginia. After Fleenor's mother found out about the bite, she insisted that he be checked by a doctor. Fleenor was then taken to a Morristown, Tennessee hospital, where he received an antivenin shot.[27] He was then flown by Lifestar helicopter to the University of Tennessee Hospital in Knoxville, where he was placed in the intensive care unit. Church members were critical of Fleenor's mother for insisting that her son be treated medically. One woman said, "If [Gerald's] mother had more faith, if she had just believed, he would have been all right." Henry Swiney, the minister of the Sneedville Holiness Church, stated that he did not believe Fleenor needed medical treatment. Swiney said, "I don't pay any attention to getting bit. . . . I never have been to a hospital or even a doctor. He probably would have been all right if his mother hadn't gotten scared."[28] Fleenor improved and attended Tess Walters's funeral a few days later.

On May 10, 1989, a thirty-four-year-old Perry County man, Alonzo Combs, was bitten by a rattlesnake and was taken to Appalachian Regional Medical Center for treatment. Combs told the *Lexington Herald Leader* that he had had a dream that the snake was going to bite him. "He bit me as quick as he touched me. I guess he got me off guard," said Combs.[29] Thurman Frye, a fifty-three-year-old Leslie County man, was bitten by a six-foot rattlesnake at the Grassy Pentecostal Church in November 1989. Bitten on the right hand, Frye was taken to the Mary Breckinridge Hospital in Hyden. Later he was transferred to the intensive care unit of the University of Kentucky's Chandler Medical Center. Following the bite, Frye's arm swelled to three times its normal size. Leslie County officials considered prosecuting Frye for violating Kentucky's anti-snake-handling laws, but the county's attorney, Phillip Lewis, explained that "law enforcement officials thought public sentiment against prosecuting people because of their religious beliefs would make a conviction improbable."[30]

Authorities have largely ignored the snake handlers in recent years unless a death has occurred. In a recent trial at Barbourville, Kentucky, Knox County attorney Mike Warren filed charges against four church members accused of violating Kentucky's anti-snake-handling law. After reviewing materials associated with the case and realizing that Kentucky's anti-snake-handling law might be overturned, Warren filed a motion to dismiss the complaint; Knox County district judge Rod Messer granted that motion. Because Warren did not argue in favor of the law, Messer refused to declare unconstitutional a law that pits state authority against religious belief. This was the first test of Kentucky's anti-snake-handling law since it was upheld in the Lawson case. Byron Crawford and Arnold Saylor's attitudes toward the law are representative of most snake handlers' convictions. Crawford states, "The Bible says take up serpents and that is what I intend to do. If it said take up grizzly bears, then I would do that." In the same vein, Saylor argued, "I believe that the laws made by man should be followed. When they conflict with the laws of God, that's a different story."

Park Saylor still relies heavily on prayer to solve illness and problems. He has seen medical doctors but contends that "God has the final say." From the early days of settlement, mountain people's life involved constant struggle with the Devil. But the battle was fought along lines set by the community or local church. Miracles took the place of what professionals and other outsiders could provide. Men like Park Saylor established a code of ethics that provided meaning for people outside the larger society, which they resisted and saw as evil. Park Saylor declares, "If God isn't in it, you're not going to be cured. I have no regrets. I was healed of cancer in the throat twenty-eight years ago. I was pleased with my life and ready to go. They dismissed me and gave me up for death. God healed me. I made a covenant. I said, Lord, if I can serve someone, I will stay. If not, I'm ready to go. I prayed for Harve Eads and he was healed of lung cancer shortly after that. You have to honor God at all times. When you really get saved you must walk, talk, and act like God."

Ten. Outmigration and Traditions

During the 1940s and 1950s, many Appalachian residents migrated to northern industrial centers like Detroit, Chicago, Cleveland, and Fort Wayne, Indiana, searching for employment. In 1958 Albert N. Votaw wrote that "70,000 newcomers" were found "among Chicago's motley population of four million."[1] Appalachians were actively recruited by the factories because of a labor shortage. About three out of five Kentucky mountain counties lost more than 15 percent of their total population. Many families moved back and forth during the bust and boom cycles associated with the coalfields, but most mountaineers finally settled in the large cities.[2] Selz C. Mayo notes, "One community after another, within Appalachia and without, is dying ever so slowly or ever so swiftly. Com-

171

munity after community and county after county are losing population. Rough boards across windows and simple locks on the doors are but symbols and signs of the depopulation."[3]

Many who did not emigrate found themselves destitute. The coal mines were still laying employees off, and jobs were scarce. In 1960, 144,000 Kentuckians received surplus food allocated by the federal government.[4] Very little work could be found in eastern Kentucky. As an article in the *Detroit Free Press Magazine* reported,

> N. B. Mills' grandson, James, moved to Detroit from Stinking Creek in 1955, when he was 17 years old and looking for work. He could have stayed in Kentucky and made a buck-and-a-half a load driving coal trucks over treacherous roads, but he wanted more out of life. So he moved in with his aunt and uncle on Third Street near downtown and within three days found work sweeping floors and cleaning machines for General Motors at the Willow Run plant in Ypsilanti. He started work on a Thursday and put in seven days a week for seven straight months, finally piling up enough money to buy a 1956 two-door Ford Fairlane—fiesta red and white, the proud colors of a Kentucky boy made good in the big city. Michigan was a good place if you were willing to work, he says. You can be willing to work here, but you still can't make no money. That's the difference.[5]

When they moved to northern cities, Appalachians brought habits that were different from those of the natives. They worked for lower wages and sometimes found semiskilled positions. Appalachians had a history of farming and coal mining, but little aptitude for auto assembly or specialized jobs. The old customs were modified, and participation in community activities increased with length of residence, but initial entry into the northern municipalities posed problems.

When the Highlanders first arrived in the industrial centers, with paltry education and few contacts or other resources, they often met a hostile environment that was impersonal and sometimes predatory in nature.[6] So for assistance in locating homes or jobs, and aid with other problems that surfaced, they turned to kin and friends who had arrived earlier.[7] Eldon Dee Smith conducted an interview with a Kentuckian regarding his reason for moving to Indianapolis. The man explained, "I had known a lot of people who came here from that area. I really never thought about any other place. Some areas are Indianapolis areas, some are Detroit or Cleveland areas. Around home is an Indianapolis area."[8]

When jobs opened, relatives in eastern Kentucky would be notified by kin who were already working in the factories. Factory owners liked this method of drawing from the mountain labor pool. Workers hired on the basis of kinfolk recommendations were generally more reliable, because family honor was at stake.[9] James S. Brown noted,

> When people go out, when people migrate, they don't go through the United States Employment Service or some recruiting agency; they go because some relative "out there" has written them and told them, or come back and told them, that there are jobs available. Or if there aren't jobs, they have told the young brothers or sisters, neighbors or friends in the mountains that they are welcome to come out and "We'll look for you a job." And they do go out and stay until they are located, and then in time another brother or sister reaches the age of migration and goes out and so on. Thus the family forms a real bridge from Beech Creek, in the case I'm describing, to Hamilton and Dayton and Cincinnati.[10]

According to Smith's research, "a total of 68 of 157 migrants reported that they had anticipated receiving help in finding a job. Fifty-three of these reported that this had some effect on their decision to come to Indianapolis."[11] Many migrants moved in advance of their families. When they had saved enough capital, they sent for their wives and children. Earl Cunningham quoted one woman as saying, "My husband was a coal miner in Molus, Kentucky, but there's no work in the mines anymore. He came to Cleveland because a friend offered to help him find a job. He got a job . . . last March and sent for us last November."[12]

In explaining how mountain transients kept family groups intact and well maintained, Brown, Schwarzweller, and Mangalam use the French sociologist Frederic Le Play's theory of the "stem family" or *famille souche.* Brown, Schwarzweller, and Mangalam refer to neighborhoods of kinfolk in the northern cities as "host communities" that helped their newly arrived kinsmen adjust to urbanization. This "branch family network" in the area of destination, which was connected to the ancestral home in the mountains, gave the newcomers the security of knowing that if problems arose, ties to the hill had not been severed. The stem family stabilized migrants and reduced their insecurity. Family members in the "host communities" and home community could be called on when difficulties surfaced.[13]

Upon their arrival in the city, the Appalachian migrants had little recreational outlet and, other than kin, "no one to turn to when . . . emotionally distressed." Religion and church activities were one of the few activities that allowed for participation in the community. The following is a letter from my friend Joyce Baker of Harmon's Lick, Kentucky, describing her family's move to Chicago when she was a child.

We (my parents and two sisters) lived in Chicago for many years. We attended a Pentecostal Church. It was a heavenly place, right there in the midst of that large, crowded, sinful city. We would get to church about 7:00. As soon as the first song—people would start shouting (dancing) and sometimes they would go on for hours. There was "praise and worship," not all this difference of opinion. I never heard about "you have to have the Holy Ghost—or you can get there without it." It was something that everyone was happy to have and the ones that didn't have it—didn't bother the ones that did. I even remember one weekend, we had visitors and they brought snakes to Church. I had never seen that, but I didn't question it. I guess what I'm trying to say is—We loved our Church enough that we had a blind-trust or whatever.[14]

The Appalachian migrants rejected the established churches in the large cities and formed denominations similar to the sects known "down home." As Votaw explained it, "Many of the newcomers regard the city churches as kin to the authorities they distrust. They either stop going to church or else frequent the store front, 'holiness' gospel centers conducted by itinerant preachers. Here they feel at home: the women are not embarrassed by the greater elegance of their neighbors; and they listen to the kind of old time religion they are used to."[15]

Many down-home preachers visited the Appalachians in their new homes and led revivals. Reverend Thea O. Carter described his experience this way:

My wife and I went to Michigan to Thelma's sister, Lucy Asher and her husband, Richard, and their nice family. They lived in the suburbs of Taylor Township. We started a revival on twenty-fourth and Begley. It lasted for several weeks. . . . We had big crowds of people to come out to every meeting. . . . We had a big baptizing in the river Risen at Monroe. . . . Two Catholic Polish men were saved. I held revivals at different places in Detroit. A great mixture of people came—Mexicans, Russians, Germans, and Indians—a Jewish lady was saved; a man from the Philippines. . . . I was led to Chicago where Rev. Claude Brock pastored on Ogden Avenue.[16]

Many of the Saylor family from the area of Straight Creek, Kentucky, moved to Fort Wayne, Indiana, in the 1950s. Arnold Saylor's father and

Arnold Saylor at the Highway Holiness Church of God, Fort Wayne, Indiana, 1989 (Photo by the author)

uncle were among them. Both of these men formed churches and preached snake handling in the eastern Kentucky style. In 1968, Arnold founded the Highway Holiness Church of God in nearby Riverhaven. Currently, his church, which is now pastored by his son Danny Kale, includes 150 members. They are a close-knit group and regard each other as family.[17] Churches such as Highway Holiness are characterized by "strong familistic bonds that unite kin members in cohesive family groups and fit individual desires into a framework of family needs."[18]

The kinship structure provides a line of communication back to eastern Kentucky. Arnold Saylor was born around Berea, Kentucky, and his son Danny Kale married a woman from that area. His oldest offspring, Arnold Jr., married a Middlesboro native. Arnold Saylor was instrumental in building a church at Harmon's Lick, Kentucky, and was pastor there for several years. He was related to practically everyone at this church and at the denominations found on Straight Creek. I have been fascinated listening to Reverend Saylor and his relatives discuss genealogical lines and common ancestors at the churches I have attended with him in eastern Kentucky.

A story Arnold Saylor once told me makes it clear that he remembered even his learning to read as a sudden and miraculous gift from God, connected with his vocation as a Holiness minister:

One day I told my daddy that I was going to start preaching. He laughed and said, "How are you going to preach, you can't even read, you have got to be able to read the Bible to be able to preach." That hurt me bad, and I prayed about it. One day the Lord spoke to me and told me to open the book of James. I looked at the pages and it said "Count it all joy, my brethren, when you meet various trials, for you know that the testing of faith produces steadfastness. And let steadfastness have its full effect, that you may be perfect and complete, lacking in nothing." I have been able to read ever since. The Lord gave me the ability to read.

Saylor served as something of a patriarch, assisting members of his church in finding jobs or locating homes when they moved from the mountains. I saw him give the needy large sums of cash, or cars, or assistance in getting a home loan, or actually providing the money for a down payment. In one memorable instance of the family's willingness to help, Saylor's wife, Myrtle, walked from door to door asking for donations to assist a family whose baby had just died. Saylor was rarely paid back for his generous deeds. Prior to his death in January of 1992 (from natural causes), he had been active in helping the hungry and disadvantaged in the Fort Wayne area. Local bakeries and produce companies donated their products for Reverend Saylor to distribute among the poor.

Arnold Saylor preserved the Holiness religious structure found in mountain churches. His church is a moral force that rejects "worldly things." He held onto the Wesleyan beliefs that his ancestors preached for generations. Saylor rejected television, elaborate dress, sporting events, cosmetics, the braiding of hair, or other practices that could be considered worldly. Saylor once said, "I went to one of my friend's house and they had that MTV playing on their television. That band was acting like they were killing someone. There is enough of that kind of filth going on in this world without putting it on the television for your babies to see."

When Saylor first arrived in Fort Wayne, the locals were hostile to him and his family. His neighbors were ignorant about his snake-handling practices and told "wild tales" about him letting poisonous snakes "crawl around in his house." These stories had no basis in truth; Arnold Saylor never kept snakes in his house. He declared, "Unless the Lord moves on me, I am scared to death of a snake. I don't want one in my house." Holiness worshipers' snakes are well secured in proper containers and pose no threat. In one case, a small copperhead escaped into Saylor's church, and services were canceled until the snake was found. In remote areas of eastern Kentucky I have seen snakes kept in homes, but they are safely

Arnold Saylor Jr. at
Berea, Kentucky, 1990
(Photo by the author)

penned in. It is true that Bradley Shell told of an old mountaineer who kept rattlesnakes in his mattress, but such examples are rare. On several occasions Arnold Saylor's neighbors tried unsuccessfully to chase him off. Saylor recalled, "They killed our pets and were mean to us. One time someone actually came into our house and poisoned my wife and daughter." When I asked whether he had called the police, he replied, "Why? They don't like us either. They have done everything in their power to stop my church."

Local police were sometimes insensitive and abusive toward the Saylor family. In 1990 Danny Kale was bitten on the hand by a rattlesnake. Instead of showing concern for Danny's welfare, the police went to his home and searched it, "claiming that they had received a report that he was letting poisonous snakes crawl around in his house, and causing danger to his children." The accusation was ridiculous. Danny Saylor is extremely protective of his children and would never place them in a life-threatening situation. In fact, on two occasions when I handled serpents and the snake acted as if it was going to bite me, Danny stuck his hand between me and the snake, offering to take the bite for me.

Newspapers have been cruel to Saylor and his church followers in Fort Wayne. Reports are typically slanted, portraying the congregation as a group of religious fanatics. Journalists have sensationalized events such as

Danny (left) and
Arnold Saylor Jr.
(right, holding snake)
at an outside service
(Photo by the author)

snakebites and appear to have made few attempts to report accurately on the history and religious beliefs of Saylor's congregation and the oppression they have suffered. I once asked Arnold Saylor, "Why do you let these people keep coming to your church when they have been so negative toward you?" He responded, "Well, I'm not in the business of telling people they can't come to my church. I'm going to be good to them. If they can live with telling lies on us, they are the ones who have to live with it."

In September of 1991, Arnold Saylor organized a school to keep his young church members out of the hostile environment of the Fort Wayne school system. While attending Fort Wayne's public schools, Saylor's church members were constantly taunted by the other children. The Fort Wayne youths made hissing sounds at Saylor's children, imitating rattlesnakes, and often struck them. Saylor would not allow his young church members to fight, which made them defenseless in these hostile surroundings.

They started by trying to make our kids wear shorts in gym classes. We don't believe in wearing shorts. The teachers didn't like our kids because of our stand. To me they ought to be getting after the kids that were bringing dope, guns and everything else into the schools and leave our kids alone. I guess they just want to pick on the weak. Many of my kids were getting bad grades. They were being taught dancing and everything else that we stand against. As you say, Dave, we teach our kids the basics and the Bible. Isn't it funny that our school is picking up members that are not even church members. It looks like others are fed up with the filth that goes on in the public schools. . . .

They told me that they would put me in jail if we took our kids out of the Fort Wayne schools. Well, they haven't yet. You should see the progress that the kids have made. They can read now. Can you believe it? We had junior high kids that couldn't read. I thank the Lord we have Sarah and Rhonda to teach them.

Attacks by the media and authorities have reinforced the Holiness people's idea that "the world" is hostile to them. Many church members regard themselves as martyrs. For example, in snakebite situations, refusing medical attention and putting their fate in the "hands of God" is a symbolic rejection of the world. Many times, denial of medical attention is a collective action representing group values and united solidarity. Arnold Saylor and his sons Danny and Arnold Jr. have been bitten by snakes. All three of these men refused to accept medical treatment and survived the bites.

Others have said that they saw their bites coming but still refused to quit. Shilo Collins of Pineville, Kentucky, who visits the Highway Holiness Church of God frequently, described the visions he experienced before he was bitten by a rattlesnake. He also recalled his first snakebite: "The first time I was serpent-bit a copperhead got me. It scared me as bad as when that coal mine caved in on me. My wife was scared too. Back then people wasn't bit that much and they looked on me like a Judas. In a couple of days I went back to that church and my hand was still swelling. All of a sudden the Lord moved on me and I was handling them again. I was so excited about it I ran all the way home and told my wife that I had handled them again."

Collins escaped the copperhead bite with no serious injury. On another occasion, though, he almost died from a rattlesnake bite. He spent nine days in bed before his condition improved. He claims that he "almost smothered" as a result of the bite and was in "terrible agony." I asked Collins, "Why did that thing bite you?," and he answered,

Andrew Hall drinking
strychnine near Man-
chester, Kentucky, 1988
(Photo by the author)

I don't know. I'm still trying to figure out why Brother Lee [Valentine] got bit. It was a strange thing. I got this big rattler over at Harlan. He was big and mean. I was afraid of him. Well, I had a dream and the Lord said that snake would not bother me, but watch out for the black one. I hadn't fasted that week. I usually fast for seventy-two hours. Anyway, I was getting ready for church and decided to clean up my snakes. I don't like to take them if they are dirty. I was in a hurry and cleaned them up with cold water. It made them mad. When church started, I went to the box, and that black rattler bit me. In just a few minutes, I was off my feet. I wasn't anointed. I got in too big of a hurry. My sister-in-law asked me if I was going to do it again. I started crying as if I was anointed then. There will always be serpent handling. If I quit, someone else will pick it up. I won't quit though.

Collins's hand still bears a scar from the bite. While his hand was still swollen and in a sling, he attended a service at John Saylor's church and handled a large yellow rattlesnake. He remarked, "Brother John [Saylor] said that he saw me in a dream wearing a white shirt handling a big yellow rattlesnake. I showed up that day in a white shirt and handled that yellow rattlesnake."

Other rituals performed in Saylor's church also have historical roots. The act of foot washing is performed frequently as an act of humility. This

Shilo Collins in Fort
Wayne, Indiana, 1990
(Photo by the author)

act reinforces the idea that the congregation is a community—not a static assembly of souls but a coherent entity in which no person is better than the other. Along with family and kinship bonds, strong moral ties are reinforced through these rituals.

The main event at Arnold Saylor's church is the annual homecoming, which is always conducted on the first Sunday in September. Homecomings tend to reinforce the communal inclinations of the Holiness people. The event usually takes the entire day. Family members from Kentucky and Ohio normally attend. The services on this occasion are always more intense, and serpents are thus handled with more frequency. Sometimes visitors to homecoming services arrive early in the morning and begin singing hymns or worshiping hours before the scheduled time. Saylor and his group also frequently attend homecoming services in Kentucky, which are conducted in the same style.

A strange thing happened in connection with the Fort Wayne homecoming in 1991. Almost a month before the event, a Kentucky woman told

Washing snakes before
church (Photo by the
author)

me that in a dream she had seen a rattlesnake strike at me. I asked, "Was I
bitten?" "I don't know," she responded, "just stay away from the snakes at
Arnold's homecoming." I forgot about the prediction and successfully
handled serpents at the homecoming. I placed a rattlesnake on top of my
head and escaped unharmed. As we were preparing to leave the church, I
was standing near a box that held an eastern diamondback rattlesnake
when the snake struck out at me. It was unable to bite me through the wire
mesh covering its container, but it did succeed in covering me with venom.
I must admit, the experience was frightening.

Homecomings of this type are not uniform. Again, local autonomy is the
rule. In eastern Kentucky, church services are conducted early in the
morning and are followed by a pitch-in dinner. After the meal, there is
usually a second service that can last well into the evening. Some homecomings are held in a revival fashion, lasting up to a week. I have attended

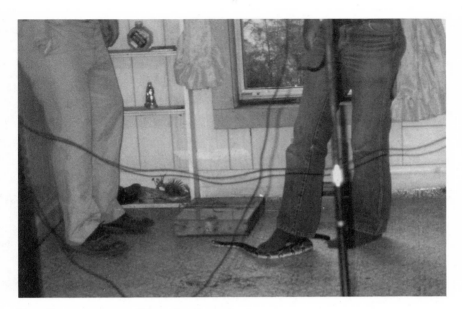

Treading on serpents (Photo by the author)

homecomings in graveyards at places like Berea, Kentucky, where the sermon centered on being reunited with dead family members.

On Sunday, August 8, 1988, I attended a homecoming ceremony with Reverend Kale Saylor at the Osborne Cemetery, near Hyden, Kentucky. Many other churches in the area attempted to get Reverend Saylor to preach their homecoming, but he has made it an annual event to preach at the Osborne Cemetery. Hyden is the county seat of Leslie County. In March of 1976, the area attracted national attention when an explosion at the Scotia Mines left over thirty coal miners dead.

This homecoming service was conducted on top of a mountain in a beautiful location. We had to be taken to the summit, where the cemetery is located, in four-wheel-drive vehicles. Some people rode horses, and the Reverend Rowe Davidson drove a Honda four-wheeler to the top. I had serious doubts that we would make it, but finally we did. Many people from as far away as Ohio and Indiana had already reached the top of the mountain. The crowd reached a total of four hundred. The service began with hymns. Skilled musicians performed beautiful songs like "I'm So Glad I Crossed Over," "It's Time to Go Back Home," and "Then I'm Going Home" in a bluegrass style. A married couple from Clay County, Kentucky, serenaded the crowd in a manner most professional musicians would have envied. Appalachia produces more than its share of gifted performers.

Arnold Saylor, 1988
(Photo by the author)

Greats such as Ricky Skaggs and Dwight Yoakam were raised not far from the site of the homecoming service.

After over a dozen songs were sung, the service was turned over to the Reverend Kale Saylor. He started the service by saying,

> I've been watching some of you people during this service. A few of you have sad faces over the loss of your loved ones. Rejoice, people, because we are only here for a short period of time. Where we are going there will be no more hurt. Your loved ones are already in heaven waiting for you to join them. That is why it is so important that you live right on this earth. You can't be part of all this sin and wickedness of this world and expect to make it to heaven. As I came up on this mountain, I saw table after table lined with food that had been prepared for us after this meeting. People, where we are going there won't be any need to prepare all this fine food, because the streets will be paved with gold and all of us that live right will be in Paradise.

As the Reverend Saylor continued with the service, many people shouted and talked in tongues. On two occasions Reverend Saylor himself began talking in tongues, and he also prophesied to a few members of the gathering. The ceremony was performed in a manner that Saylor's ancestors, including Solomon, John, Josiah, "Frosty John," and Henry, would have been content with. Folklorist Elaine J. Lawless summarized this kind of worship thus:

The author handling a rattlesnake at Jolo, West Virginia, September 3, 1994 (Photo courtesy of Anthony Feyer)

Pentecostalism is based on things that happen to people. And the essence of the experiences, as well as their interpretation, must be communicated to the other members of the group. It is on that foundation that all doctrine rests. Pentecostalism is an oral religion. All members learn to speak a special religious language. It is within the context of the church service that the tenets of the faith are conveyed, interpreted, and stabilized. Stories passed down from grandparents about the early days of traveling preachers who brought the Pentecostal message lay a firm historical foundation for the beliefs of the modern church. A testimony about how someone received the Holy Ghost and spoke in tongues proves to listeners that this experience can happen and elaborates a model for their own conversion experience.[19]

By keeping close ties with family and friends in the mountains, the Holiness churches in places like Fort Wayne have preserved their lay religion and heritage, including serpent handling. When they entered the industrial centers, Appalachians again adapted their religion to their environment by establishing storefront churches in an attempt to give order and meaning to their society. Their churches provided the spiritualism and emotionalism that dull and cold city churches did not provide. Holiness religion brought a sense of worth to a depersonalized populace.

Conclusion

Snake handling emerged in eastern Kentucky during the early 1930s in response to the social anomie that resulted from industrialization. Industrial capitalism destroyed the habitat and society of the native population. From the settlement of Solomon Saylor in present-day Harlan County around 1805, the Saylor family's society was organized around close kinship associations: the group acted as an economic unit in a subsistence-based agricultural network. As sociologist Harry Schwarzweller points out, "Subsistence farming was a family enterprise; family life and the occupation of farming were inextricably interwoven."[1]

In this subsistence agricultural setting, the collective welfare of the family and of the kin group as a whole was of paramount importance.

Individual needs were subordinated to the requirements of the family. In this way the Saylor family was representative of most lineages in Harlan County. Kinship units tended to be culturally and economically insular, functioning independently of mountain society as a whole. A man's standing in the social hierarchy was determined mainly by localistic standards or ascriptive values, the most important of which was kinship association.

The religion found at Forrester's Creek was also organized according to kinship in response to family needs. Highly intellectual sermons delivered by educated Presbyterian ministers from the East did not suit eastern Kentucky society. Mountaineers demanded a folk religion, and from their ranks arose lay preachers who could deliver sermons that they identified with. The Saylor family discarded their Presbyterian heritage and became associated with the Baptists, who appeared in the Kentucky highlands during the settlement period. Highly emotional sermons from pioneer preachers appealed to the Saylors as a response to the realities of a harsh life on the eastern Kentucky frontier.

Knowledge of the Bible was often fragmentary on the frontier, and unlettered preachers transmitted a religion that developed its own oral tradition. Many sermons were delivered from the standpoint of social needs and in response to local standards. The Holiness serpent-handler faith can be traced directly to the pioneer preachers, popular frontier revivals, and backwoods camp meetings of the nineteenth century and to the Methodism of John Wesley. As Steven M. Kane explains, "The snake handling rite itself represents an intensification and elaboration of traditional patterns, not a radical deviation or departure from them."[2]

At the beginning of the twentieth century, industrial capitalism caused a rapid social transformation in Harlan County. Communities in areas like Forrester's Creek quickly traded subsistence agriculture for a profit-oriented, cash-based, coal mining economy. Kinship networks that mountaineers had depended on for assistance during hard times became fragmented, and society became market-organized and geared to the accumulation of goods. Profit seeking was placed ahead of people and traditional values. Individuals became commodities in the system. The land owned by the Saylor family for generations was lost to the enterprising capitalists, and men such as John Austen Saylor moved into the coal camps found throughout Appalachia. Conditions were horrible in the mining communities; poor nourishment, violence, and mining accidents threatened their lives every day.

During the early 1900s, many people in Appalachia became frustrated with the established churches because of their lack of emotionalism and their insensitivity to existing problems. As a result, they joined emerging sects such as the Church of God, Pentecostal and Holiness churches, and Free Will Baptist churches. Many of the preachers in these emerging sects were fellow workers. Workers were more willing to listen to a preacher who could identify with their problems than to a minister who had little time for them. The new churches and preachers offered the participants the freedom for self-expression and gave members the opportunity to identify with a greater power.

As a response to the conditions capitalism had created, mountain evangelists such as George W. Hensley, Sherman Lawson, Bradley Shell, the Eads family, and Park Saylor began to preach on the five Bible signs described in Mark 16. Reports of miracles being performed—levitations, fire handling, serpent handling, the drinking of poisons, and the resurrection of the dead—spread through the hills. These miracles symbolized the power of God over the evil disruptions that an uncontrolled society posed.

The sociologist Emile Durkheim created a "nonobvious theory of religion, in which the key to religion is not its beliefs but the social rituals that its members perform. Religion is a key to social solidarity, and religious beliefs are important, not in their own right, but as symbols of social groups."[3] Thus, religion becomes sociologically and culturally important, playing a significant role in the social life of Holiness worshipers. Except for his use of the loaded term "cult," J. Wayne Flynt described the snake handlers perfectly: "The cult was an enigma, a classic confrontation between cultures. Snake handling occurred most frequently not in the most isolated regions of Appalachia, but in peripheral areas undergoing change from subsistence agriculture to industry. The cult helped its members cope with the humiliation attendant to being poor and hillbilly. One way to adjust to threatening new values was to reject them, and the snake-handling group demonstrated the tension of people torn from decades of isolation and thrust into the modern world."[4]

The snake handlers' religious world is segregated into two basic classifications: good and evil. Unifying symbols that are preached on constantly from Holiness pulpits are represented in this dichotomy in such forms as gospel songs, good works, the signs, and the presence of the Spirit. Evil is represented by the changing social world, and "following the signs," including serpent handling, becomes a ritual that displays God's power over evil. Ritual is strictly determined, goal-oriented behavior; in studying society, Durkheim "gave priority to rituals over beliefs."[5] For example, when a church is in collective prayer, which is common among Holiness congregations, people behave in similar ways. When the Holy Ghost moves, a sort of emotional contagion results, providing both sociological and psychological unity that makes up for the lack of other sources of social integration. Participation in church rituals is modified by members' grasping how others feel and acting accordingly. The members look to others for cues on how to modify their behavior. That is, if a worshiper begins shouting or crying, others begin to act similarly. Of course, different personalities show different degrees of suggestibility. Arnold Saylor described the situation in this way: "If the Holy Ghost moves on one person, He is likely to move on all of us. . . . This is also true of serpent handling. If someone handles a serpent someone else will probably get it." Generally, the rituals that the snake handlers perform illustrate a homogeneity of experience with shared backgrounds. Since the time of settlement in the Kentucky highlands, when hardships arose, the Saylor family bonded together through religion and common worship practice.

During the 1940s, Appalachians moved out of the highlands to industrial centers in the North. They took with them their kinship practices and religion, which were used as a means of coping and explaining an alien outside world that threatened their existence. These people still draw on traditional cultural patterns for help in adjusting to new patterns of life.

The Holiness snake handlers are not crazy, neurotic, or psychotic. Their actions outside of church functions are consistent with the communities in which they live and work.[6] Except for their modest dress and rejection of "worldly pleasures," they exhibit no behavior that distinguishes them from non-serpent-handling people. The many serpent handlers I have become acquainted with are normal people by Appalachian standards and are well adjusted to their environment.

Park Saylor and his family are millennialists who believe that the thousand years of peace described in Revelation could happen at any moment. They encourage their congregations to "live right." Belief in the millennium gives them a sense of order and security in a world that appears to be collapsing. Their fatalistic views attribute poverty, illness, and death to "the Lord's will." Fear of uncontrolled social change has made believers such as Park, Kale, and Arnold Saylor align themselves with God in order to have a privileged position in the Kingdom of Heaven.

Notes

Introduction

1. Interview with Liston Pack, August 15, 1987, Carson Springs, Tenn.

2. Mark Nichols, "Rattlers Bit Two Who Disobeyed, Pastor Says," *Indianapolis Star*, September 10, 1987, p. 1.

3. Arnold Saylor died of a heart attack on January 3, 1992, at the age of fifty-one.

4. Interview with Kale Saylor, March 7, 1988, Harlan County, Ky.

5. Applying the label "snake-handling" can be tricky. Many of the congregations perform the ritual on an intermittent basis. Others have handled snakes only on a single occasion or allowed a visiting preacher to perform the ceremony. Others handle many snakes every night of the week.

6. Roth, "Hired Hand Research," 190–96.

7. McCauley, "Appalachian Mountain Religion," 13.

8. This is an old custom in some Appalachian churches. Ministers have a member of the congregation read scriptural passages for a brief period, then they suddenly stop the reader and preach or comment on the reading. This routine commonly leads into an emotional and lengthy sermon that lasts for hours.

9. Due to the emotionalism in Holiness churches, it is very hard to resist becoming involved in the meetings. Like me, professional photographer Shelby Adams has become so absorbed in the church services that he has handled snakes.

10. Dakin and Tennant, "Consistency of Response," 73–84.

11. Bodnar, "Power and Memory in Oral History," 1201–21.

12. Thompson, *Voice of the Past*, 50.

13. Schrager, "What is Social in Oral History?," 78.

14. Henige, *Oral Historiography*, 34.

15. "Reptile in the Meetin'," *Chattanooga Daily Times*, September 21, 1914, p. 3.

16. Wachtal, "Memory and History," 209.

17. Montell, *Saga of Coe Ridge*, viii, xviii.

18. Dorson, "Debate over the Trustworthiness of Oral Traditional History," 21; Montell, *Saga of Coe Ridge*, xix.

Chapter 1

1. As I mentioned in the Introduction, most scholars have given George Went Hensley credit for founding the snake-handling movement; however, these scholars offer little or no evidence for their claim, and the scholarship itself reflects much confusion over the movement's origin. Most earlier studies claim that Hensley instituted serpent handling in 1909. (See La Barre, *They Shall Take Up Serpents*; Sims, "Snake Handlers"; Stekert, "Snake-Handling Sect of Harlan

County, Kentucky"; and J. B. Collins, *Tennessee Snake Handlers.*) Hensley himself gave different dates of origin. In a March 9, 1936 interview with the *Tampa Morning Tribune* ("Preacher Juggles Snake Again, Says It Bit Him"), Hensley claimed that he had been handling snakes for twenty-three years. That would make the date of origin 1913. Probably the most reliable interview with George Hensley that included questions on when snake handling began was conducted by Keith Kerman of the *St. Louis Post-Dispatch* in the summer of 1938 at Harlan County, Ky. Hensley informed Kerman that he "had introduced the practice twenty-eight years before in Sale Creek, Tennessee" (Kerman, "Rattlesnake Religion," 101). This would make the date of origin 1910. Another interview that supports 1910 as the date of origin was an article by Charles Crane of the *Chattanooga News–Free Press* for July 20, 1945 ("Demonstrations of Faith with Gyrations Held in Dolly Pond Church"). The column stated that George Hensley was credited with founding the cult in the area "about 35 years ago."

Other evidence, however, suggests that Hensley was not the first person to handle snakes in Appalachia. For example, Homer A. Tomlinson states that the ritual of taking up serpents in religious services began in 1908 (*Shout of a King*, 39). Also, I have received isolated reports of serpent handling before Hensley, although I have been unable to satisfactorily document them. In an interview at Cleveland, Tenn., on February 19, 1988, George Hensley's son, James Roscoe Hensley, stated that his father had seen a man handle poisonous snakes at a religious service. He claimed that this experience is what caused his father to become a snake handler. If Hensley was not the first to handle serpents, he was responsible for the spread of the snake-handling movement. Once he started preaching snake handling, the movement boomed throughout Appalachia.

2. Kane, "Snake Handlers of Southern Appalachia," 94.

3. In 1947, Joe Creason of the *Louisville Courier-Journal* reported that he saw some snake boxes that were made from wood scraps taken from the coal mines, which were appropriately stenciled "Dynamite." See Joe Creason, "The Grapevine," *Louisville Courier-Journal*, October 26, 1947, magazine sec., p. 4.

4. When Holiness preachers reach an emotional height, they frequently punctuate each sentence with an "Ah" or a deep breath. In this excited state they stride back and forth and their voices rise and fall, fluctuating between a roar and a whisper. Deborah Vansau McCauley refers to this type of preaching as the "holy tone."

5. Generally, snake-handling preachers such as Park Saylor do not claim credit for healing if a miracle occurs; they give full honor to God. It is also necessary for the sick to have faith that they will be healed by the "laying on of hands." Holiness beliefs hold that if the anointing is strong enough in the minister, and if it is God's desire, the sick will be healed. I have viewed two means of healing: the laying on of hands, as described in Mark 16:17, and the use of prayer cloths, as described in Acts 19:11–12.

A prayer cloth was passed around the church at Crockett, Ky., in an attempt to heal the daughter of Kale Saylor. His daughter had been injured in a terrible automobile accident in December 1987. She was taken to Knoxville, Tenn., for medical attention, and there was a consensus among the doctors that she would die. On March 6, 1988, the prayer cloth was passed among Crockett's congregation of 350 people. Each person prayed over the fabric, and serpents were actually passed over it in some instances. As Brother Asher passed the prayer cloth from aisle to aisle, in the same way that offering plates are conveyed in other churches, he held a giant rattlesnake in his hands. It was a very moving event. On that day Kale Saylor's daughter's condition improved. She is now out of the hospital and living in the Straight Creek area.

6. Robertson, *That Old-Time Religion*, 74–75.

7. Supplied by Mrs. Ben Brock of Berea, Ky.

8. Kane, "Holiness Ritual Fire-Handling," 371.

9. Ibid., 372.

10. "Snake Bite Is Fatal to Cultist: Another Struck Down by Rattler," *Chattanooga Times*, August 27, 1946, p. 9.

11. Richard Golden, "Kentuckians Have More Faith: 'Snake-Handling' Woman Bitten Because of Lack of Faith, She Declares," *Knoxville News-Sentinel*, September 19, 1939, home ed., 1.

12. "Snake Defiers Jailed," *New York Times*, August 1, 1940, p. 18.

13. "Snake-Rite Leaders Fast," *New York Times*, August 4, 1940, p. 31.

14. "Snake Defiers Jailed."

15. "Snake-Bitten Child Remains Untreated," *New York Times*, August 3, 1940, p. 28.

16. Ibid.

17. "Snake Tests Barred to Preacher's Son," *New York Times*, September 2, 1934, sec. 2, p. 1.

18. Ibid.

19. "Rattler May Bite Father Here But Law Plans to Protect Boy," *Nashville Tennessean*, September 1, 1934, p. 1.

20. Joe Creason, "Snake Handlers: Leaders Claim Kentucky Has 1,000 Cult Members," *Louisville Courier-Journal*, October 26, 1947, magazine sec., pp. 6–9.

21. *Middlesboro Daily News*, n.d.

22. Ibid.

23. M. C. Garrott, "Death of Man from Snake-Handling Bite Brings to Mind a Frightening Experience," *Murray Ledger and Times*, n.d. [1983].

24. "Girl, 14, Is Bitten by Snake at Cult," *Chattanooga Times*, August 23, 1948, p. 3. Pauline's relative Berlin Barbee died from a rattlesnake bite. "City Man Dies of Snake Bite," *Chattanooga Times*, October 25, 1976, p. 1.

25. "Snake Bites Man and Dies," *New York Times*, July 23, 1945, p. 21.

26. The method of baptism can itself cause much controversy. Generally speaking, most Holiness churches practice the rite in a creek or river. I received the following statement from a Kentucky woman: "I was baptized in Straight Creek

by Brother Kale. If the Jordon [*sic*] River was good enough for Jesus, then Straight Creek is good enough for me. We don't need those ol' fancy tubs to be baptized in. It should be done in running water." I have seen the ice being broken on a creek in preparation for a baptism. I was told that "the water feels warm if you are deep enough in the Spirit." On several occasions I have witnessed snakes being handled in the water or on the bank during the baptism.

27. Most people in the Chattanooga area who knew him referred to Perry Bettis as "Brother Perry." People who met him liked him immediately. Even the "sinner people" around his hometown were quick to defend him. Bettis was born in 1927 and was a Jesus' Name preacher. In the past few years Bettis suffered from diabetes, which caused him to lose half of one foot and two toes on the other. He also had heart problems, and they claimed his life on December 11, 1991. Although Brother Perry was in poor health during his final years, nothing could dampen his spirit. For many who knew him, he represented a model Christian who stuck to his beliefs.

28. The late Tess Walters of Blackmont, Ky., stated that the reason snake handlers have failed to organize is that if they did, their sovereignty would be reduced: "If we would organize into something like the Assembly of God, then we would receive our messages from the main office holders instead of God. I don't want that. I'll take care of my church just like Kale will take care of his. We don't need someone far away, who is not sensitive to our needs, telling us how to run our churches." In fact, the church's resistance extends to Sunday schools. Walters commented, "Sunday schools are taught with man-made materials, with man's ideas. Most of that stuff has no scriptural basis. You have to teach them the Word straight from the book. When they hear it enough they will finally grasp what it means. One time a man from New York brought a bunch of that Sunday school junk with him, trying to get me to use it. I looked at it, and then put him on the road. New York sermons don't apply to our ways and customs down here."

29. "Women Arrivals Kissed at Church," *Chattanooga Times*, December 20, 1973, p. 44.

30. Golden, "Kentuckians Have More Faith," 1. I have seen relatively few snakebites in the church services I have attended. Only one of the people bitten received medical attention, and that was at my insistence.

31. Kane, "Snake Handlers of Southern Appalachia," 132.

Chapter 2

1. George Went Hensley was probably born in the hills of eastern Tennessee in 1880. However, listings of Hensley's birthplace vary. Steven M. Kane conducted an interview with Hensley's oldest son, Franklin, during the 1970s and was informed that George was born in Kentucky. Hensley's other children's birth certificates list Virginia and West Virginia as the site of his birth. No birth certificate exists, so it is impossible to locate his birthplace. Hensley's ancestors

may have come to Tennessee from Pennsylvania. Hensley was one of thirteen children born to Emanuel and Susan Jane Hensley. He received little education during his childhood and never learned to read or write (Kane, "Snake Handlers of Southern Appalachia," 31). Hensley was born in the Baptist faith but never adhered to the religion devoutly or with much seriousness. In the early 1900s, Hensley practiced no religion. He married Amanda Wininger at Lenoir City, Tenn., on May 5, 1901 (Burton, *Serpent-Handling Believers*, 150). The Hensleys lived the first years of their marriage at Owl Hollow, between Cleveland and Chattanooga. They had a total of seven children while they lived together: Bessie Jane (1903), Mae Marie (1904), Katie Pearl (1907), Rosa Frances (1909), Jesse Franklin (1913), James Roscoe (1915), and Esther Lee (1918). An eighth child, William Hillman (1923), was born to the Hensleys seven months after George and Amanda were separated.

Hensley farmed, worked at a sawmill on occasion, and made moonshine whiskey, while "supplementing his income by digging iron ore from the hillsides and selling it to the Chattanooga Paint Company" (Kane, "Snake Handlers of Southern Appalachia," 31).

2. J. B. Collins, *Tennessee Snake Handlers*, 1. Polly Ann Long of Rose Hill, Va., related a conversation she had with Hensley during the 1930s. Ms. Long stated that Hensley claimed God actually ordered him to "take 'em up." Hensley said, "You mean those things that crawl around on the ground?" According to Hensley, God answered, "Yes, those things that crawl on the ground."

3. La Barre, *They Shall Take Up Serpents*, 11.

4. Interview with Perry Bettis, February 19, 1988, Birchwood, Tenn.

5. J. B. Collins, *Tennessee Snake Handlers*, 2.

6. Almost all of George Hensley's associates refer to him as "Little George."

7. J. B. Collins, *Tennessee Snake Handlers*, 2.

8. Interview with Park Saylor, May 27, 1988, Path Fork, Ky.

9. Kane, "Snake Handlers of Southern Appalachia," 32.

10. A. J. Tomlinson was the first general overseer of the Church of God, Cleveland. He held the office from 1909 to 1923 (Conn, *Our First 100 Years*, 71).

11. Homer A. Tomlinson, *Shout of a King*, 39.

12. Ibid.

13. This is a very common practice among the Holiness churches. I have never seen a minister use notes of any kind to deliver a sermon. The messages are totally unrehearsed. Park Saylor informed me that the Holy Ghost moves on him to preach the gospel. He stated, "I have never used notes in my life. These college-educated ministers of today do, and I tell them that their messages are as old as a year-old bird nest. The Lord has to move on you to preach the Word. You can't get that from a textbook" (interview with Park Saylor, May 27, 1988, Path Fork, Ky.).

14. Kane, "Snake Handlers of Southern Appalachia," 36.

15. The following three *Church of God Evangel* articles found by Steven M. Kane comment on Hensley's evangelical works in the Chattanooga area:

Bro. George Hensley is conducting a revival at the tabernacle in Cleveland, Tennessee. It began the last Sunday in Aug. and is still continuing with increasing interest. The power has been falling and Souls crying out to God. Twice during the meeting. Serpents have been handled by the Saints. Bro. Hensley is being assisted by Bro. M.S. Haynes and others. (September 12, 1914, p. 2)

It is reported that thirty or more have received the Holy Ghost at Harrison Tenn. in the revival conducted by Bro. George Hensley recently. (February 5, 1916, p. 2)

Birchwood, Tennessee: A letter from William Headrick said: "I thank God for ever sending Brother George Hensley to this place to preach holiness. He gave us the light on the Church of God. Praise the Lord." (April 13, 1918, p. 2)

16. *Church of God Evangel,* May 9, 1914, p. 8; Kane, "Snake Handlers of Southern Appalachia," 37.

17. "He Can Handle Snakes But Will He Walk the River?," *Chattanooga Daily Times,* September 24, 1914, p. 3.

18. "Religion and Snakes," *Cleveland (Tenn.) Herald,* September 24, 1914, p. 7.

19. *Pentecostal Holiness Advocate,* October 11, 1917, pp. 2–3.

20. *Church of God Evangel,* June 29, 1918, p. 1.

21. Homer A. Tomlinson, *Shout of a King,* 41.

22. Ibid., 42.

23. A. J. Tomlinson, *Church of God Evangel,* September 19, 1914, p. 2.

24. "Reptile in the Meetin'," *Chattanooga Daily Times,* September 21, 1914, p. 3.

25. Interview with James R. Hensley, February 19, 1988, Cleveland, Tenn.

26. J. B. Collins, *Tennessee Snake Handlers,* 2 (both quotes).

27. "Proselyting with Snakes," *Chattanooga Daily Times,* September 16, 1914, p. 3.

28. *Church of God Evangel,* October 4, 1914, p. 6.

29. The handwriting on the certificate was clearly Amanda Hensley's.

30. *Church of God Evangel,* April 4, 1914, p. 7.

31. No written records exist that suggest the neighbor and Amanda were having an affair. Amanda's suitor certainly made his intentions known, according to church members; however, after George and Amanda were separated, she did not have anything to do with him.

32. Interview with Flora Bettis (John Roberts's daughter) Birchwood, Tenn., February 19, 1988.

33. Telephone interview with George Hensley's granddaughter, La Creta Simmons, July 3, 1988. George and Amanda were separated on August 8, 1922, and were divorced on November 9, 1926. See Burton, *Serpent-Handling Believers,* 155.

34. Kane, "Snake Handlers of Southern Appalachia," 56.

35. Park Saylor said of Klunzinger, "She knew the Bible like she wrote it herself" (interview with Park Saylor, May 27, 1988, Path Fork, Ky.).

36. Telephone interview with Loyal Hensley, April 11, 1990. Loyal said it is possible that Irene suffered from epilepsy. He stated that she did have "fits" in her youth, though he never witnessed any seizures. Loyal Hensley informed me that his mother constantly complained of this curse. When she murmured about her hex in front of George Hensley, he would reply, "Oh, bullshit, Irene." Irene would then state, "But it is in the Bible." At that point George Hensley would "just be quiet," according to his son.

37. Burton, *Serpent-Handling Believers*, 44.

38. Irene gave birth to five children by George Hensley: Faith Lillian (1928), Loyal (1929), Vinette (1932), Emma Jean (1935), and John, who died as an infant.

Chapter 3

1. Going up on a mountain to pray has been a common practice for many religious groups in Appalachia, and it remains common today. "It makes me feel closer to God," I was told by a seventy-four-year-old snake-handling preacher. Sherman Lawson was born in 1884 at Ewing, Va. He lived to be seventy-two years old and died in 1956. Lawson was not raised in the Holiness faith. One day in the early 1920s, Lawson went to the mountains and returned talking in tongues. He made a habit of going to the mountains for prayer. Sometimes he would stay for days. On occasion, after Hensley introduced serpent handling in Kentucky, Lawson would handle serpents in the wilderness. On a bright sunny day in June of 1934, Lawson came upon a group of Baptists who were enjoying a nature walk far into the mountains. After conversing with the party, the friendly Lawson joined them. The group came upon a large rattlesnake that began to buzz ferociously, frightening everyone. Sherman Lawson calmly walked up to the snake and picked it up without being bitten. The small Baptist gathering was shocked at the display. I asked Lawson's son, Lawrence, if his father was showing off in front of the Baptists. "No," replied Lawson, "my father had tremendous power with God. Unless God was with him he would never mess with snakes." (Interview with Lawrence Lawson, January 2, 1988, Florence, Ky.)

Lawson was never the regular preacher for any church. He was always an evangelist and usually accompanied his friend Sill Eads to revivals and other religious meeting throughout the mountains.

2. Sherman Lawson was an unlettered man; he depended on his wife and others to read for him. Mrs. Lawson was a midwife and was said to have "immense power with God." I have been told that on many occasions she would simply lay hands on a woman in childbirth and the pains would go away. Mrs. Lawson was struck by rattlesnakes on several occasions without apparent suffering.

3. Interview with Park Saylor, May 27, 1988, Path Fork, Ky. Jim Jackson ran a sawmill in the Pineville area. A deeply religious man, Jackson spent a great deal of his time hunting lost treasures and rare minerals. He lived to be 104 years old.

4. When Hensley arrived in eastern Kentucky, the only shirt that he owned bore some fifty patches.

5. Interview with Park Saylor, May 27, 1988, Path Fork, Ky. Park Saylor's uncles, Sill and Harve Eads, had a large role in establishing the church. Shortly after Hensley's arrival, Jackson offered Hensley a job as the church's regular preacher, which Hensley accepted. He also gave Hensley a room in the back of the church to live in. Jackson later built Hensley a room on the back of a large log truck. Hensley traveled throughout the South in that truck, preaching and evangelizing. The building was used as a church until 1941, when Mr. Wyatt Woody bought it for two hundred dollars. Woody lived in the structure until 1943, when he sold it to a railroad worker named Sam Anderson. Shortly after Anderson bought the building he sold it back to Jim Jackson, who started church services again. The church was torn down in the 1960s, when US 119 was built through its site.

6. Ibid.

7. Ibid. This is a common experience among the snake handlers. I have been told by many members that they have "been so wrapped up in the power" that they never knew they handled snakes at a particular meeting.

8. People from rural areas would travel to the county seat on Saturday mornings in order to conduct business, visit, or go to the movies in a festive atmosphere. David McConnell Graybeal observed the same types of gatherings during this period in Morristown, Tenn., which lies sixty miles from Pineville. Among the crowd in Morristown on many such occasions, eagerly waiting to see a movie at the Princess Theater, was my father, Lester ("Bill") Kimbrough. David McConnell Graybeal, "Analysis of the Influence of Cultural Change," 148–50.

9. Shortly after this event, in the summer of 1932, Hensley was conducting another meeting at the Pineville courthouse. When the meeting reached an emotional height, the church people began singing songs, clapping hands, shouting, and handling serpents in front of many unbelievers. When the town drunk approached the crowd and observed the ceremony, he joined in the service, handling rattlesnakes with Hensley and the other worshipers. The inebriated gentleman luckily did not receive a bite. Hensley was unaware that the man was drunk, and was amazed at his ability to handle serpents.

After the music died down and the snakes were put back in their boxes, the drunk left the service. Hensley became upset that he had not been introduced to the man and asked his church brother George Eads, "Who was that man that handled them big rattlesnakes with me, George? Now he had the power. I have never seen a man so filled with the power." Before Eads could answer Hensley, an unbeliever in the crowd shouted, "He sure did [have the power], preacher, about 90 proof."

10. Guest pastors and visiting evangelists are common in Holiness churches. I have attended church services where ten preachers have spoken to the congregation. To quote one preacher from Indiana, "I really don't like to go down to

Kentucky and preach, Dave. It might be evening before those boys will let you get up and say anything."

11. Mossie Simpson still resides in an area known as Jenson. She is well into her eighties. I have spent many hours talking to her about the early snake-handling churches. Ms. Simpson has strictly adhered to the Holiness faith her entire life.

12. I have found no one who disputes the fact that it was George Hensley who introduced snake handling in eastern Kentucky. Bradley Shell maintains, "I never saw anyone handle serpents in Kentucky until George Hensley came," and Kale Saylor concurs: "Hensley was the first to handle snakes in the mountains."

13. Holiness preacher Denver Short informed me in January of 1989 that Hensley had another encounter at a country store near Harlan with a local who hated the Holiness people, especially snake handlers. The hostile mountaineer walked up to Hensley and shouted, "You snake handlers are crazy!" Hensley simply "paid the man no attention," and by ignoring him Hensley only made the confrontation more intense. The man kicked Hensley in the leg and said, "Take that, preacher! Did your God protect you from that?" Hensley replied, "In short time, you will lose your leg because of that." In a matter of weeks, Hensley's prediction proved true: the mountaineer cut his leg off in a logging accident.

14. I have seen pictures of women and men riding to church on the backs of mules. Women would ride side-saddle to accommodate the long dresses they wore.

15. Carter, *Sixty Years of Ministry*, 8.

16. In the early years of the snake-handling movement, non–church members or "sinner men" brought the snakes to the churches. Most people wanted to either be entertained or actually see a person receive a bite. Usually, as a mountain man named Dexter Callahan informed me, the unbeliever would torment the snakes by whipping them with sticks, shaking up the snake box, burning them with cigarettes, or cutting off the tips of their tail. Park Saylor stated, "We preached it and the sinner men carried in the snakes. I never saw a Christian carry a snake to church until the people from Alabama did."

Today it is a common practice for the church members to bring the snakes to church. They acquire the serpents by a variety of means. Some people go out in the surrounding woods to catch the snakes. Others purchase them from merchants who deal in reptiles or wild animals. On occasion the snakes are donated to the churches by locals. The prices of the snakes that are purchased vary considerably. On one occasion I was offered a beautiful king cobra for fifty dollars. Other snakes, such as copperheads, are sold for as low as two dollars.

Many church members object to the purchase of snakes. For example, Mrs. Perry Bettis stated, "Since snake handling is a small part of our service, I think it is wrong for people to to be out buying them. If a snake shows up in church it is all right to handle it then. It's wrong to be out buying them for church, though." When I asked how else they would acquire them, she replied, "The Lord will provide them. One time Perry prayed for a snake for weeks. Finally a copperhead showed up in the yard. I took a [garden] hoe and killed it. Boy, Perry was mad."

17. Interview with Park Saylor, May 27, 1988, Path Fork, Ky.

18. This was a common practice in early times. People in remote areas did not have telephones or receive newspapers. It was essential for them to depend on their neighbors for world and local news.

19. Because of improvements in transportation, the churches in eastern Kentucky are now frequently visited by friends and relatives from Michigan, Indiana, and adjacent states.

20. Park Saylor stated that he "wore out a 1928 Chevrolet hauling Hensley around" to various churches throughout the mountains.

21. Interview with Park Saylor, May 27, 1988, Path Fork, Ky.

22. I have had snakes go limp in my hands. I have seen them actually die in church members' hands.

Chapter 4

1. Solomon Saylor was born in the 1760s on Snider Creek in Mecklenberg County, N.C. His parents were Joseph and Catharine Saylor (Fee, *Saylor Family Footprints*, 1). Most of the initial settlers in eastern Kentucky were, like the Saylors, of Scotch-Irish descent. Others who migrated to the Appalachian highlands were "from England, Scotland, and the north of Ireland, with a tincture of French Huguenot blood and a German strain coming through Pennsylvania and Delaware." See Frost, "God's Plan for the Southern Mountains," 407.

Sarah Salyer Saylor was born around 1770 in western North Carolina. Sarah died in Harlan County, Ky., in 1855.

2. Faragher, *Sugar Creek*, 4.

3. Kulikoff, "Migration and Cultural Diffusion in Early America," 163.

4. Salyer, *Salyer Family*, 408.

5. Henretta, "Families and Farms," 4.

6. Salyer, *Salyer Family*, 408.

7. Interview with Park Saylor, May 27, 1988, Path Fork, Ky.

8. Eller, "Land and Family," 94.

9. Fee, *Saylor Family Footprints*, 1.

10. Egerton, *Generations*, 49.

11. Warner, "Comments on Kentucky," 256.

12. Pudup, "Social Class and Economic Development in Southeast Kentucky," 244.

13. Ibid., 235.

14. Brown, *Beech Creek*.

15. Billings, Blee, and Swanson, "Culture, Family, and Community in Preindustrial Appalachia," 159

16. Eller, "Land and Family," 86.

17. Raine, *Land of Saddle-Bags*, 2.

18. Henretta, "Families and Farms," 15.

19. Faragher, "Open-Country Community," 245.

20. Mary Beth Pudup argues that "class distinctions did exist in the larger community, country and region. . . . The southern mountain country contained a minority of wealthier, landed families whose economic power and political influence set them off as an elite group. . . . These wealthier families provided the local political leadership in the mountains and often controlled local commercial enterprises. . . . Their political influence, access to resources, and contacts with the outside placed mountain elites in a strategic position to benefit from economic change" ("Social Class and Economic Development," 238). See also Eller, "Land and Family," 83–109.

21. Hahn, " 'Unmaking' of the Southern Yeomanry," 183.

22. Frost, "Our Contemporary Ancestors in the Southern Mountains," 309.

23. Albanese, *America, Religions, and Religion*, 235.

24. Eller, "Land and Family," 102.

25. Caudill, *Night Comes to the Cumberlands*, 55.

26. Surface, *The Hollow*, 142; Jones, "Mountain Religion," 403.

27. Quoted in Jones, "Mountain Religion," 403.

28. Ibid.

29. Goodykoontz, *Home Missions on the Frontier*, 157.

30. Bruce, *And They All Sang Hallelujah*, 37.

31. Ibid., 41.

32. Ibid., 36.

33. Albanese, *America, Religions, and Religion*, 226–36.

34. Caudill, *Night Comes to the Cumberlands*, 26.

35. Haney, *Mountain People of Kentucky*, 160.

36. Albanese, *America, Religions, and Religion*, 239.

37. Posey, *Development of Methodism*, 42.

38. Mathews, *Religion in the Old South*, 104, 105.

39. Albanese, *America, Religions, and Religion*, 238.

40. Miyakawa, *Protestants and Pioneers*, 145.

41. Interview with Arnold Saylor, August 15, 1988, Stanford, Ind.

42. Miles, *Spirit of the Mountains*, 138–39.

43. Eller, "Land and Family," 84.

44. Pioneers practiced what is termed "sibling-exchange marriages." Local historians such as Harry Caudill have been critical of these marriages; Caudill contends that "the inbreeding with its attendant genetic pitfall contributed much in later years to the erosion of the highlander's self reliance" (*Night Comes to the Cumberlands*, 85). I am skeptical of Caudill's claim. He has failed to produce any evidence that these unions produced "genetic pitfalls" or eroded "the highlander's self reliance." It was virtually impossible for mountaineers to find spouses outside the confines of their settlement due to geographic seclusion. These endogamous marriages strengthened family ties and kinship networks. However, they further

narrowed the flow of information and techniques to the mountains and further restricted movement.

45. Fee, *Saylor Family Footprints*, 3.

46. Pudup, "Land before Coal," 136.

47. Eller, "Land and Family," 87–88.

48. Miles, *Spirit of the Mountains*, 119–20.

49. Dalton, "Camp Meeting Revivals of 1797–1805," 59.

50. McCauley, "Appalachian Mountain Religion," 52.

51. Eller, *Miners, Millhands, and Mountaineers*, 30.

52. Mullen, "Ritual and Sacred Narrative in the Blue Ridge Mountains," 17–38; quotes p. 21.

Chapter 5

1. Fee, *Saylor Family Footprints*, 15.

2. Weller, *Yesterday's People*, 125–26.

3. Bryant, *We're All Kin*, 92–93.

4. McCauley, "Appalachian Mountain Religion," 138.

5. Ibid., 184.

6. Ibid., 200.

7. Ibid., 179.

8. Ahlstrom, *Religious History of the American People*, 818.

9. McCauley, "Appalachian Mountain Religion," 277.

10. Ibid., 290.

11. Scott, "Shall They Take Up Serpents?," 5.

12. Holt, "Holiness Religion," 741.

13. Lawless, *God's Peculiar People*, 27.

14. Cash, *Mind of the South*, 296.

15. Carrier, *Flight of the Dove*, 88.

16. Interview with Park Saylor, January 31, 1990, Path Fork, Ky.

17. Carrier, *Flight of the Dove*, 38–39.

18. Lawless, *God's Peculiar People*, 29–30.

19. Carrier, *Flight of the Dove*, 84–85.

20. Z. B. and Dan Brock's preaching was received with mixed reactions. In their sermons they contended that it was essential to receive the Holy Ghost to gain salvation. The Brocks' convictions became known as "Brock doctrine," and the creed is still found today in churches along St. Creek. Park Saylor is adamantly opposed to Brock doctrine and maintains that it is not necessary to talk in tongues to "make it to heaven." Arnold and Kale Saylor accept Brock doctrine. The issue has divided many mountain churches.

21. Carrier, *Flight of the Dove*, 170.

22. Interview with Park Saylor, May 27, 1988, Path Fork, Ky.

23. Jean Comaroff, *Body of Power, Spirit of Resistance*, 129, 27.

24. Waller, *Feud*, 34.

25. Douglass, *Christian Reconstruction in the South*, 303–34, 335–66, cited in McCauley, "Appalachian Mountain Religion," 274.

26. Jillson, "History of the Coal Industry in Kentucky," 25.

27. Banks, "Land and Capital in Eastern Kentucky," 9.

28. "Governor's Message," *Kentucky Senate Journal*, 1828; Banks, "Coal Miners and Firebrick Workers," 87.

29. Banks, "Coal Miners and Firebrick Workers," 87.

30. Ibid., 88.

31. Hevener, *Which Side Are You On?*, 3–4.

32. Caudill, *Theirs Be the Power*, 7.

33. Gaventa, *Power and Powerlessness*, 52.

34. Scott, "Where There Is No Middle Ground," 60.

35. Fee, *Saylor Family Footprints*, 3.

36. Eller, "Coal Barons of the Appalachian South," 196.

37. Ibid.

38. Scott, "Shall They Take Up Serpents?," 3.

39. Hevener, *Which Side Are You On?*, 3.

40. Photiadis, *Community and Family Change in Rural Appalachia*, 14.

41. Gillenwater, "Cultural and Historical Geography of Mining Settlements," 2.

42. Ibid., 105.

43. Raine, *Land of Saddle-bags*, 236; Lewis, Kobak, and Johnson, "Family, Religion, and Colonialism in Central Appalachia," 118.

44. Lewis, Kobak, and Johnson, "Family, Religion, and Colonialism in Central Appalachia," 122.

45. Flynt, *Dixie's Forgotten People*, 154.

46. McGaw, *Most Wonderful Machine*, 260–61.

47. Caudill, *Night Comes to the Cumberlands*, 100.

48. Ibid., 113.

49. Corbin, *Life, Work, and Rebellion in the Coal Fields*, 10.

50. Ibid.

51. Seltzer, *Fire in the Hole*, 19.

52. Ibid.

53. Caudill, *Night Comes to the Cumberlands*, 115.

54. Corbin, *Life, Work, and Rebellion in the Coal Fields*, 15.

55. Ibid.

56. Carroll Saylor—Park Saylor's brother—said, "We might voice some opposition to their policies out here in the rural areas. The closer they got to Harlan, the meaner they got." When I said that I would have expected them to become more cautious as they got closer to the cities, he explained, "The police was in with them. They protected the company thugs. If someone got killed they just turned their heads." Interview with Carroll Saylor, July 25, 1991, Path Fork, Ky.

57. U.S. Congress, Senate, *Report of the U.S. Coal Commission*, part 3, 1428, cited in Eller, *Miners, Millhands, and Mountaineers*, 183.

58. Park Saylor remembered, "I was only four years old then, but remember the event very well. A man came on a black mule and told us the story about my grandpa being killed, before my father got home."

59. Hevener, *Which Side Are You On?*, 25.

60. Ibid., 20, 11, 25–26, 23.

61. Ibid., 23

62. Ibid., 10.

63. Miller, "Child Health in Mining Camps and Village," 6–7.

64. Ibid., 8.

65. Ibid., 5.

66. Flynt, *Dixie's Forgotten People*, 157. I highly recommend Malone, *Country Music U.S.A.*, and Whisnant, *All That Is Native and Fine*, for informative reading on Appalachian music and handicrafts.

67. Carter, *Sixty Years of Ministry*, 45.

68. Billings, Blee, and Swanson, "Culture, Family, and Community in Preindustrial Appalachia," 157.

Chapter 6

1. Kane, "Appalachian Snake Handlers," 117.

2. Interview with Park Saylor, May 27, 1988, Path Fork, Ky.

3. When asked about his snake-handling reputation, Shell commented, "I handled any of them that was brought to me, but Brother George Hensley was the best snake handler." Shell's own background is somewhat unique among the snake handlers:

> Kimbrough: Were you religious all of your life?
> Shell: Heavens no, I was raised with drunks. There was a Baptist preacher that came through one time. When he looked at that bunch I grew up around he said, "The only thing that will do this bunch any good is powder and lead."
> Kimbrough: When was you first saved?
> Shell: There was this evangelical preacher that was roaming through the mountains preaching on foot. We didn't have many cars back then. All we had was wagon roads. Well, this preacher stopped and asked my Grandpa [Squire] Browning if he could use his porch to preach on. My grandpa said it was all right, so the old preacher held his service. He would preach awhile then he would cry awhile. I told my mother, "This man has something." He made an altar call and fifty-seven of us was saved. Only two of us are still living.
> Kimbrough: Was that the first time you handled a serpent?
> Shell: No, but I did shortly after. My mother and I was out in the garden hoeing and I said, "Mommy, someone will bring a rattler to church tomorrow

and I will handle it." She said, "Honey, what are you talking about?" I said, "The Lord told me that someone will bring a serpent tomorrow and I will take him up." She said, "Honey, your mind is bad." The next morning a man came to church with a box under his arm. The power hit me just like that. I raised the lid and have handled them ever since.

4. Interview with Denver Short, January 5, 1989, Ages, Ky.

5. When I asked him whether he had seen people handle fire, Park Saylor replied, "Yes, many times. I have seen Bradley Shell eat and drink bottles of poison. You can hold a blowtorch on him and he will keep on dancing. I have seen Jim Jackson and George Hensley drink strychnine and handle fire."

6. I asked Bradley Shell, "Were you afraid when he started shooting at you?" He replied, "No, I wasn't afraid. If it was meant for me to be shot, I would have been."

7. One of the most famous local episodes of prophecy, recounted to me by several eastern Kentucky old-timers, occurred in 1946, when Sill Eads actually predicted the time of his death. Eads had been ill for approximately one year, but one morning he told his wife, Lucy, "At six o'clock today, I'm leaving." In response, she summoned many of the church members to her home to pray for her husband. Many people believed that Eads's illness had been brought on by psychological problems and that he was "talking out of his head." A large gathering of church brethren came to the Eads home, including the prophet Lee Johnson. The house was full of guests who kept watching the clock. Sill Eads's bed was positioned so that he could not possibly check the time himself. When the clock hit "straight on six o'clock," Eads said, "Well, Brother Lee, here's the gate. Aren't you coming in with me?" He then closed his eyes and died. Lee Johnson was stunned by the event and sank to the floor. The brethren who saw what happened declared, "Brother Lee, you will be next." The prediction proved to be accurate: Lee Johnson died one month later.

8. Telephone conversation with Mrs. Rowe Collins, August 10, 1988. Shortly after this incident Rowe Collins became a preacher. He still has a church in eastern Kentucky.

9. Morrow, "Seventy-Seven Years," 38.

10. "Wave Rattler in Frenzy," *New York Times*, August 19, 1935, p. 17.

11. "Harlan Holiness Church Disciple Bitten by Snake during Ritual," *Louisville Courier-Journal*, May 25, 1939, p. 2.

12. "Pastor Here Whirls Snake, It Escapes, People Flee," *Tampa Morning Tribune*, March 2, 1936, p. 1.

13. Ibid.

14. "Preacher Juggles Snake Again, Says It Bit Him," *Tampa Morning Tribune*, March 9, 1936, p. 1.

15. Ibid.

16. Ibid.

17. "Snake Expert Warns People Preacher's Rattlers Poisonous," *Tampa Morn-*

ing Tribune, March 11, 1936, p. 7. End had actually sold the snake for two dollars to a Mr. L. J. Stone; a "good lively medium-sized snake," it was capable of delivering a lethal shot of venom. Stone then gave the snake to Hensley.

18. Bill Abbott, "Man Bitten by Preacher's Snake Dies," *Tampa Morning Tribune*, May 5, 1936, p. 1.

19. Ibid.

20. "'Faith' Service Snake-Bite Fatal," *New York Times*, May 5, 1936, p. 25.

21. Bill Abbott, "Man Bitten by Preacher's Snake Dies," *Tampa Morning Tribune*, May 5, 1936, p. 1. During the inquest Mrs. J. R. King interrupted the meeting by shouting "Glory to God!" and "Hallelujah!"

22. "County Buries Snake Victim; Shows Banned," *Tampa Morning Tribune*, May 6, 1936, p. 7.

23. "'Faith' Failed," *Tampa Morning Tribune*, May 6, 1936, p. 8.

24. "County Buries Snake Victim; Shows Banned."

25. Day, *Bloody Ground*, 7. In most areas Day's book is accurate, according to Thomas D. Clark. I discussed Day's work with Professor Clark in Bloomington, Ind., in April 1993. Regardless of Day's correctness, he was insensitive and derogatory toward the snake handlers.

26. "Church Fights Law against Snakes," *Louisville Courier-Journal*, April 9, 1940, sec. 2, p. 1.

27. "Snake Cult Facing Legislative Prohibition in State," *Louisville Courier-Journal*, March 5, 1940, sec. 2, p. 1.

28. Ibid.

29. Ibid.

30. Ed Edstrom, "Snake-Tossing Preachers Offer to Let Hearers Pick 'Em Up; Find No Takers," *Louisville Courier-Journal*, September 15, 1939, sec. 3, p. 12.

31. *Louisville Courier-Journal*, March 5, 1940, sec. 2, p. 1; Kentucky Acts 1940, 290, cited in Kane, "Snake Handlers of Southern Appalachia," 65.

32. "Church Fights Law against Snakes."

33. "Snake-Handling Sect Asks Court for Protection," *Louisville Courier-Journal*, August 22, 1940, sec. 1, p. 11.

34. *Lawson v. Commonwealth* (1942), 291 Ky. 437, 164 S.W. 2d 972, cited in Kane, "Snake Handlers of Southern Appalachia," 67.

35. I learned of these deaths through Steven M. Kane.

36. Telephone interview with Henry Swiney, August 1, 1989, Sneedville, Tenn.

37. "Snakes Kill Preacher," *New York Times*, October 1, 1936, p. 15.

38. "No Law against Handling Snakes," *Big Stone Gap (Va.) Post*, October 8, 1936, p. 1.

39. Mary Breckinridge, "Snake's Victim Dies Although Given Antivenin Serum," *Louisville Courier-Journal*, September 10, 1940, p. 7.

40. Day, *Bloody Ground*, 8–9.

41. Ibid., 9. This trial was initiated when Jim Cochran's brother pressed charges against Bowling and the church members for his brother's death. In the

1960s, the son of a man killed by snakebite in Tess Walters's church at Blackmont swore to kill Walters, because Walters had allegedly handed his father the rattlesnake that killed him. Fortunately, cooler heads prevailed, and the young man did not act on his threat. Tess Walters never backed down to authorities or threats. Warrants were sworn against him in Alabama for his snake handling, but they did not deter him. At one meeting, he literally walked barefooted on rattlesnakes in front of the authorities.

42. "Nine to Face Charges in Snake-Bite Death," *Louisville Courier-Journal*, August 28, 1940, sec. 2, p. 1.

43. Ibid.

44. "Eleven Snake Cultists Jailed: Refused to Pay $57 Fines," *Louisville Courier-Journal*, September 8, 1940, p. 1.

45. Ibid.

46. Ibid.

47. "Snake Handling Sect Prays for Jail Doors to Fall," *Louisville Courier-Journal*, September 9, 1940, sec. 1, p. 2.

48. Kentucky State Board of Health records for the 1940s report two other deaths from snakebite. They were not associated with church services. A Harlan County housewife died of a rattlesnake bite in 1940, and in Hopkins County a "year-old infant died of a copperhead bite in June 1946." See "Snake Rites Fatal to Four since 1940," *Louisville Courier-Journal*, October 29, 1947.

49. The source for this story wishes to remain anonymous.

50. "Snake Sect Demands Three Be Released," clipping file of Austin Long, n.d.

51. Interview with Sweet Ball, January 31, 1990, Harlan, Ky.

52. Robertson, *That Old-Time Religion*, 170.

53. "Three Rattlesnakes Refuse to Bite Six Handlers, Two from Kentucky," *Louisville Courier-Journal*, June 3, 1935.

54. Telephone interview with Emma Jean Hensley Potts, June 13, 1988. She is the daughter of George and Irene Hensley.

55. Telephone interview with Loyal Hensley, June 14, 1988. He is the son of George and Irene Hensley.

56. Interview with Denver Short, January 31, 1990, Ages, Ky. Short commented, "I thought [Hensley] was going to die. He swelled up and turned black. Blood was oozing from his mouth."

Reverend Short has been a powerful leader among the Holiness in eastern Kentucky. While preaching at Tess Walters's church at Blackmont in the 1950s, Short reached an anointed state, ran through the church, and jumped out of a window twelve feet above the ground. He landed in "briars and stickers." When Short hit the ground he kept on preaching. He recalled the event during our interview: "I'll never forget it; a young boy ran to the window and looked out to see where I landed. He was so short all I could see was his eyes and nose peering over the window." Tragedy struck Short in January of 1989. His son, Ernest "Wayne," was bitten by a three-foot rattlesnake at the Ages Pentecostal Church and killed. Wayne Short was always kind and courteous to me and assisted me in my research. I regarded him as a true friend. His wife was pregnant with their baby at the time of his death. She also lost her first husband, James Saylor, to a snakebite, in 1967 at Covington, Ky.

57. Morrow, "Seventy-Seven Years," 75.

58. " 'Deadly' Snakes Passed around in Revival Meet at Church Here," *Knoxville News-Sentinel*, September 10, 1939, home ed., A9.

59. "Snake Custodian, Chided by Pastor at Farewell Demonstration, Thrusts Copperhead Down Throat," *Knoxville News-Sentinel*, September 25, 1939, home ed., p. 12.

60. Ibid.

61. Robertson, *That Old-Time Religion*, 171.

62. Burton, *Serpent-Handling Believers*, 46.

63. Ibid., 46–47.

Chapter 7

1. Telephone interview with Emma Jean Hensley Potts (George Hensley's daughter), August 16, 1988.

2. J. B. Collins, *Tennessee Snake Handlers*, 16.

3. Vance, "History of Serpent Handlers," 86–87.

4. J. B. Collins, *Tennessee Snake Handlers*, 9.

5. Charles Crane, "Demonstrations of Faith with Gyrations Held in Dolly Pond Church," *Chattanooga News–Free Press*, July 20, 1945, pp. 1–2.

6. J. B. Collins, *Tennessee Snake Handlers*, 17.

7. Ibid., 17–20.

8. Charles Pennington, "Snake-Handling 'Preacher' Dies of Rattler's Bite in Ceremony," *Chattanooga Times*, September 6, 1945, p. 1.

9. Ibid.

10. Ibid. The newspaper article identified Alice as Hayes's wife, but Alice was his daughter; his wife was named Cora. The article also mistakenly referred to Mrs. "Arthur" Hutton, rather than Mrs. Oscar Hutton, as the one who was bitten.

11. Charles Pennington, "Ford, Rattler's Victim, Buried; Flock Handles Snakes in Ritual," *Chattanooga Times*, September 9, 1945, p. 1.

12. Ibid.

13. Ibid.

14. Ibid. According to an account given by Mr. and Mrs. Carl Swafford, Mr. and Mrs. Charles Hall, and Ida Harden, "When the snakes came in contact with the corpse, they 'rolled on their backs with their bellies in the air,' " as if they were dead. See Vance, "History of Serpent Handlers," 92.

15. Pennington, "Ford, Rattler's Victim, Buried." Shortly after Ford's death, Ressie had announced to news reporters that she would "have members of the faith take part in snake handling at his funeral. See "Tennessee Preacher, Virginia

Woman Die of Snake Bites in Rites of Religious Sect," *New York Times*, September 5, 1945, p. 25.

16. Ibid.

17. Alex Corliss, "Two 'Faith-Healing' Ministers Held for Handling Snake in City Limits," *Chattanooga Times*, September 24, 1945, p. 1.

18. Ibid.

19. Vance, "History of Serpent Handlers," 92.

20. J. B. Collins, *Tennessee Snake Handlers*, 22.

21. Ibid., 23.

22. Alex Corliss, "Snake Bite during Church Rites Proves Fatal to Daisy Worshiper," *Chattanooga Times*, July 15, 1946, p. 1.

23. Ibid.

24. "Boy Badly Bitten during Snake Rite: Harry Skelton of Cleveland in Critical Condition," *Chattanooga Times*, August 19, 1946, p. 7.

25. "Snake Bite Is Fatal to Cultist: Another Struck Down by Rattler," *Chattanooga Times*, August 27, 1946, p. 9.

26. "Walter Henry, 51, Bitten by Rattler," *Chattanooga News–Free Press*, August 26, 1946, p. 2.

27. "Third Snake Cultist Dies in Cleveland," *Chattanooga Times*, September 3, 1946, p. 15.

28. Ibid.

29. "Bradley Paper Seeks to 'Ban' Snake Handling," *Chattanooga News–Free Press*, September 4, 1946, p. 5.

30. "Rites without Snakes Held for Cult Member," *Chattanooga Times*, September 5, 1946, p. 13.

31. Burton, *Serpent-Handling Believers*, 54.

32. Quoted in J. B. Collins, *Tennessee Snake Handlers*, 24.

33. Ibid.

34. "Dolly Pond Sect Quiet under New State Law," *Chattanooga News–Free Press*, March 31, 1947, p. 1.

35. J. B. Collins, *Tennessee Snake Handlers*, 25.

36. "Dolly Pond Sect Quiet under New State Law."

37. J. B. Collins, *Tennessee Snake Handlers*, 25.

38. Ibid.

39. "Dolly Pond Sect Quiet under New State Law."

40. J. B. Collins, *Tennessee Snake Handlers*, 27.

41. Ibid.

42. Ibid.

43. Ibid., 28.

44. "Snakehandler Case Opens as Statute Case," *Chattanooga News–Free Press*, November 12, 1947, p. 5.

45. J. B. Collins, *Tennessee Snake Handlers*, 29.

46. Ibid., 32.

47. Ibid., 34.

48. Ibid.

49. "Snake-Handling Trial Postponed to October 20," *Chattanooga Times*, October 12, 1947, p. 3.

50. "Snake Handlers of Georgia, Kentucky to Attend Trial Here; Snakes Barred," *Chattanooga Times*, November 12, 1947, p. 1–2.

51. Ibid.

52. Vance, "History of Serpent Handlers," 99.

53. Vaughn Smartt, "Snake Cult Jury Split 6–6; Mistrial of 12 Is Expected," *Chattanooga Times*, November 13, 1947, p. 1.

54. "Jury Deadlock to Mean Later Test for Law," *Chattanooga News–Free Press*, November 13, 1947, p. 1.

55. Ibid.

56. "Snake Cult Case Called Mistrial," *Chattanooga Times*, November 14, 1947, p. 3.

57. "Ten Cultists Ruled Guilty; Get $50 Fines," *Chattanooga Times*, February 12, 1948, p. 1.

58. Lee Anderson, "County Group Fined $50 Each for Offenses," *Chattanooga News–Free Press*, February 11, 1948, p. 1.

59. Ibid.

60. Vance, "History of Serpent Handlers," 101.

61. Letter to Paul R. L. Vance from Henry Haile, assistant attorney general of the State of Tennessee, dated March 27, 1972, cited in Vance, "History of Serpent Handlers," 49–50.

62. "Five Held on Charge of Snake Handling," *Chattanooga Times*, June 14, 1948, p. 3.

63. "Snakebite Victim at Church Is Dead," *Chattanooga Times*, August 10, 1948, p. 3.

64. "Dolly Ponders Quit Handling Snakes; Trustee 'Doesn't Have Faith Enough,'" *Chattanooga Times*, August 1948, clipping file of Chattanooga–Hamilton County Bicentennial Library.

65. "Girl, Fourteen, Is Bitten by Snake at Cult," *Chattanooga Times*, August 23, 1948, p. 3.

66. "Snake Cult Opens Church on Sunday," *Chattanooga Times*, December 13, 1947, p. 3.

67. Robertson, *That Old-Time Religion*, 170.

68. Ibid.

69. Ibid., 171.

70. Burton, *Serpent-Handling Believers*, 56.

71. Don Kimsey, "The Jaws of Death," *Atlanta Journal*, January 8, 1973, p. D9.

72. "Cultist Dies of Snakebite; Believed Dolley Pond Leader," *Chattanooga Times*, July 25, 1955, p. 3.

Chapter 8

1. Womeldorf, "Rattlesnake Religion," 1517–18.

2. "Holiness Faith Healers," 59–62.

3. "Police Raid Virginia Snake Sect and Kill Four of Their Eight Rattlers," *New York Times*, July 30, 1945, p. 21.

4. Ibid.

5. Ibid. The newspaper does not name Shell as the man who was arrested. He admitted to me in August of 1989 that he was the person arrested and that he put the snake in his shirt to conceal it from the police.

6. "Take Sect's Snakes Alive," *New York Times*, August 6, 1945, p. 17.

7. Kane, "Snake Handlers of Southern Appalachia," 74.

8. Ibid.

9. "Paralyzing Prayers," 23.

10. "Tennessee Preacher, Virginia Woman Die of Snake Bites in Rites of Religious Sect," *New York Times*, September 5, 1945, p. 25.

11. Kane, "Snake Handlers of Southern Appalachia," 74.

12. Ibid.

13. Jon Greer, "Prayers Failed to Heal Snake's Bite; Man Dies," *Kingsport Times-News*, August 31, 1976, p. 1.

14. Ibid.

15. Kane, "Snake Handlers of Southern Appalachia," 74.

16. Ibid., 74–75.

17. Ibid., 75.

18. Ibid., 68.

19. "Any Deadly Thing," 25.

20. Joe Creason, "Snake Handlers: Leaders Claim Kentucky Has 1,000 Cult Members," *Louisville Courier-Journal*, October 26, 1947, magazine sec., p. 8.

21. "3,000 Watch at Snake-Cult Meeting; Girl Handles Rattler That Bit Her," *Louisville Courier-Journal*, October 13, 1947.

22. Joe Creason, "Faith Lets Him Handle the Snakes," *Louisville Courier-Journal*, August 16, 1948.

23. "3,000 Watch at Snake-Cult Meeting."

24. Ibid.

25. Ibid. On one occasion Hayes was bitten on top of his head.

26. Ibid.

27. Ibid.

28. "Defiant Cult Handling Snake in Harlan Fined," *Louisville Courier-Journal*, October 16, 1947.

29. Ibid.

30. "Six Snake-Cultists Fined $100 Each at Harlan," *Louisville Courier-Journal*, October 29, 1947.

31. Joe Creason, "They Must Have Faith to Handle the Snakes," *Louisville Courier-Journal*, September 20, 1948.

32. "Faith Lets Him Handle the Snakes."

33. "Oblivion Is a Good Idea for the Snake-Handlers," *Louisville Courier-Journal*, February 23, 1948.

34. Ibid.

35. Joe Creason, "Snake Handlers: A Dying Cult," *Louisville Courier-Journal*, September 10, 1950.

36. Interview with Arnold Saylor, November 22, 1987, Fort Wayne, Ind.

37. Interview with Shilo Collins, September 17, 1988, Pineville, Ky.

38. Interview with Tess Walters, May 27, 1988, Blackmont, Ky.

39. Ibid.

40. Interview with Shilo Collins, September 17, 1988, Pineville, Ky.

41. Ibid.

42. "Crowd of 2,000 Attends Funeral for Rev. Valentine," *Middlesboro Daily News*, August 17, 1955, p. 1.

43. Interview with Kale Saylor, July 19, 1993, Bledsoe, Ky.

44. Interview with Shilo Collins, September 17, 1988, Pineville, Ky.

45. "Crowd of 2,000 Attends Funeral for Rev. Valentine."

46. "Faith Rites to Be Held Tomorrow," *Middlesboro Daily News*, August 20, 1955, p. 1.

47. Kobler, "America's Strangest Religion," 27.

48. Golden, "Snake Church," 50.

49. "Police Arrest Virginia Preacher Handling Snakes at Service," *Middlesboro Daily News*, August 22, 1955, p. 1.

50. Ibid.

51. Ibid.

52. "Snake-Cult Handler Bitten by Rattler Refuses Doctor Despite Pain, Swelling," *Louisville Courier-Journal*, July 20, 1959.

53. Ibid.

54. "Snake-Bitten Arjay Man Is Better; Handles Four-Foot Rattler to Prove It," *Middlesboro Daily News*, clipping file of Tess Walters, n.d.

55. Paul R. Jordan, "Snake-Handling Cult Meets Openly in Clay," *Louisville Courier-Journal*, July 6, 1959, p. 1.

56. Ibid.

57. "Harlan Man Gets Medical Aid after Being Bitten," *Middlesboro Daily News*, clipping file of Tess Walters, n.d.

58. "Rattler-Bitten Cultist under Hospital Care," clipping file of Tess Walters, n.d.

59. "Judge Confesses He's Rattled by Rattlesnakes," *Louisville Courier-Journal*, August 5, 1965.

60. "Snake-Handling Minister Gets Fine, Lecture," *Louisville Times*, August 26, 1965.

61. "Three Accused in Snake Case Are Acquitted," *Louisville Courier-Journal*, April 16, 1967.

62. "Snake-Rite Cases Delayed at Covington," *Louisville Courier-Journal*, March 8, 1967.

63. Ibid.

64. "Judge Grants Snake Handlers Trial by Jury," *Louisville Times*, April 5, 1967.

65. "Three Accused Snake Handlers Win Jury Trial," *Louisville Courier-Journal*, April 6, 1967.

66. "Three Accused in Snake Case Are Acquitted."

67. Hank Burchard, "Grief, Joy Mingle at Snake Handler's Funeral," *Louisville Courier-Journal*, August 26, 1968.

68. "Virginia Snake-Handling Law to Be Tested," 22.

69. Morrow, "Seventy-Seven Years," 38.

70. "Jury Acquits Minister in Snake-Handling Death," *Louisville Courier-Journal*, October 24, 1968.

71. Jon Greer, "Prayers Failed To Heal Snake's Bite; Man Dies," *Kingsport Times-News*, August 31, 1976, p. 1.

72. Ibid.

73. Bryan Wilkins, " 'If God Doesn't Move, You'll Die,' Veteran Snake Handler Says," *Lexington Herald-Leader*, June 1, 1978.

74. "Harlan County Man Dies of Snakebite Apparently Suffered in Church Service," *Louisville Times*, June 1, 1978.

75. Rita S. Gatton, "Fatal Snake Bite Linked to Religious Ceremony," *Louisville Courier-Journal*, May 31, 1978.

76. Wilkins, " 'If God Doesn't Move, You'll Die.' "

77. Ibid.

78. Gary Lee Tussey, "Doctrine of Snake Handling," *Richmond Register*, April 13, 1979.

79. Fortunato, "Snake Handlers," 58, 123.

80. George W. Hackett, "Snake Handling Still Persists in the Mountains," *Richmond Register*, April 6, 1979, p. 7. In 1975, Davidson and a few other brethren had been arrested for snake handling. They were fined fifty dollars and court costs, but they refused to pay the fines and took the case to the court of appeals. The judge refused to hear the case.

81. "Snake Handler Dies of Bites," clipping file of Tess Walters, n.d.

82. "Rattlesnake Bite Kills Man after Leslie Church Service," *Whitesburg (Ky.) Mountain Eagle*, September 18, 1980.

83. "Snake Handler Dies from Bite," *Richmond Register*, September 16, 1980.

84. Andrew Wolfson, "Daring the Devil . . . Church Snake Handlers Undaunted by Death of Man Who Didn't Have Enough Faith," *Louisville Times*, September 22, 1980, p. B1.

85. Andy Mead, "Handler Dies of Snakebite at Services," *Lexington Herald-Leader*, September 16, 1980, p. 1.

86. Ibid.

87. "Kentuckian Dies of Rattlesnake Bite after a Religious Service in Leslie," *Louisville Courier-Journal*, September 17, 1980.

88. "Spurning Aid, Preacher Dies of Snake Bite," *Louisville Courier-Journal*, August 25, 1982.

89. Oppie Gulley, " 'Savage Rituals of the Rattlesnake Religionists,' " *Louisville Courier-Journal*, September 13, 1982.

90. "Woman's Snake Bite Is Treated," *Louisville Courier-Journal*, February 25, 1983.

91. "Phelps Man Dies from Snake Bite during Ritual in West Virginia," *Louisville Courier-Journal*, August 30, 1983, B1.

Chapter 9

1. Joe Creason, "Snake Handlers: Leaders Claim Kentucky Has 1,000 Cult Members," *Louisville Courier-Journal*, October 26, 1947, magazine sec., p. 7.

2. Interview with Park Saylor, May 27, 1988, Path Fork, Ky.

3. Ibid.

4. There are many accounts of people levitating in church. A preacher named "Happy" Tom Brooks was said to have been caught up in a fiery sermon on a Sunday in the 1930s. Lawrence Lawson (Sherman's son) reminisces, "I will never forget it. Brooks came clear out of his high-topped shoes. When church was over my dad asked him to go eat with us. He said, 'Let me get my shoes.' His shoes were still there, where he came out of them, still laced up and tied." Vincent Synan mentions levitations in his works (see "Pentecostal Movement in the United States," 242).

5. Bissell McWilliams Jr., "Snake Found in Fatal Crash Car," clipping file of Wyatt Woody, January 1961.

6. Butler, *Awash in a Sea of Faith*, 68.

7. Interview with Mrs. Coots, June 1989, Middlesboro, Ky.

8. Quoted in Carden and Pelton, *Persecuted Prophets*, 162.

9. Interview with Liston Pack, August 15, 1987, Carson Springs, Tenn.

10. Interview with Bradley Shell, August 15, 1987, Harlan County, Ky.

11. Ibid.

12. Rex Bailey, "Sect Believes that Serpent-Handling Has Spiritual Role Despite Man's Death," *Louisville Courier-Journal*, November 5, 1973.

13. Rob Kasper, "Faith Survives the Rattler's Bite," *Louisville Times*, November 1, 1973, p. 1.

14. Rex Bailey, "Death Doesn't Deter Sect from Handling Serpents," *Louisville Courier-Journal*, November 5, 1973, p. 1.

15. Ibid.

16. Ibid.

17. Kasper, "Faith Survives the Rattler's Bite."

18. I have witnessed this on occasion. At the deathbed of A. D. Saylor, Reverend Kenneth Saylor (Kale's son) stuck his head in a snake box and danced.

19. In the late summer of 1988, Joe Short of Mayking, Ky., was bitten by a rattlesnake. The preacher, Andrew Hall, informed me that Short was struck because of fighting and confusion in the church.

20. "Death of Snake Handler Should Not Deter Believers, Leader Says," *Richmond Register*, February 15, 1986.

21. "Harlan County Attorney Won't File Charges in Snake-Handling Death," *Louisville Courier-Journal*, February 19, 1986.

22. Judy Jones Lewis, "Bell County Woman Refuses to Be Treated for Snakebite," *Lexington Herald-Leader*, July 2, 1987, p. B1.

23. "Snake Bite at Church Kills Man," *Evansville Courier*, January 31, 1989.

24. "Man Killed by Snake Led Church Where Tennessean Was Bitten," *Louisville Courier-Journal*, January 31, 1989.

25. Wayne Short, a carpenter by trade, was well liked in the community. Short was always kind to me and made me feel welcome at his church. His friends and family have asked me not to elaborate on his death, and I will not. However, I will mention that his death was heroic: he actually stepped in and took a bite that was intended for another person. A good account of Wayne's death can be found in Bill Estep and Todd Pack, "Pastor's Death Won't End Snake-Handling at Church," *Lexington Herald-Leader*, January 31, 1989, p. A1.

26. "Minister Bitten by Snake out of Hospital," *Lexington Herald-Leader*, November 29, 1988.

27. Betsy Kauffman, "Church Members Say Snake Victim's Kin Lacked Faith," *Knoxville News-Sentinel*, November 22, 1988, p. A1.

28. Ibid.

29. "Man Bitten by Rattler during Church Service," *Richmond Register*, May 10, 1989.

30. Amy Brooke Baker, "Leslie Man Bitten by Snake in Church May Not Be Charged," *Lexington Herald-Leader*, November 15, 1989, p. B1.

Chapter 10

1. Votaw, "Hillbillies Invade Chicago," 64.

2. Albert N. Votaw commented that the moving back and forth caused problems with the children's education: "If the family goes home for the winter, the children are so much further behind on their return that they must either be demoted or carried as a more or less passive and unassimilated segment in the class" ("Hillbillies Invade Chicago," 65). Votaw's article has merit but makes many reckless generalizations about Appalachians. For a critique of Votaw, see Batteau, *Invention of Appalachia*, 145–46.

3. Mayo, "Appalachian-Urban Crisis," 29.

4. Cunningham, "Religious Concerns of Southern Appalachian Migrants," 37.

5. Duane Noriyuki, "On Stinking Creek," *Detroit Free Press Magazine*, September 9, 1990, pp. 11–13.

6. Mayo, "Appalachian-Urban Crisis," 25–26.

7. Sharp, "Migration and Social Participation," 9. The manner in which Appalachians relied on kinships for assistance coincides with what John Bodnar found among European immigrants (see Bodnar, *The Transplanted*).

8. Smith, "Migration and Adjustment Experience," 88.

9. Schwarzweller, Brown, and Mangalam, *Mountain Families in Transition*, 153–54.

10. Brown, "Family behind the Migrant," 153.

11. Smith, "Migration and Adjustment Experience," 92.

12. Julian Krawcheck, "Smile When You Say Hillbilly!" (reprints from the *Cleveland Press*, January 29–February 4, 1958), cited in Cunningham, "Religious Concerns of Southern Appalachian Migrants," 39.

13. Cunningham, "Religious Concerns of Southern Appalachian Migrants," 9. In reference to the "stem family," see also Zimmerman and Frampton, *Family and Society*; Schwarzweller, Brown, and Mangalam, *Mountain Families in Transition*, 90.

14. Letter from Joyce Baker to David L. Kimbrough, November 7, 1988.

15. Votaw, "Hillbillies Invade Chicago," 66.

16. Carter, *Sixty Years of Ministry*, 26–27.

17. Appalachians commonly accept people with close social bonds as kin, regardless of whether they have blood ties. F. Carlene Bryant gives an accurate portrayal of this tendency in *We're All Kin*.

18. Brown, Schwarzweller, and Mangalam, "Kentucky Mountain Migration and the Stem-Family," 49.

19. Lawless, *God's Peculiar People*, 33.

Conclusion

1. Schwarzweller, "Social Change and the Individual," 53.

2. Kane, "Appalachian Snake Handlers," 116.

3. Randall Collins, *Sociological Insight*, 32.

4. Flynt, *Dixie's Forgotten People*, 156.

5. Randall Collins, *Sociological Insight*, 34.

6. Kane, "Ritual Possession in a Southern Appalachian Religious Sect," 293–302.

Bibliography

Ahlstrom, Sydney E. *A Religious History of the American People.* New Haven: Yale University Press, 1972.

"Ain't It the Truth," *Louisville Courier-Journal,* October 26, 1947, magazine sec., p. 4.

Albanese, Catherine L. *America, Religions, and Religion.* Belmont, Calif.: Wadsworth Publishing Company, 1981.

"Any Deadly Thing." *Time,* September 8, 1947, p. 28.

Banks, Alan. "Land and Capital in Eastern Kentucky, 1890–1915." *Appalachian Journal* 8, no. 1 (Autumn 1980): 8–18.

——. "Coal Miners and Firebrick Workers: The Structure of Work Relations in Two Eastern Kentucky Communities." *Appalachian Journal* 11, nos. 1 and 2 (Autumn/Winter 1983–84): 85–102.

Batteau, Allen W. *The Invention of Appalachia.* Tucson: University of Arizona Press, 1990.

Billings, Dwight B. "Religion as Opposition: A Gramscian Analysis." *American Journal of Sociology* 96, no. 1 (July 1990): 1–31.

Billings, Dwight B., Kathleen Blee, and Louis Swanson. "Culture, Family, and Community in Preindustrial Appalachia." *Appalachian Journal* 13, no. 2 (Winter 1986): 154–70.

Bodnar, John. *The Transplanted: A History of Immigrants in Urban America.* Bloomington: Indiana University Press, 1985.

——. "Power and Memory in Oral History: Workers and Managers at Studebaker." *Journal of American History* 75, no. 4 (March 1989): 1201–21.

Brown, James S. "The Family behind the Migrant." In *Appalachia in the Sixties: Decade of Reawakening,* ed. David S. Walls and John B. Stephenson. Lexington: University Press of Kentucky, 1972.

——. *Beech Creek: A Study of a Kentucky Mountain Neighborhood.* Berea: Berea College Press, 1988.

Brown, James S., Harry Schwarzweller, and Joseph Mangalam. "Kentucky Mountain Migration and the Stem-Family: An American Variation on a Theme by Le Play." *Rural Sociology* 28 (March 1963): 48–69.

Bruce, Dickson D., Jr. *And They All Sang Hallelujah: Plain-Folk Camp-Meeting Religion, 1800–1845.* Knoxville: University of Tennessee Press, 1974.

Bryant, F. Carlene. *We're All Kin: A Cultural Study of a Mountain Neighborhood.* Knoxville: University of Tennessee Press, 1981.

Burton, Thomas. *Serpent-Handling Believers.* Knoxville: University of Tennessee Press, 1993.

Butler, Jon. *Awash in a Sea of Faith: Christianizing the American People.* Cambridge: Harvard University Press, 1990.

Campbell, John C. *The Southern Highlander and His Homeland.* New York: Russell Sage Foundation, 1921. Reprint, Lexington: University Press of Kentucky, 1969.

Carden, Karen W., and Robert Pelton. *The Persecuted Prophets.* Cranbury, N.J.: A. S. Barnes and Company, 1976.

Carrier, Alfred. *The Flight of the Dove: Roots of Pentecost in Eastern Kentucky.* Hustonville, Ky.: n.p., 1988.

Carter, Thea O. *Sixty Years of Ministry: An Autobiography.* Pineville, Ky.: n.p., 1991.

Cash, W. J. *The Mind of the South.* New York: Alfred A. Knopf, 1941. Reprint, New York: Random House, 1969.

Caudill, Harry M. *Night Comes to the Cumberlands: A Biography of a Depressed Area.* Boston: Little, Brown and Company, 1962.

———. *Theirs Be the Power: The Moguls of Eastern Kentucky.* Urbana: University of Illinois Press, 1983.

The Church of God, Evangel (Cleveland, Tenn.). April 4, 1914, p. 7.

———. September 12, 1914, p. 2.

———. October 4, 1914, p. 3.

———. February 5, 1916, p. 2.

———. April 13, 1918, p. 2.

———. June 29, 1918, p. 1.

Collins, J. B. *Tennessee Snake Handlers.* Chattanooga: Chattanooga Magazine Company, 1947.

Collins, Randall. *Sociological Insight: An Introduction to Non-Obvious Sociology.* New York: Oxford University Press, 1982.

Comaroff, Jean. *Body of Power, Spirit of Resistance: The Culture and History of a South African People.* Chicago: University of Chicago Press, 1985.

Conlin, Wendy. "Perry Man Bitten by Snake in Service." *Louisville Courier-Journal,* May 11, 1989.

Conn, Charles W. *Our First 100 Years: 1886–1986.* Cleveland, Tenn.: Church of God Publishing House, 1955.

Corbin, David. *Life, Work, and Rebellion in the Coal Fields.* Urbana: University of Illinois Press, 1981.

Crawford, Byron. "'Serpent-Handlin' Is as Real as Heaven Is.'" *Louisville Courier-Journal,* September 22, 1980.

Creason, Joe. "Publicity Gave Snake Cult New Life." *Louisville Courier-Journal,* August 25, 1955.

Cressey, Paul Fredrick. "Social Disorganization and Reorganization in Harlan County, Kentucky." *American Sociological Review* 14 (1949): 389–94.

Cunningham, Earl. "Religious Concerns of Southern Appalachian Migrants in a North Central City." Ph.D. diss., Boston University, 1962.

Dakin, Ralph E., and Donald Tennant. "Consistency of Response by Event-Recall Intervals and Characteristics of Respondents." *Sociological Quarterly* 9 (1968): 73–84.

Dalton, James S. "The Camp Meeting Revivals of 1797–1805, as Rites of Initiation." Ph.D. diss., University of Chicago, 1973.

Day, John F. *Bloody Ground*. New York: Doubleday, Doran and Company, 1941. Reprint, Lexington: University Press of Kentucky, 1981.

Dorson, Richard M. "The Debate over the Trustworthiness of Oral Traditional History." In *Volksüberkieferung: Festschrift für Kurt Ranke*, ed. Fritz Harkort (Göttingen: 1968), 21. Cited in William Lynwood Montell, *The Saga of Coe Ridge: A Study in Oral History* (Knoxville: University of Tennessee Press, 1970), x.

Douglass, H. Paul. *Christian Reconstruction in the South*. Boston, 1909.

Egerton, John. *Generations: An American Family*. Lexington: University Press of Kentucky, 1983.

Eller, Ronald. "The Coal Barons of the Appalachian South, 1880–1930." *Appalachian Journal* 4, nos. 3 and 4 (Spring/Summer 1977): 195–215.

———. "Land and Family: An Historical View of Preindustrial Appalachia." *Appalachian Journal* 6 (Winter 1979): 83–109.

———. *Miners, Millhands, and Mountaineers: Industrialization of the Appalachian South, 1880–1930*. Knoxville: University of Tennessee Press, 1982.

Estep, Bill. "No Charges Will Be Filed in Snake Case." *Lexington Herald-Leader*, February 18, 1986, p. B1

———. "Knox Church Members Charged with Snake Handling." *Lexington Herald-Leader*, June 2, 1988, p. B1.

———. "Snake-Handling Case Dismissed in Knox County." *Lexington Herald-Leader*, September 28, 1988, p. B1.

Faragher, John Mack. "Open-Country Community: Sugar Creek, Illinois, 1820–1850." In *The Countryside in the Age of Capitalist Transformation: Essays in the Social History of Rural America*, ed. Steven Hahn and Jonathan Prude (Chapel Hill: University of North Carolina Press, 1985), 233–58.

———. *Sugar Creek: Life on the Illinois Prairie*. New Haven: Yale University Press, 1986.

Fee, Holly. *Saylor Family Footprints: Being the Family and Descendants of Solomon and Sarah Saylor*. Harlan: self-published, 1987.

Fetterman, John. *Stinking Creek: The Portrait of a Small Mountain Community in Appalachia*. New York: E.P. Dutton, 1970.

"Five Killed in Bell County's Most Tragic Accident." Clipping file of Wyatt Woody, January 21, 1960, p. 1.

Flynt, J. Wayne. *Dixie's Forgotten People: The South's Poor Whites*. Bloomington: Indiana University Press, 1979.

Fortunato, Frank. "Snake Handlers: Risking Death as a Test of Faith." *Hustler*, April 1980.

"Four Charged with Handling Snakes." *Louisville Courier-Journal*, June 6, 1988.

"Four Fined for Public Snake-Handling." *Louisville Courier-Journal*, clipping file of Tess Walters, n.d.

Frost, William Goodell. "Our Contemporary Ancestors in the Southern Mountains." *Atlantic Monthly* 83 (March 1899): 311–19.

———. "The Southern Mountaineer: Our Kindred of the Boone and Lincoln Type." *American Monthly Review of Reviews* 21 (March 1900): 303–11.

———. "God's Plan for the Southern Mountains." *Biblical Review* 6 (July 1921): 405–25.

Gaventa, John. *Power and Powerlessness: Quiescence and Rebellion in an Appalachian Valley*. Urbana: University of Illinois Press, 1980.

Gillenwater, Mack Henry. "Cultural and Historical Geography of Mining Settlements in the Pocahontas Coal Fields of Southern West Virginia, 1880–1930." Ph.D. diss., University of Tennessee, 1972.

Glaser, Barney G., and Anselm Strauss. *The Discovery of Grounded Theory: Strategies for Qualitative Research*. New York: Aldine Publishing Company, 1967.

Golden, Richard. "Snake Church: A Kentucky Sect Uses Poisonous Snakes to Fortify Religious Faith." *Pageant* 11, no. 9 (March 1956): 49–51.

Goodykoontz, Colin Brummitt. *Home Missions on the Frontier: With Particular Reference to the American Home Missionary Society*. Caldwell, Idaho: The Caxton Printers, 1939.

Graybeal, David McConnell. "An Analysis of the Influence of Cultural Change upon the Protestant Churches of a Southern Appalachian Town." Ph.D. diss., Yale University, 1952.

Griffin, Gerald. "In the Name of Religion, the Serpent Takes Its Toll." *Louisville Courier-Journal*, September 2, 1940.

Hahn, Steven. "The 'Unmaking' of the Southern Yeomanry: The Transformation of the Georgia Upcountry, 1860–1890." In *The Countryside in the Age of Capitalist Transformation*, ed. Steven Hahn and Jonathan Prude (Chapel Hill: University of North Carolina Press, 1985).

Hall, C. Ray. "The Law, the Lord, and the Snake-Handlers: Why a Knox County Congregation Defies the State, the Devil and Death." *Louisville Courier-Journal*, August 21, 1988.

Hamada, Tarek. "Two Critical after Snakebites." *Fort Wayne (Ind.) News-Sentinel*, September 7, 1987.

———. "Snakebite Victim's Move Was Uninspired." *Fort Wayne (Ind.) News-Sentinel*, September 10, 1987, p. 1.

Haney, William H. *The Mountain People of Kentucky*. Cincinnati: Robert Clarke Company, 1906.

"Harlan Police Nab Seven Handling Snakes." *Louisville Courier-Journal*, October 27, 1947.

Haukebo, Kirsten. "Snake-Handlers Defy Ban, Plan Services at Church." *Louisville Courier-Journal*, May 26, 1991, p. 1.

Henige, David. *Oral Historiography*. New York: Longman Group Limited, 1982.

Henretta, James A. "Families and Farms: *Mentalité* in Pre-Industrial America." *William and Mary Quarterly* 35 (1978): 3–32.

Hevener, John W. *Which Side Are You On?: The Harlan County Coal Miners, 1931–1939*. Urbana: University of Illinois Press, 1980.

"Holiness Faith Healers: Virginia Mountaineers Handle Snakes to Prove Their Piety." *Life*, July 3, 1944, 59–62.

Holt, John B. "Holiness Religion: Cultural Shock and Social Reorganization." *American Sociological Review* 5 (October 1940): 740–47.

"Investigation Continues into Death of Woman from Snake Handling." *Lexington Herald-Leader*, February 15, 1986.

Jillson, Willard Rouse. *The Kentucky Land Grants: A Systematic Index to All of the Land Grants Recorded in the State Land Office at Frankfort, Kentucky, 1792–1924*. Louisville: Filson Club Publications, 1925.

Jones, Loyal. "Mountain Religion: The Outsider's View." In *Religion in Appalachia: Theological, Social, and Psychological Dimensions and Correlates*, ed. John D. Photiadis (Morgantown: West Virginia University, 1978).

Kane, Steven M. "Holy Ghost People: The Snake-Handlers of Southern Appalachia." *Appalachian Journal* 4 (Spring 1974): 255–62.

———. "Ritual Possession in a Southern Appalachian Religious Sect." *Journal of American Folklore* 87 (October–December 1974): 293–302.

———. "Snake Handlers of Southern Appalachia." Ph.D. diss., Princeton University, 1979.

———. "Holiness Ritual Fire-Handling: Ethnographic and Psychophysiological Considerations." *Ethos* 10, no. 4 (1982): 369–84.

———. "Appalachian Snake Handlers." In *Perspectives on the American South*, vol. 4, ed. James C. Cobb and Charles R. Wilson (New York: Gordon and Breach, 1987), 4:115–27.

Karlsen, Carol F. *The Devil in the Shape of a Woman: Witchcraft in Colonial New England*. New York: Vintage Books, 1987.

Keesler, William. "Ohio Woman Who Held Rattler at Uncle's Wake Dies after Being Bitten." *Louisville Courier-Journal*, February 14, 1986, p. B1.

"Kentucky Man Killed by Rattler in Rite of Snake-Handling Cult." *New York Times*, October 30, 1973.

Kerman, Keith. "Rattlesnake Religion." In *Eve's Stepchildren*, ed. Lealon Jones. Caldwell, Idaho: The Caxton Printers, 1942.

Kimbrough, David L. "Solomon and Sarah Saylor: The Emergence of Lay Religion in Eastern Kentucky." *Appalachian Heritage* 21, no. 3 (Summer 1993): 49–57.

Kobler, John. "America's Strangest Religion." *Saturday Evening Post*, September 28, 1957, pp. 25–30.

Kulikoff, Alan. "Migration and Cultural Diffusion in Early America, 1600–1860: A Review Essay." *Historical Methods* 19 (1986): 153–69.

La Barre, Weston. *They Shall Take Up Serpents.* Minneapolis: University of Minnesota Press, 1962.

Lawless, Elaine J. *God's Peculiar People: Women's Voice and Folk Tradition in a Pentecostal Church.* Lexington: University Press of Kentucky, 1988.

Lawson, Gil. "Snake-Handling Charges against Four Men are Dismissed." *Louisville Courier-Journal,* September 28, 1988.

———. "Snake-Handling Charges Are Dismissed." *Louisville Courier-Journal,* September 29, 1988.

Lewis, Helen Matthews, Sue Easterling Kobak, and Linda Johnson. "Family, Religion, and Colonialism in Central Appalachia, or Bury My Rifle at Big Stone Gap." In *Colonialism in Modern America: The Appalachian Case,* ed. Helen Lewis, Linda Johnson, and Donald Askins (Boone, N.C.: Appalachian Consortium Press, 1978).

Lewis, Judy Jones. "Minister Relents, Gets Treatment for Snakebite." *Lexington Herald-Leader,* November 22, 1988, p. B1.

Lightfoot, William E. "Folklore of the Big Sandy Valley of Eastern Kentucky." Ph.D. diss., Indiana University, 1976.

McCauley, Deborah Vansau. "Appalachian Mountain Religion: A Study in American Religious History." Ph.D. diss., Columbia University, 1990.

McGaw, Judith A. *Most Wonderful Machine: Mechanization and Social Change in Berkshire Paper Making, 1801–1885.* Princeton: Princeton University Press, 1987.

Malone, Bill C. *Country Music U.S.A.: A Fifty-Year History.* Austin: University of Texas Press, 1968.

"Man Bitten While Handling Snakes at Church Dies." *Louisville Times,* September 17, 1980.

Mathews, Donald G. *Religion in the Old South.* Chicago: University of Chicago Press, 1977.

Mayo, Selz G. "The Appalachian Urban Crisis." In *Appalachia in Transition,* ed. Max E. Glenn (St. Louis, Mo.: Bethany Press, 1970), 25–33.

Miles, Emma Bell. *The Spirit of the Mountains.* New York: James Pott, 1905. Reprint, Knoxville: University of Tennessee Press, 1975.

Miller, Iva M. "Child Health in Mining Camps and Village." *Mountain Life and Work* 4, no. 8 (January 1933): 5–8.

Miyakawa, T. Scott. *Protestants and Pioneers: Individualism and Conformity on the American Frontier.* Chicago: University of Chicago Press, 1964.

Montell, William Lynwood. *The Saga of Coe Ridge: A Study in Oral History.* Knoxville: University of Tennessee Press, 1970.

Moore, Tyrel G. "Economic Development in Appalachian Kentucky, 1800–1860." In *Appalachian Frontiers: Settlement, Society, and Development in the Preindustrial Era,* ed. Robert D. Mitchell (Lexington: University Press of Kentucky, 1991), 222–34.

Morgan, John. "Log House Construction in Blount County, East Tennessee." In *Appalachian Frontiers: Settlement, Society, and Development in the Preindustrial Era*, ed. Robert D. Mitchell (Lexington: University Press of Kentucky, 1991), 201–21.

Morrow, Reverend Jimmy. "Seventy-Seven Years—The History of Serpent-Handling Churches (1909–1985)." Unpublished manuscript.

Mullen, Patrick B. "Ritual and Sacred Narrative in the Blue Ridge Mountains." *Papers in Comparative Studies* 2 (1983): 17–38.

"Paralyzing Prayers." *Time*, September 17, 1945, pp. 23–24.

Partadiredja, Atje. "Helvetia, West Virginia: A Study of Pioneer Development and Community Survival in the Appalachia." Ph.D. diss., University of Wisconsin, 1966.

Peacock, James L., and Ruel W. Tyson, Jr. *Pilgrims of Paradox: Calvinism and Experience among the Primitive Baptists of the Blue Ridge*. Washington: Smithsonian Institution Press, 1989.

Pennington, Charles. "Snakes Figured in Pagan Religions But Only Lately in Christian Rites." *Chattanooga Times*, September 16, 1945, p. 21.

Pentecostal Holiness Advocate, October 11, 1917, pp. 2–3.

Photiadis, John D. *Religion in Appalachia: Theological, Social, and Psychological Dimensions and Correlates*. Morgantown: West Virginia University, 1978.

——. *Community and Family Change in Rural Appalachia*. Morgantown: West Virginia University Center for Extension and Continuing Education, 1985.

Posey, Walter Brownlow. *The Development of Methodism in the Old Southwest: 1783–1824*. Ph.D. diss., Vanderbilt University, 1933.

"Preacher Fined $50 for Handling Snakes." *Louisville Courier-Journal*, September 4, 1940, sec. 2, p. 8.

Pudup, Mary Beth. "Land before Coal." Ph.D. diss., University of California at Berkeley, 1987.

——. "Social Class and Economic Development in Southeast Kentucky, 1820–1880." In *Appalachian Frontiers: Settlement, Society, and Development in the Preindustrial Era*, ed. Robert D. Mitchell (Lexington: University Press of Kentucky, 1991), 235–60.

Raine, James W. *The Land of Saddle-Bags: A Study of the Mountain People of Appalachia*. New York: Council of Women for Home Missions and Missionary Education Movement of the United States and Canada, 1924. Reprint, Detroit: Singing Tree Press, Book Tower, 1969.

"Rattlesnake Bite Kills Man, 32, after Service." *Louisville Courier-Journal*, September 17, 1980, n.p.

Raulston, J. Leonard, and James Livingood. *Sequatchie: A Story of the Southern Cumberlands*. Knoxville: University of Tennessee Press, 1974.

Redfield, Robert. *The Little Community* and *Peasant Society and Culture*. Reprint (2 vols. in 1), Chicago: University of Chicago Press, 1989.

Robertson, Archie. *That Old-Time Religion*. Boston: Houghton Mifflin, 1950.

Roth, Julius A. "Hired Hand Research." *American Sociologist* 1 (August 1966): 190–96.

Salyer, Elisabeth. *The Salyer Family: Genealogy and Records of Their First 250 Years in America*. Stuart, Fla.: self-published, 1982.

Schrager, Samuel. "What Is Social in Oral History?" *History and Anthropology* 4 (June 1983): 76–98.

Schwarzweller, Harry K. "Social Change and the Individual in Rural Appalachia." In *Change in Rural Appalachia: Implication for Action Programs*, ed. John D. Photiadis and Harry K. Schwarzweller (Philadelphia: University of Pennsylvania Press, 1971).

Schwarzweller, Harry K., James S. Brown, and J. J. Mangalam. *Mountain Families in Transition: A Case Study of Appalachian Migration*. University Park: Pennsylvania State University Press, 1971.

Scott, Shaunna Lynn. "Shall They Take Up Serpents?: A Crisis in Community and Class Solidarity." Unpublished paper, University of California at Berkeley, 1987.

———. "Where There Is No Middle Ground: Community and Class Consciousness in Harlan County, Kentucky." Ph.D. diss., University of California at Berkeley, 1988.

Seltzer, Curtis. *Fire in the Hole: Miners and Managers in the American Coal Industry*. Lexington: University Press of Kentucky, 1985.

Semple, Ellen Churchill. "The Anglo-Saxons of the Kentucky Mountains: A Study in Anthropogeography." *Geographical Journal* 17 (1901): 588–623. Reprinted in the *Bulletin of the American Geographical Society* 42 (1910): 1–34.

Sharp, Harry P. "Migration and Social Participation in the Detroit Area." Ph.D. diss., University of Michigan, 1954.

Sims, Patsy. *Can Somebody Shout AMEN?* New York: St. Martins, 1988.

Smith, Eldon Dee. "Migration and Adjustment Experience of Rural Migrant Workers in Indianapolis." Ph.D. diss., University of Wisconsin, 1953.

"Snakebite Death Doesn't Shake Beliefs of Church." *Louisville Courier-Journal*, February 15, 1986.

"Snake-handler Bitten, Dies Praising Lord." *Louisville Courier-Journal*, August 12, 1974.

"Snake Handlers Pass Challenge of Blow Torch." *Chattanooga News–Free Press*, July 23, 1945, p. 21.

"Snakehandlers' Song Still Shakes the Hills." *Troublesome Creek Times*, January 14, 1987.

"Snake-Handling Kentucky Man Bitten Three Times, Refuses Aid, Dies." Clipping file of Tess Walters, n.d.

"'Snake Sect' Loses Battle." Clipping file of Tess Walters, October 2, 1942.

"Snake Sect Prays for Jail Doors to Open." *Louisville Courier-Journal*, September 10, 1947, p. 7.

"Snakes in Demand." *Cleveland (Tenn.) Herald,* September 17, 1914, p. 1.

"State Police Arrest Virginia Preacher." *Middlesboro Three States,* August 25, 1955, p. 1.

Stekert, Ellen. "The Snake-Handling Sect of Harlan County, Kentucky: Its Influence on Folk Tradition." *Southern Folklore Quarterly* 27 (1963): 316–22.

Surface, Bill. *The Hollow.* New York: Coward-McCann, 1971.

Sutton, Thad, George L. Mehaffy, and O. L. Davis Jr. *Oral History, A Guide for Teachers (and Others).* Austin: University of Texas Press, 1983.

Sweet, William W. *Methodism in American History.* New York: Abingdon-Cokesbury Press, 1933.

Synan, Vincent. "The Pentecostal Movement in the United States." Ph.D. diss., University of Georgia, 1967.

Taussig, Michael. *The Devil and Commodity Fetishism in South America.* Chapel Hill: University of North Carolina Press, 1980.

"Tennessee Snake Handlers Seized." *New York Times,* September 24, 1945, p. 10.

Thompson, Paul. *The Voice of the Past: Oral History.* New York: Oxford University Press, 1986.

Tomlinson, A. J. *The Church of God, Evangel* (Cleveland, Tenn.). September 19, 1914, p. 2.

Tomlinson, Homer A. *The Shout of a King.* Queens Village, N.Y.: Church of God, U.S.A., 1968.

Vance, Paul. "A History of Serpent Handlers in Georgia, North Alabama, and Southeastern Tennessee." Master's thesis, Georgia State University, 1975.

Verhoeff, Mary E. *The Kentucky River Navigation.* Louisville: Filson Club Publications, 1917.

Vincent, George E. "A Retarded Frontier." *American Journal of Sociology* 4 (July 1898): 1–20.

"Virginia Snake-Handling Law to Be Tested." *Mountain Life and Work* 44, no. 10 (November 1968): 22.

Votaw, Albert N. "The Hillbillies Invade Chicago." *Harper's,* February 1958, 64–67.

Wachtal, Nathan. "Memory and History: An Introduction." *History and Anthropology* 2 (October 1986): 207–24.

Waller, Altina. *Feud: Hatfields, McCoys, and Social Change in Appalachia.* Chapel Hill: University of North Carolina Press, 1988.

Warner, Charles Dudley. "Comments on Kentucky." *Harper's New Monthly Magazine* 78 (December 1888–May 1889): 255–71.

Watson, Judge. "The Economic and Cultural Development of Eastern Kentucky from 1910 to the Present." Ph.D. diss., Indiana University, 1963.

Weller, Jack E. *Yesterday's People: Life in Contemporary Appalachia.* Lexington: University Press of Kentucky, 1965.

"West Virginia Minister Dies from Bite by Rattlesnake He Handled." *Richmond Register,* August 25, 1982.

Whisnant, David E. *All That Is Native and Fine: The Politics of Culture in an American Region*. Chapel Hill: University of North Carolina Press, 1983.

Whitaker, Fess. *History of Corporal Fess Whitaker: Life in the Kentucky Mountains, Mexico, and Texas*. Louisville: Standard Printing Company, 1918.

Williams, Lillian Walker. "In the Kentucky Mountains: Colonial Customs That are Still Existing in That Famous Section of the Country." *New England Magazine* 30 (March 1904): 37–45.

"Woman Dies from Rattlesnake Bite." *Richmond Register*, February 14, 1986.

"Woman Dies of Snakebite Received at Harlan Church." *Lexington Herald Leader*, February 14, 1986, p. 1.

Womeldorf, John A. "Rattlesnake Religion." *Christian Century* 64 (December 10, 1947): 1517–18.

"Worshiper Dies of Rattlesnake Bite." *Knoxville News-Sentinel*, January 31, 1989, p. A1.

Zimmerman, Carle C., and Merle E. Frampton. *Family and Society*. New York: D. Van Nostrand Company, 1935.

Index

Agriculture. *See* Farmers and farming

Alcohol, 33, 92; moonshine, 47

Anointing/anointment, 25–26, 51, 56, 156, 163, 180

Anti-snake-handling legislation, 2, 106, 107, 110, 126, 137, 168

Appalachians: language of, 3; and status of children, 5; communal lifestyle of, 9, 60, 187–88; and family cohesion, 10, 11, 61–63, 173–75, 187–90; "stem family," 11, 173; as early settlers, 59–72; preindustrial life of, 61–62; values of, 61–63, 85; and self-sufficiency, 62–63; work ethic of, 63, 82, 172; and division of labor, 63–64; and church life, 64–65, 67; societal structure, 70; breakdown of societal structure, 85, 89–93, 95, 171–72; and family feuds, 88–89; fundamentalist response to anomie, 93, 96, 187. *See also* Attitudes, fundamentalist; Children; Oral tradition

Appearance, personal: fundamentalist preferences in, 32–33, 77, 179; of lay preachers, 66. *See also* Holiness church: and rejection of worldliness

Arminianism, 65, 71, 75

Assemblies of God, 194 (n. 28). *See also* Church of God; Holiness church

Attitudes, fundamentalist: toward women, 15–16, 27, 33–34, 67; toward homosexuality, 21; toward drugs, 21; toward television, 21; toward alcohol, 33, 92; toward tobacco, 33, 92; toward the super-natural, 69; toward capitalism, 92. *See also* Appalachians: values of; Holiness church: and rejection of worldliness; Snake handlers: harassment of; Snake handling: sensationalized

Baptism, 68, 75, 78, 157, 193–94 (n. 26); and conversion, 72. *See also* Baptists; Salvation

Baptists: early churches, 64–66; Hardshell, 68; Missionary, 68; Primitive, 68; splits among, 68; and Calvinism, 71; Free Will, 77. *See also* Baptism

Bible, 4, 41, 191 (n. 8); snake handling, biblical basis of, 2, 8, 11, 14–15, 40, 56, 97; "scripture jargon," 3; "five signs," 8, 22–23, 30, 40, 49–50, 57, 101, 189; literal interpretation of, 65

Calvinism, 68, 71

Camp meetings (revivals), 54, 65, 71, 72

Capitalism: effect on Appalachian economy, 10–11, 81, 82, 188; and intensified snake handling, 11, 92, 96. *See also* Coal industry; Economy; Farmers and farming; Industrialization

Casting out demons, 96, 162, 163, 164

Childbirth, 63, 66, 197 (n. 2)

Children: at snake-handling services, 6, 19, 27, 28, 29, 43–44, 102, 138; education of, 63, 73, 86, 179, 215 (n. 2). *See also* Appalachians

Christianity, Victorian, 76

Gender differences: regarding snake handling, 15–16, 27; regarding "holy kiss," 33–34; division of labor among Appalachians, 63–64; in frontier churches, 67; and egalitarianism, 67, 70

Glossolalia (speaking in tongues), 6, 14, 18, 29, 44, 78–80, 197 (n. 1), 202 (n. 20)

Godhead, Holiness interpretation of, 31

Healing, 14, 30; laying on of hands, 109, 158, 160, 192 (n. 5), 197 (n. 2). *See also* Miracles

Hensley, George W., 2, 4, 5, 128, 129, 132; marriages and divorces of, 4, 45–47, 48, 125, 133, 195 (n. 1), 196 (n. 31); as self-proclaimed prophet, 7; evangelism of, 9, 11, 45, 103, 104, 112–15, 131, 133, 195–96 (n. 15); as founder of snake-handling church, 11, 39–40, 53, 115–16, 199 (n. 12); and Church of God ministry, 40, 42, 46–47; skepticism surrounding, 43, 51, 52, 53; and lack of education, 46, 132; arrest and indictment for moonshining, 47; escape from chain gang, 47; move to Ohio, 47–48; move to Kentucky, 50–51; multiple snakebites of, 111; as indifferent father, 115–16; and attitude toward authorities, 132–33; death of, 133; birth and childhood of, 194–95 (n. 1). *See also* Church of God; Dolly Pond church; Snake handlers; Snake handling; Snake-handling churches

Holiness church, 6, 13, 29, 43; Presbyterian foundations of, 13, 14, 65–65, 188; and rejection of worldliness, 21, 32–33, 77, 92, 176, 179, 189, 190; common beliefs of, 29–30; and split from Baptists and Methodists, 76–77; and persecution of members, 79, 177–79; urban, 174–76; community contributions of, 176; and good-evil dichotomy, 176. *See also* Church of God; Snake-handling churches

Holy Ghost, 25, 31, 202 (n. 20)

"Holy kiss," 15, 33–34, 74, 166

Holy trinity, 31

Home Missions, 76, 81

Home remedies, 63. *See also* Disease

Hymns, 17–18, 20, 22, 23, 55, 183. *See also* Music and musicians

Illiteracy, 46, 56, 63, 132, 197 (n. 2); and education, 73, 86, 179, 215 (n. 2). *See also* Oral tradition

Individualism, religious, 74

Industrialization: and spread of Holiness sects, 78; and spread of violence, 79, 87, 88–89; and spread of disease, 90. *See also* Capitalism; Coal industry; Economy

Land: shortage of, 10; preindustrial availability of, 59; legal control of, 82; and logging industry, 84. *See also* Capitalism; Coal industry; Farmers and farming; Industrialization

Law and law enforcement: communal, 71. *See also* Snake handlers: arrest/incarceration of; Snake handlers: prosecution/conviction of; Snake handling: laws against

Laying on of hands, 109, 158, 160, 192 (n. 5), 197 (n. 2); and healing, 14, 30. *See also* Miracles

Lay religion, 64, 65; storefront churches, 174, 175, 186

Levitation, 15, 189, 214 (n. 4)

Arnold Saylor as urban church patriarch, 176, 177

Sermons: and "scripture jargon," 3; preparation and delivery of, 21, 66–67, 71, 192 (n. 4); intellectual vs. unrehearsed, 75, 76, 78, 79, 195 (n. 13). *See also* Memory; Oral tradition; Preachers; Snake-handling churches: typical worship services in

Shell, Bradley, 204–5 (n. 3)

Signs, five biblical, 8, 22–23, 30, 40, 49–50, 57, 101, 189

Sins: snakebite as punishment for sin, 36, 107, 151; of the flesh, 67; confession of, 67, 155

Snakebite: lethal, 4–5, 26, 45, 104–5, 119, 124, 125, 126, 133, 137, 150, 151, 152, 165, 207 (n. 48); and refusal of medical treatment, 27, 34, 102, 105, 150, 167; allergy to, 35; as punishment for sin, 36, 107, 151; media accounts of, 104, 105, 111, 124, 125, 131, 151; touted as arthritis cure, 108; survival of, 122, 138, 148; prayer for, 157, 159. *See also* Snake handlers; Snake-handling churches; Snakes

Snake handlers: harassment of, 2, 11, 14, 43, 51, 99, 127, 138, 139, 147, 177–78; arrest/incarceration of, 2, 14, 27, 28–29, 106, 109, 111, 123, 127, 135–36, 139, 140, 147, 151; and suspicion of outsiders, 8; religious beliefs of, 14, 30; estimated number of, 29; two factions of, 31, 32; lawsuits against, 102; and response to anti-snake-handling laws, 107; fining of, 107, 109, 111, 140, 141; prosecution/conviction of, 109, 128–29, 130, 131, 137, 149, 168, 206–7 (n. 41); legal representation of, 128. *See also* Children;

Hensley, George W.; Saylor family; Shell, Bradley; Snakebite; Snake handling; Snake-handling churches; Valentine, Lee

Snake handling: media accounts of, vii–viii, 2, 6, 7, 28, 29, 43, 45, 114, 135, 136, 137, 138; biblical basis of, 2, 8, 11, 14–15, 40, 56, 97; laws against, 2, 106, 107, 110, 126, 137, 168; and participant observers, 4, 8; oral tradition in, 4–8; emergence and spread of, 8, 9, 114–15, 187, 191–92 (n. 1); sensationalized, 13, 177–78; individual styles of, 18, 19, 40, 42–45, 55, 96, 98, 100; opposition to, Holiness, 30, 31, 42–43; as secondary worship, 30–31; as "Devil's diversion," 43; decrease in Tennessee, 45; and religious freedom, 106, 123, 139, 147–48, 149, 150, 168; emotional contagion of, 190. *See also* Fire handling; "Five signs"; Poison drinking; Snakebite; Snake handlers; Snake-handling churches; Snakes

Snake-handling churches: renowned, vii, 53–55; autonomy of, 3, 33, 194 (n. 28); variations among, 8, 9; family preservation of, 11; urban, 11, 172, 174–76; typical worship services in, 15–22, 66, 67; decline in Tennessee, 45. *See also* Snakebite; Snake handlers; Snake handling; Snakes

Snakes: treading on, 18; taming of, 34; rendered less harmful, 34–35, 51; intentional provocation of, 112, 199 (n. 16); examination by authorities, 136; overhandling of, 145; transportation of, 199 (n. 16). *See also* Snakebite; Snake handlers; Snake handling; Snake-handling churches

Speaking in tongues (glossolalia), 6, 14, 18, 29, 44, 78–80, 197 (n. 1), 202 (n. 20)

"Stem family," 11, 173; and family cohesion among Appalachians, 10, 11, 61–63, 173–75, 187–90

Strychnine. *See* Poison drinking

Superstitions, 69

Television, 21. *See also* Holiness church: and rejection of worldliness

Testimony, religious, 21; "hot," 75, 78, 99

Theology, 67, 71

Tobacco, 33, 92

Tomlinson, A. J., 40, 42, 43. *See also* Church of God

Valentine, Lee: death of, 143–45; legendary conversion of, 145–46

Violence, spread of, 79, 87, 88. *See also* Appalachians: and family feuds; Law and law enforcement; Snake handlers: harassment of

Witchcraft, 48, 162. *See also* Demons

Work ethic, Appalachian, 63, 82, 172. *See also* Appalachians: values of; Capitalism; Coal industry

Worship: typical services in snake-handling churches, 15–22, 66, 67